Allhen—
On your bad days with
D+A— these stories
will make 'em feel
like good days!

Sister to Sister
...

edited by Patricia Foster

MINDING THE BODY

Sister to Sister

Women Write About the Unbreakable Bond

• • •

edited by Patricia Foster

ANCHOR BOOKS
DOUBLEDAY
New York · London · Toronto
Sydney · Auckland

AN ANCHOR BOOK

PUBLISHED BY DOUBLEDAY
a division of Bantam Doubleday Dell Publishing Group, Inc.
1540 Broadway, New York, New York 10036

Sister to Sister was originally published in hardcover by Anchor Books in 1995.

Book design by Susan Yuran

The Library of Congress has cataloged the Anchor hardcover edition of this work as follows:
Sister to sister: women write about the unbreakable bond / edited by Patricia Foster.
p. cm.
1. American prose literature—Women authors.
2. American prose literature—20th century.
3. Femininity (Psychology)—Fiction.
4. Femininity (Psychology) 5. Sisters—Fiction.
6. Women—Fiction. 7. Sisters. 8. Women.
I. Foster, Patricia.
PS647.W6S57 1995
818′.540808352045—dc20 95-10486
CIP

ISBN 0-385-47129-7

Printed in the United States of America
First Anchor Books Trade Paperback Edition: January 1997

1 2 3 4 5 6 7 8 9 10

To my sister, Jean,
who taught me to love stories.

Acknowledgments

My thanks to the contributors in this book whose stories have deepened my understanding of the relationship between sisters. I am grateful to my agent, Kimberly Witherspoon, and to my editor, Deb Futter, her assistant Lee Boudreaux, her former assistant Wendy Hubbert, and to friends Lynne Taetzsch, Kris Vervaecke, Mary Allen, and Honor Moore for their willingness to read, listen, and advise. Special thanks to my husband, David Wilder, for his computer expertise, and to my mother's sisters, Barbara, Mary Jo, Eloise, and Tiny, whose experience of sisterhood is complex and sustaining.

A Florida Arts Council grant provided the time to work on this book.

Contents

Sister to Sister

...

Patricia Foster

Introduction

AT AGE FIVE, I stood at the opposite end of a high school stage from my six-year-old sister, both of us dressed in identical corduroy cowgirl suits, holsters snug around our hips, red cowgirl hats tilted rakishly on our heads.

I can't live on ricochet romance
I can't live on ricochet love . . .

We sang in our flat, flirtatious voices, holding a rope taut between us, a straw man tied prisoner-style in the middle. Though we stared at the audience, we could just as well have been singing to each other, our hands pressed up against one another's as if we were mirrors. What seemed inevitable to me—so natural, it wasn't even questioned—was this link between my sister and me, the two of us performing together, yin and yang, I blond and pale, she brunette and olive. My sister said we were like Snow White and Rose Red, then later, Betty and Veronica in the Archie comics; I accepted her pronouncement without question, for early in my life I knew she was the mouth and I was the body, our roles so entwined, they locked us together in a knot. "The girls," we were referred to by our family as if tied by the same umbilical cord. If one moved, the other was bound to follow. To the outside world, the only difference between us seemed to be our coloring: dark-haired dolls went to her, fair-haired ones to me. Yet in reality, I was the one attracted to the dark, to the scary edges of life. Later in life, I'd let go my end of the rope, not waiting for consequences, while my sister invariably held on, choosing middle ground.

But at age five, I was in transitional allegiance, moving from the protection of my mother to this merger with my sister. "I'm you," I said to her one night, feeling the weight of these words on the tip of my tongue. For a long time I pretended we were the same person, a mind stretched between two bodies, only separated by air. It felt intimate, practical: we could always take baths together, could sleep beside each other for the rest of our lives, the same furry animal slippers waiting for us on the floor.

"We're me," she agreed, shaking her brown wavy hair in total acceptance as we settled in twin canopy beds with white-dotted Swiss canopies, dust ruffles to match.

I ran my hand up and down the covers. My toes pinched the sheet. "Sometimes I'm me," I said to test her patience. I sat up in bed, staring at her. She rarely wiggled in bed, but lay very still like a patient or a statue.

"No, you're not," she said, giving me a pout. "We're always *me.*"

"Not always," I said, putting the pillow over my head.

"Always," she said, but when she looked at me I pretended to be asleep.

MORE THAN THIRTY YEARS later in the December grayness of a Tallahassee morning, I sit at my desk and write these words: *I am not my sister.* A creaking silence fills my head as I reread this sentence, wondering if it can possibly be true. Of course I know objectively that I'm not fused with my sister, and yet beneath the regular heartbeat of rationality, I live a more primitive life, vacillating with emotional tides that seem beyond my control. In this subterranean place, a fine membrane divides my sister and me so that we drift together—not parasite and host, but twin sea anemones floating on the ocean floor. My sister has lived so long, so restlessly in my psyche that it occurs to me only as an aberration that we are not joined. Yet I need to be clear, to understand who I am if I'm not my sister.

Who am I if I am not my sister? This book was a result of that question to myself, a question that provoked other questions about the relationship between sisters, both biological sisters and the larger cultural movement of feminism. When I began reading about sisters, I realized that this sense of merger between sisters, what Charlotte Brontë called "the web in childhood," was neither uncommon nor without its accompanying antagonism. In *The Game* A. S. Byatt writes about two such sisters, Cassandra and Julia:

> When we were children, we were not quite separate. We shared a common vision, we created a common myth. And this, maybe, contained and resolved our difficulties. We wove a web in childhood, a web of sunny air . . . But there is no innocent vision, we are not indistinguishable. We create each other, separate. It is not done with love. Or not with pure love. Nor with detachment. . . . We are food for thought. The web is sticky. I trail dirty shreds of it. (New York: Vintage, 1992)

By the time this book became a reality I had spent years trying to understand my relationship to my sister's personality and politics. Like Lily Briscoe looking at Mrs. Ramsay in *To the Lighthouse,* I needed not only to see my sister's profoundness as heroic but also to recognize that her vision wasn't primal, wasn't the only game in town. I wanted desperately to become my own heroine, to be the central character in my own private drama. I realize now that one becomes a heroine only by defining a point of view and recognizing that the struggle to develop such discrimination matters. Such assessment of our eccentricity is, after all, what invokes an individual consciousness.

And yet for me to recognize my difference often felt like betrayal. "You'll never have anything unless you get things in order," my sister said to me once when she noticed the complete disarray of the utensil drawer in my kitchen. It wasn't just messy but filthy, tomato sauce spilled and dried in blotchy streaks. I looked at it dispassionately, wanting to shout, "I don't care about this drawer. I don't care about having anything right now. I'm just trying to finish my Ph.D." But I was flustered and said nothing, as if she would never really understand the depth of my worries. Together we cleaned out my filthy drawer while the inevitable questions stalked my confused mind: *Why don't you want what I want? Why can't I tell you what I want?* As a result of these ambivalent feelings, I became curious how other sisters negotiate not only sameness and difference but the often ambiguous loop of love and hatred that characterizes sibling ties. What would happen, I wondered, if we split open the cracks in familial sisterhood and looked at what was exposed? How *do* sisters work out issues of identity and difference? And how, I asked, might this help us to understand the possibilities for sisterhood in a larger context?

Since feminism proposed a new family of sisters, few writers have looked closely at the issues which unite and disrupt real sisters, at the difference in interpretation of the female role by women brought up with similar ideas and cultural cues about what it means to be a woman. What exactly are the stories about sisters? And why have women not been encouraged to critique this relationship with the same intensity as that of the mother/daughter role? It occurs to me that the silence surrounding sisters suggests the difficulty of critiquing someone of your own generation, someone with no cultural distance to separate you from this closest female tie. And yet when I talked with contributors, with women students and friends, they all had sister stories to tell.

"It's the big secret," one contributor confessed, "what we think about our sisters. She's the person I've known most intimately throughout my life, but still don't really know." Hearing this, I thought how often my own sister has been my mirror, my touchstone, an example of whom to become and how to see myself. Other writers felt "absolute terror" at having their sisters read their essays. "That was the scariest moment in my life," one writer said when she left her essay in her sister's hands. "What if she hates me for telling my side of the story? What if she says it's a bunch of lies?"

When I began studying art in the 1970s, my sister was finishing up medical school at the University of Alabama Medical Center in Birmingham. Often I drove from Tuscaloosa to Birmingham to visit her on the weekend, where we'd sit on the floor, eating pizza, drinking Cokes, and watching movies, then late at night we'd talk about the secrets of our lives, drawn as always into the intimacy of family knowledge. One evening while we were watching *Five Easy Pieces*, my sister said suddenly, "You might as well know this. I want to have a baby."

I sat up, stunned. "But you've got to finish medical school," I said, crunching the popcorn already in my mouth. I knew she'd worked long and hard for this choice of career, had been one of few women admitted to her class. I also wondered—though I was careful not to say it—whether a baby would replace me in her emotional life. "And your husband's got to finish law school."

She lay her head back on the chair and grinned at me. "But I'll only be *pregnant* in medical school, silly. I'll arrange it so that the baby will be born just after graduation."

"Arrange it? Are you crazy?"

"Yes," she nodded, smiling a secret smile.

I turned off the movie and just stared at her. I was amazed at and slightly jealous of her audacity. In her twenties, she was not afraid to walk high in the air without a net, to trust in possibility even if that meant occasionally coming up with zero; in contrast, my entire training had taught me to steer clear of the edge though I always seemed to be negotiating some precipice.

That night after everyone went to bed, I crept back into the living room and lay on the floor in the dark. The house creaked and shuddered, throbbing with internal nerves. I breathed deeply, pulling in air like an undertow, then letting it out slowly as if I were breathing a silken membrane into the room. I remembered reading somewhere that Rilke had said that an essential portion of any artist's labor was not creation so much as invocation. As I lay on the floor, my bare heels rubbing the nubby new carpet, my eyes closed, I began to question myself, to pull apart like stitches from a quilt, opening from inside out. In attempting to follow the rules of the dutiful daughter, I knew that I had avoided my own fury. I'd married early, divorced soon afterward, become anorexic and depressed; after the divorce, I lost my hair and what was left of my self-esteem. I was, in my own eyes, a mess! This fact of my passive disasters had always embarrassed me. Such mistakes were so unlike my sister's choices, acts which to my mind seemed bold and impulsive. And yet in that moment in the dark I knew that my fall—its peculiar motion, its private repercussions—was what I had to tell. A great weight fell from my shoulders as it occurred to me that I no longer had to resist my past, no longer had to see myself as "less than" my sister, but as moving in a world where the most deceptive barriers are often unmarked.

When I opened my eyes, I was surprised to see my sister standing hesitantly at the door, her face loose and curious as if a bolt had been thrown open in her mind. I knew she was watching me just as I was watching her, and I was amazed at that. I thought I was the only secret observer, the silent voyeur. I had always assumed that she took me as a given, a sidekick in her life, the younger sister always ready to tag along, follow in her footsteps, whereas to me she embodied the world. Yet her presence suggested something different, a narrative that fixed me in the center of her vision, just as I'd fixed her in the center of mine. I smiled at that thought, knowing we were still so hyper-aware of each other we noticed even the slight scrunching of the brow, the jut of a hip, the smallest intimacy of displeasure or joy.

BEFORE I ASKED CONTRIBUTORS to respond with their own personal stories and analysis about sisters, I wanted first to consider the connection for me between literal and cultural sisterhood. I realized that my relationship to feminism, to other women, was deeply affected by my relationship to my sister. Since adulthood I've had an intense longing for affinity with other women, to the private space of female sorrow and joy, to a shared consciousness of building new shapes for a female life. In many ways I've idealized this longing, making of it a desire too romantic to bear the weight of reality. I wanted sisterhood without the pain of competition and rivalry, the needs for differentiation and separation. Even more than a lover, I longed (in my twenties) for a close-knit friendship with my own sex, a fusion like that with my sister in childhood. I see now that I was trying to reinvent and possibly complete the old narrative of family: to hold each other so tight, nothing could disrupt the circle.

But this, of course, cannot be, neither in the biological circle of sisters nor in the larger cultural sphere of women. Feminism succeeds only when women's coming together blossoms with the wealth of separate stories, stories which admit to the diversity of female connection, including feelings of fear and fury at one's own sex. Instead of idolizing women as nurturers and emotional saviors, I find myself longing now for a more healthy competition, a more invigorating debate. In the past, women's stories have been ignored by culture—particularly stories about sisters, for female siblings have little power in the world—yet today that mythology is irrelevant, outdated. Sisterhood, both biological and social, is not simply about sharing feelings but involves the revelation of passionate truth, an encouragement to tell those stories buried deep inside. And if sisters do not go through the process of separation, their stories are diminished, reduced, the anxiety palpable in what gets repressed.

It is with this emphasis—to find the stories buried deep inside—that this anthology came to life.

Although the silence surrounding sisters in our culture suggests that this relationship is believed to be less significant psychologically than other relationships in the family romance, the stories collected here indicate that girls become keen interpreters not only of themselves together but of the family as a whole. Often in these essays and stories, sisters feel simultaneously threatened by and closely involved in parental dynamics. They see clearly what is not meant to be seen: *the family mythology laid bare.* Maria Flook in "The Boat Train" writes eloquently, "This was the challenge of our household—how to maintain family life against a backdrop of carnal spectacles. Our mother's roiling jealousies and hungers swarmed the calendar. She was not Cinderella who had lost a slipper—she *was* the empty slipper. Her beauty created a lifelong fiasco for our father, and for us [my sister and me]. We lived in our mother's element the way fish can live in a mesh bucket in the river, zigzagging with the current in the confines of a trap." Joy Harjo in "The Gift of Margaret" tries to understand the different routes she and her sister took in response to their parents' abusive relationship. She remembers her father throwing her mother against the bathroom walls, trying to choke her while she pounded at his jeans, begging him to stop. When her mother later married a second abusive man, Harjo openly rebelled, "hiding knives, making plans," while her sister Margaret lived "with grace through the dangerous years." Both Flook and Harjo are attempting to assess how the family dynamics affected the sisterly connection, how one sister survived trauma differently—though not necessarily more successfully—than the other.

Just as girls notice and analyze conflict, they also remember moments of family connection, even when that intimacy involves —as it does in Debra Spark's essay—giving comfort to a twenty-six-year-old sister dying from cancer. The twin sisters in "Last Things" give their sister Cyndy foot rubs and head massages, hoping temporarily to relieve some of the disturbing symptoms of brain cancer; they survive on girl talk about masturbation and shared pleasure, then flop on Cyndy's bed to watch her video from graduate school at UCLA. They do as a family what we all long to do for each other—to be *there* in the most profound sense of awareness, to give spontaneously without any expectation of tomorrow.

As feminist theorists have articulated in numerous books, the mother is frequently the most significant model for young girls. In sister plots, the mother also plays a dominant role, pulling the daughters closer together in their rebellion against the older generation or, more often, drawing one daughter closer, binding her more tightly to the mother's values and desires while allowing the other sister or sisters to swing free, exploring another version of femininity. This can result in what Erika Duncan calls "daughter splitting" in her essay "What Is Cinderella's Burden?" "As a child," Duncan writes, "so carefully bearing the self-hatred my mother couldn't bear, when I looked at my freer and lovelier sister, how could I have known that there was no room for my sister in that mission, and that my sister's seeming freedom was not, originally, a choice?" For Duncan, the strong bond with the mother eclipsed the sister, made her Other, a sister in the shadows, separate, unaligned. Thus, the sister journey is fractured, polarized by the mother, who stands, an imperial force, between the daughters. In bell hooks's "Girls Together: Sustained Sisterhood," the mother—who had been pregnant as a teenager—is the policing agent of young girls' sexuality, the one "who inspected underwear . . . and noticed missed periods," the one "who desired an end to desire," who wanted a different life for her six girls. Yet her fear is so strong, the girls learn instead to betray each other, terrified of bringing the mother's wrath (through the force of the father) "into the sanctuary of our pink rooms." Still, the mother's role is not simple, reducible to a single attribute, for Rosa Bell is also the one who asserts " 'feminist' values," encouraging autonomy and individuality. Sometimes the mother is more absent than present, as in Donna Gordon's "Temporary Shelter," her absence requiring the sisters to treat her more like an older sister than a mother, helping her dress for dates and dances, to attract men in her silver and gold gowns with matching metallic shoes, and most tellingly to follow in her footsteps. "As young women, my sister and I were taught to follow our mother's example—an example which she inherited from her mother—to believe that if we were pretty enough, our respective princes would come. Only years later did I come to understand that this belief in our beauty was a belief in our powerlessness." Yet it's clear in all of the essays that mothers do not form us alone, but themselves bear the weight of cultural training, which in each generation opens doors to certain ideas while shutting tight the possibility of alternative dreams.

IN THE SMALL TOWN where I grew up, I was always conscious of groups of sisters, of the way girls came to adolescence in pairs and threesomes. Particularly I was enthralled by the Van Wezel girls, who lived nearby in Magnolia Springs: smart, sophisticated, dark-haired intellectuals, destined, my sister and I thought, for a more privileged life. They went to a private school in Mobile, and in their elusive knowledge of Latin and Hebrew, they seemed out of our league, girls whose lives we could fantasize about as we rode our bikes down dirt roads, through ditches full of kudzu.

More intimately, we knew the Provost sisters—Susie, Wyline, and Louise—who lived next door to us and were close to us in age. For at least five years we spent endless summer days together, reading under the mimosa trees, making paper dolls, cooking spaghetti, and swimming like lone torpedoes underwater at the neighborhood pool. The Provost girls caroused with my sister and me in a way that made girlhood a dominant sphere where boys were incidental, a disruption in the rites of girls. "Get out of here," we'd yell at their brother Tom when he came crashing into our games. "Go away and leave us alone. We don't want any boys!"

I watched these sisters fight and barter with each other, become friends and then enemies in a split second. Like my sister and me, they each developed some sphere of influence within the family, though one sister ultimately functioned as the narrative voice for them all, claiming dominance, the one who said, "All right, let's do it *this* way," and then took the lead.

The refrain of leader/follower, master/devotee, surfaces in many of the essays collected here, how one sister directs the agenda in the sisters' lives, controlling the narrative plot. Often, but not always, this is the older sister, and if so, the younger remains ambivalent about her feelings of rivalry even when she's successful in the competition. Inevitably this brings up the question of whether emotional connection is so strongly emphasized for girls that overt confrontation and competition remain taboo. Nobody says to girls, "Go on outside and fight it out." Instead, girls are more often encouraged not to express conflict, to withhold—and ultimately, even deny—what they want in order to create harmony. Often the sister admired, esteemed, becomes the other sister's totem, her reference point for whom to become. Bonnie Friedman in "My Gertrude Stein" writes of her sister Anita, "My training was in appreciation. Like Alice Toklas, that's what I felt I did best. I was good at admiring the other's art—Anita's illustrations, the beautiful light blue and dark blue afghan which, before she went to Israel, flowed from her needles in opulent woolen waves. . . . I carry her in my mind as the real one, the original, the *aleph* to my *beth,* the word to which I am the rhyme, the person whose vision is clear while mine blurs with distortion."

In a similar vein, Robin Behn describes in "The Early Days of Her Conversion" how the younger sister is preconceived by teachers who've had the older sister a year, two years before. "My sister's large smiling face had blazed a trail through the air," a trail the younger sister cannot erase. Later in her essay, Behn philosophizes about her sister deserting their close emotional bond by going off to the Buddhists: "Maybe when we're young we need some genie to believe in, something in bright shining robes to augment the quotidian forms. I know we need something to follow. Somehow or somewhere there is a way to feel entitled to the mood of eternity, that beingness among beings . . . I tried to follow her to it. My genie was *her,* and together, for a little while, our mutual genie was music." Likewise, in her story "Earth," Jesse Lee Kercheval's narrator, Julie Watts, depends on her sister Kay to be her spiritual mentor, to keep the family together, to put up a Christmas tree and eat together in the dining room on Thanksgiving, when "my father would rather stay at his office, I in my room, my mother in her bed."

When one sister leaves—either physically or psychically—there exists a narrative void, one no one can ever fill. Yet in the heart, the desire to hurt and be hurt, to fight and still remain friends, underscores the desire for sisterhood, the hope that every emotion, no matter how awful, how brutally honest, will be revealed. As Friedman suggests toward the end of her essay: "This is the dream that goes unfulfilled: that I can break her and she'll remain, that I can topple her and she'll still be triumphant, that I can rip and punch and bite her and she'll know this is the demon me, the puny me, not the me who loves her, who really loves her —not politely, not for show, but savagely."

Just as I wanted writers to reveal the personal relationship between sisters, I was also eager for writers to explore the political landscape of sisterhood in our cultural stories. In "Leah Behind the Veil," Lori Hope Lefkovitz examines how the erotic triangle—presented in the story of the biblical Jacob and the sisters Leah and Rachel, as well as in such films as *Hannah and Her Sisters*—deprives sisters of the loyalty necessary for betrayal, making of them shadow sisters, their intimacy diminished, hidden behind the veil of sexual desire. "While other readers were interested in the love story between Jacob and Rachel and in the motif of the trickster tricked," Lefkovitz writes, "*I* wondered about the sisters in the story: What was Leah thinking when she was at the altar in her sister's place? Did Rachel know about the rule that elder sisters must marry first, and did she approve the plan? Was Rachel sad, bitter, resigned, or is it possible to imagine that she was pleased?" What Lefkovitz wonders is why the story of the sisters' relationship is absent from the story, and who benefits from this absence.

Such questions resurface when Lefkovitz, her husband, and her sister go to see Woody Allen's *Hannah and Her Sisters,* a film whose plot involves the sexual seduction of a wife's sister, an act which Lefkovitz asserts "reassures the hero, whose masculinity is weak . . . that his virility is indeed adequate." Here, in the Allen film, the old gender stereotypes—in which men desire and women are seduced—appear when "sexual taboos are twice violated, as three men prove that they know what women want, managing to win sisters and best friends with no consequence to themselves." What assumes importance in these stories is male virility rather than female intimacy. Why, one wonders, was this never noticed by reviewers?

As a child reading *Little Women,* I remember how thrilled I was to be among so many girls. The March sisters were like my sister and me, like my female neighbors, girls bound together yet divergent, strikingly different in ways that made them unique to each other. I felt the same thrill when I read Marilynne Robinson's *Housekeeping,* pleased to be within a world I knew as intimate. It was not that I became tired of the heterosexual love plot that prevailed in the rest of my reading—how could one grow tired of the likes of *Anna Karenina, Villette,* or *Wuthering Heights?*—but rather that I longed for recognition as if I were inside the book rather than a shadow on its page. When I read books about sisters, about women together—mothers and daughters, aunts and nieces, friends, cousins—I knew that I'd entered a territory of my own. As a young girl I didn't know if I'd have a great love, one that would make me throw all caution to the wind, a love that bound me body and soul to another as Cathy was to Heathcliff. But I did know what it meant to have a sister.

And yet that sister was someone I often took for granted, never thinking about what it would be like if she weren't there. Instead I shared space with her—both mental and physical—and wished only that she'd stay put on her side of the bed instead of kicking me with her bony foot. I'll never know what it would be like to be in her position, the older sister, the original daughter as Joan Wickersham explores in "The Shadow of the Mountain." "I was free to make choices and decisions, to stride out on unmarked sands. But wherever she walked, there were my footprints; she couldn't not see them, and she was always having to decide whether to step in them or not." Nor will I know the difficulties of twinship as Lucy Grealy describes in her essay "The Other Half." Although when she was a young child she once told someone that her name was "Sarah and Lucy" so frequently were the twins bound together as a pair, Grealy deconstructs the myth of twinship, breaking apart the mirror of the "twin as missing clue" to one's essential nature. To Grealy, twinship is not doubling, but two women with separate stories that only tangentially overlap. "The story of having a twin is really about something very different from what other people think it is about," Grealy says. What it's about, of course, is as complex and ambiguous as language. To look at one's sister is to look at the other and realize that even with the most unflinching scrutiny, all bets are off. To know a sister is to know paradox; to try to describe her is to tangle with the subjectivity of language, the inherent lies of story. And yet we still try. We must.

I have come back full circle to my own sister, to the value of traversing an often troubling relationship, one that has fractured and sustained me, but most important, has helped me piece together the story of myself.

After a visit to my family last year, my husband and I returned home and began to unpack. As he put away some books and magazines he'd been reading, he turned to me and said with quiet exasperation, "You know, I watched you on this visit, and I realize you'll do anything for your sister. If she says, 'Come over,' you break your neck to get there as if it's an order. You agree with everything she says and hardly ever argue with her. You never do that with me. You argue about everything!"

I was both puzzled and surprised. When I called my sister that week—as adults we like to report back to each other, to compare notes—I told her about my husband's outburst.

"Mirror worlds," she said, laughing with relief. "Mine said almost the same thing." And she related to me how her own husband criticized her for making all her plans around me when I come home to Alabama, and more important, for ignoring him. "When Pat's here, you act like I'm not even in the room."

"What's with these men?" I asked. "Don't they know anything about the craziness of sisters?"

MY SISTER AND I call each other frequently; we're keenly aware of the process of each other's lives, the ups and downs of marriage and work, family and health, the yearly decisions about vacations and Christmas. "What's happening?" my sister says when I pick up the phone. On my desk, I have papers to grade, the first page of a story I'm trying to write. I hear her children arguing in the background, then doors slamming, the intimate noises of family life. Yet for the moment I know she's shut them out, focused totally on me. I feel her waiting, her breath drawing me closer.

I sit back in my chair, prop my feet up on the stool. "You just won't believe this," I begin. And I feel the tug of our secret life.

Robin Behn

The Early Days of Her Conversion

WHEN I WAS sixteen and she was eighteen, I believed I had lost my sister forever. There she is in front of me, lying in her bed in our parents' house—it's Christmas vacation—and beneath the covers I can see the triangular outline of her legs locked into a full lotus: the knees' sharp points, the calves' crossbar, and the rest of her stick-straight above it, except for her arms descending to a nest of fingers on top of her belly. Her head snaps left when I open her bedroom door, turning her body into a kind of note, a mark I recognize from high school band scores: ♪. Instead of playing music, it seems she has reduced herself or been reduced to this figure for percussion, this unsingable alphabet chunk, quick snare drum hit, symbol crash, the sound of something falling, hitting. What I have just asked is would she like to play duets with me? But since she is this new note in the pages of white sheets, there's no one there to reply. I close the door behind me, one fast click.

What had she been devoted to before she went off to the Buddhists? I had never given it a thought. Boys, I suppose? Interchangeable boys? A string of best friends? Jazz? No. I had been the most constant landing point of her attentions. Even when it came to music, our mutual first love, her focus turned to me. She had started on piano, then migrated to clarinet, and from there to saxophone, accumulating instruments as she went, mastering them all. Lately, she'd become the lead sax, and the only girl, soloing in front of the high school jazz band. She *said* it was because she was a real reed player now, and reed players had to "double," that she asked me to teach her the flute. And since the flute is what I was—I was up to practicing six hours every day—her asking me to teach her was the highest possible praise.

I approached the job like a god, starting her off with the basics—just the barrel-shaped mouthpiece on which, through a practiced pout, she came to make a tone pure as Eden-air; then, gradually, I gave her the body of keys, the tangle of silver undergrowth that lets you say anything. Soon she was playing passable electric flute in the front row of the Rithum Machine, but at home, I kept after her to be better. I taught her to read the ladders of ledger lines up to the highest notes; I taught her to open her throat to get there, to maintain the frown to get there, not to pinch off beauty with a smile. She was already an accomplished musician; her piano lessons, of course, had started two years before mine. And so it wasn't very long before she was ready for Telemann's *Tafelmusik,* the tabletop duets.

There we are at the table, sitting across from one another, the single sheet of notes laid out like one supper between us. In this world everything is right side up, no matter how you look at it. Reading from opposite sides, one upside down from the other, we start to play the matched flutes—the melody switches back and forth—and it is then that I relax and become as mortal as she is, both of us servants to the body of sound in between. In the air is a loom and we make up the pattern as we weave it, and it is the story of the struggle of the world. There is one brief note in the middle of the middle, a fleeting unison where whatever has been bubbling up from the underworld sees the light of day and changes places with it and keeps on dancing. If you practice the piece alone you will never hear it. But that was one of our pacts: we forbade each other to practice it. Ours was a frenzy of sight-reading where everything you know is in the future. We made each other keep up. For a few minutes, we could both be gods, mutual makers of inviolate time, with the joint power to conjure something bigger than ourselves that both of us thrilled to hear.

Back on earth we occupied ordinary dimensions, except that she had always been more *there:* her nine-year-old body level with the lethal ironing board, the hot black cord dangling from the dangerous world above, her accomplished fingers careful with the pleats of the dress that would be mine in a few years, when I would catch up and be allowed to iron. Each day marked, in some small way, a point where I could erase the mystery of what she had been doing two years, three months, and five days before. Her large hands wrapped around the softball bat, the steering wheel—everything had its day when I would grow into the size and the privileges of those hands. But she must have sensed my panting after her, my eagerness. "Guess who's older?" she asked everyone, especially important-looking strangers, the kind our parents were friendly with at church. Invariably came the dreaded answer, "Robin?"

In my impatience I learned seriousness sooner. I wore my iron face through the hallways of successive schools where other big girls in uniform (Girl Scout, cheerleader) accosted me with "Smile!" But I didn't need to smile. Each time I arrived at a new grade, new class, the teacher recognized my last name and knew how well I'd do. My sister's large smiling face had blazed a trail through the air. She stood up in front of the band, wailing jazz. I came along behind and, in front of the orchestra, played "classical." And then she'd turned around and needed me to teach her my classical flute for her jazz. It was an accident, really. She'd led the way for years until she needed me to teach her. A few months more and there, across the table, we succumbed to something big that led, that leveled, us both.

But music, by its nature, is temporary. You can play and play, but it will be over and over. The lessons didn't last. She got good enough at the flute to suit her purposes. The brief period of her following my instruction came to an end. She needed something else to follow. I should have been prepared.

THERE HAD BEEN one inkling, when she was twelve, that I would lose her. In summers, our parents—displaced, landlocked people, seekers of significance—liked to drive us great distances (gas station, motel, gas station, picnic, motel with a pool *please)* to view monstrous forms. Days and days in the backseat, slumped against her shoulder until she grew impatient and condemned me to lie on the hot, humped floor. But finally, there it was on the horizon. Cumulus, haze, mirage . . . But of course my sister was the first to say "Mountains!" Is it a good thing to see the truth first? Good thing for whom? In a few hours we believed her, though I had not yet come to appreciate her visions. I didn't see it first, I said, because she had me pinned on the floor.

It was the sixties and the Unitarians who ran the family mountain camp said it was cool to believe whatever you chose to believe. Still, they insisted on age groups. What I did, condemned to the ten-year-olds' crafts class, was chisel a wooden peace sign with a kitchen knife, day after day, molecule by molecule, into a wearable shape. She never said what it was the big kids did. She'd leave after dinner wearing her woven poncho. It looked like the kind of garb you could cross a desert in—that look of being on a journey, the poncho a liquid shape so you could drink yourself if you had to, right down to the secret places underneath—she was becoming like that. She wore her long straight hair in a leather strap secured with a wooden pick. She was elemental. Like a caveperson. Someone from illustrated Bible stories we imagined but had never seen.

I waited for her to come back. I polished off the last twenty pages of another *Nancy Drew*, but Nancy wasn't half as interesting as I imagined my sister's life to be. After our parents went to sleep I sat in the dark smelling the wood smell rising up out of the porch. I chewed on the thong suspending the giant peace sign from my neck. I thought about universal love. Celestial harmonies. The moon in the seventh house. Nothing worked; still, she did not come. There must be candles, I thought. They're out there, maybe they're singing songs they all know the words to. No one leads, but they sing all together. Someone among them has perfect pitch and hums the starting note so softly it sounds like it's coming from the trees and then they know to start right on that pitch all together. Maybe there's a bonfire the fireflies here are sparks of: the screen was rough, just like her legs a day after she shaved. It tasted of sour metal. Is that what her braces taste like?

There was some laughing in the distance. I thought surely now she's coming back. I opened the book to the middle, I adopted a nonchalant pose slumped in the chair. But then the laughter died away again, if laughter is what it was. They must have moved farther off into the woods. The print in my book became an endless thicket through which I pursued them until I fell asleep.

I awoke to heavy footsteps. Something not-her coming toward the cabin—someone tall with a backpack getting louder and louder and then saying "Shhh! Open the door!" He carried her into the porch, limp as a spirit, in the nest of his handsome arms. I was right about the candles. There really was a bonfire. The rest—no one ever said. The stranger, not a counselor, not a recognizable anyone, told me they'd conjured up a séance for the dead. Then what? What arrived? Was it as good as music? Why did she have to follow it, why couldn't she quite come back? She came to just enough to stumble silently to bed.

I know she saw things in the air after that, although she never spoke about it. She started breaking curfew, she saw boys who didn't have last names, she got bored, sometimes, with duets. Her eyes that glassed over in the midst of a saxophone solo started glassing over for an audience of air. But from her gaze I knew: there is a better life somewhere, as though a secret perfect family dwells in the air, out there. And she had glimpsed herself among them. And they were better than us.

These were still the early days of her conversion when her devotions to the unnamable were young. She still dwelled among us; she was perfectly good, still, for recipes, advice. She let me borrow her earrings. She let people use her tempera paints to add to the graffiti on her bedroom walls. Her friends from school came over and painted their names and their boyfriends' names. Cute stuff—little bears, a try at all four Beatles. She actually let me try it. I painted two flutes to scale, poised in a V-shape like wings; I painted the bell of her saxophone blooming from the corner. I painted a passable likeness of Big Bird and beneath it my logo, a robin. I added a few spiders to her glow-in-the-dark web, some blobs on the ceiling to protest the authority of the establishment constellations. A peace sign, two infinity signs, a mandala I didn't know the name for. It was amazing, the way she let us do this. She didn't seem to be territorial about her space anymore.

Inch by inch, color by color, she was relegating her material space to the universe, but we didn't see that. She was still my cool big sister. She was the Midwest in all its grandeur, the straight part parting her hair the divider between rows of perfect corn. Whatever she derived from the invisible humid air, well, that was her own thing, and one just didn't ask her.

She went off to college for her freshman year, but of course she also came back. That first summer she rejoined us, she worked in the local health food store, becoming an expert on what the body wants—what pellets, what natural greens, what new age-old *what* heals *what.* She brought home a book from the store, a book about meditation. But if she tried the directions, she tried them in private. There were long silences from behind her bedroom door that filled up the house like clear sand; you had to trudge through it and prevail against some unseen heavy obstacle to get to the point of knocking. Her life was divided between work—the day shift, sometimes seven days a week—and this unspecified silence. Still, she ate dinner with us, holding forth, if asked, about natural cures for diseases. Lecithin, I remember. Quercetin, silybum marianum . . . It sounded like a foreign language, a country where everyone is sick. Unrememberable words, she'd say them once if you asked her, and then the words fell back into the great silent pit.

But the house had plenty of what passed for music. I had a home industry going: I taught thirty-minute flute lessons, back-to-back, to hopeful neighborhood girls. I knew just how to do it. I started, again, with the headjoint, I gradually let them have their shiny keys. I taught them all to count. And they did play tolerably well, better and better all summer. But when I tried to play with them, a little easy Bach, a Kuhlau duet, as soon as I joined in with them, they crumbled, embarrassed, overwhelmed. It was as if the only way they could imagine playing was tooting their boring little toot in the middle of a desert surrounded by deaf sheep. To play *with* someone, to make a thing grander than they themselves could make, seemed to undo them. They perished under a giggling wave.

I tried, then, saying in words how to play a phrase. At this point in Bach's Sonata in E Minor, it is like two sisters. Here is the main sister, hear her?, I'd say, the big grounding note you keep hearing in your head no matter what else you do. Meanwhile, here's the little dizzy sixteenth-note sister, she arpeggios like crazy to catch up but every time she almost does the big-note moves. It worked. They got quite musical. My girls climbed and climbed up through the junior high and high school band's roster; one even made first chair. It pleased their mothers to see them filled with such confidence. They wanted to pay for hour-long lessons now; they didn't mind waiting at the curb in their Muzak-filled, air-conditioned cars. I raised my rate from $3.50 to $4.00 a lesson, taking the wads of small bills to the bank each week, where the balance in my passbook eked up toward a thousand dollars, the price of a solid-silver Haynes flute. Girl by girl, note by note, I was building my future. In the fall I would go to Oberlin Conservatory and from there to the stages of the world. But still I couldn't get my girls to hold up their end of the duets. They could keep up in band practice, sometimes they succeeded in cutesy pairs with one another when I conducted them, but when I tried to play duets with them, they fell apart. It seemed they could take my advice, but not the glint of my flute sidling up alongside them, not the pairing, not the arm-in-arm musical walk. Their sound was a following sound. If I let them catch up they choked.

My sister's silence, though, was inexplicable. How could she learn that much quiet from a book filled up with words? It had to do, she said when I interrogated her, with emptying one's mind. Emptying it of what? What was in there that you needed to get rid of? Nothing, she said. Nothing was the point.

Except for the expensive green vitamins she bought at the 40 percent employee discount, she didn't buy anything all summer. She squirreled away her wages in some special account, and then, in the fall, instead of going back to school, she bought herself a ticket and flew off to a Buddhist retreat. Before she left she wrote down on a card her name, followed by an unpronounceable word in front of the word *Institute,* and then a very American-sounding address somewhere in Pennsylvania.

I took that card and my flute, a suitcase, and went off to college, where I tried to forget her. I managed to fill up the days till Thanksgiving, practicing mostly, following my new famous flute teacher's methods, and then when the break came I got out the map. I was already halfway there.

What did I bring with me? For how long did I think I was

going to be a guest? It looked on the map like a day's drive. I had written her a postcard, carefully reproducing all the intricate vowels of her new address. I might stop by on my way, I said. As if I actually could be en route to someplace else.

Most of Ohio was pretty easy. I kept the heater on, played classical flute tapes I had brought. In the back of the atlas I'd found the tiny town, population 1,200 natives, plus who knows how many Buddhists. It wore on toward afternoon. I crossed into Pennsylvania under a steel-gray sky, knocked about by wind. And then the flakes began, and then the double lane of cars began to be scored by tire marks, four wet lines, one short of a musical staff, and I was a note traveling on it. Flutists like the melody; sticking out on top of the orchestra, we get it most of the time. We are the tune you hum on your way home from the concert. But now the radio turned to static, fuzzy, gray, unhummable. It got hard to see the other cars. I stopped for gas. Word was, the troopers were about to close the road.

But I was intent on following my original plan. I crawled back onto the interstate, and in a few miles the fog began. Then snow in fog, white on white. And then the staff in front of me vanished. Suddenly I was in front of a jazz band, all the white lights on me, no music to read, just the bass drone of tires underneath. Choiceless, terrified, I made up my way, the wipers grinding like forearms shoving away white tears. I hugged the faint rise of the road and counted on it to keep going toward her. I had nothing to say, to sing. I tried to drive a straight line like one long boring note to save my life. I didn't have enough money for a motel even if I could have seen one. I counted on myself to reach her. I counted on her to take me in.

THE CARS IN THE LOT had tags from hip states like Vermont, Colorado, California. None had been moved since the snow first started. I dragged my outsider status like a dirty word behind me

—the only tracks were mine. I had a small daypack—aptly named, I thought. A neutral change of clothes—what do you wear to be quiet?—a toothbrush, the map.

It didn't look like a monastery. It looked like a cross between a farm and a rich vacationer's Adirondack lodge. I stood at the door with the snow behind me, shivering in my red jacket, saying her name with a question mark after it. I felt like a dot of blood on the snowy lip of silence. But I must have been shy enough, or frozen enough; whoever it was let me in.

IT TURNED OUT I was the lone outsider to have crossed the threshold in months. On the other side of the door I stepped into a hush. It was the same quiet that I had been keeping at bay, turning up the radio's giant comforting static like a man-made snow to keep out the killer outside whiteness. But now here it was, its paleness swirling inside the building, milking over everything, disturbed only by the occasional padding of stocking feet. I felt sick. I summoned my clattering voice, I said her two-syllable name again and sat down near the door. The silence settled over me and I remembered to breathe: I let it in.

I looked up and finally saw her. There she was not in the floaty toga I'd expected but in a prim gold business suit among the others of her kind against a background of shiny gold drapes, all of them sipping out of thimbles something that looked like blanched blood. When she'd finished hers and bowed, to what or whom I could not tell, they told her I was out there. She turned her head slightly and a look passed over her—deep but opaque, like a pool just shocked green with chlorine you have to hope you'll smell before you dive in and it burns your skin off, so much does it want to cleanse you—and then it seemed to pass away and she came out to greet me.

I stayed on until supper, a macrobiotic rice and vegetable stew for which much thanks was due. Around me the perfect family-in-the-air settled down to their benches—everyone slightly fluid in the joints, slightly beaming, poised in front of their chopsticks, elbow-to-elbow like intricate, damp paper dolls. It was a really big big-kids' club. Someone whose turn it was led an unintelligible chant—goobledygoobledygook—as, phrase by phrase, everyone but me answered—gookgookgook—and then we all ate in silence under the giant photographed gaze of the absent important toga-clad man.

Telemann is absent too, of course, but when you play, especially the duets, you feel like he is in the room. You feel what he must have felt and you add your *today*. It is a cumulative thing—the more you fill the silence, the more the silence gets filled. The lapping of the two worlds, the silver surfing in between that makes more and more waves until you almost can't bear it, and then you turn the page and do it all over again. It is like a hunger, and the more you pursue it, the more there is for everyone to eat.

But when they'd finished eating, every last one, they froze again in the silence. The chopsticks, by some miracle of physics or acrobatics, had made the food disappear. The whole room was less and less, and then the emptiness was broken by the same suited chanter starting up another chant, this time a low-in-the-throat one, like a record winding down after you've pulled the plug, and then the meal was over, the great silence fed.

She wrote on a napkin that she was glad to see me, but what could I write back? I'd followed her as far as I could. The god in this place was silence. I simply couldn't hear. I slept briefly on a pallet in one of the honeycomb's empty rooms, and slipped out early the next morning past the great gold hall where the numerous huddled figures were already sitting on rows of *zafus* like birds on a wire facing into some cruel quiet wind. Outside, it had cleared some. A few shards of broken blue tore at the white sky. The car choked then started. I fishhooked to the end of the blurry drive, then rejoined the road that, during the course of the night, had been plowed.

WHEN MY SISTER ran out of money four months later—it was an expensive silence—she came back home from the Buddhists'. But she did not really come back. In place of her liveliness, her temper, her glorious moody moods, in place of the nicknames, the music, was something she called *peace.* But it was not really her own, I thought, not like the noise of the saxophone had been hers, jammed in her mouth, her on stage, jamming. This quietness was too sudden, too complete, not of her. It wore her like a mantle, it told her what to do. Here is your sake, here is your brown rice, here is your new name, here is your boredom with your Western sister.

What happened after that? Years went by. She grew quieter, older. Sometimes she was a waitress. Sometimes she went to school. She had boyfriends who played bass, became doctors. But what was she really doing in those early years of her quietness? At home for brief visits, she baked, shopped, talked—a version of the usual things. But at night a deep hush issued from her room no knocking on the door could bring her out of. Sometimes it was punctuated—thwack—by prostrations. Thwack. But I could never see. Sometimes she wore a small brace—something about the cartilage in her knee.

It was as if she sailed an endless becalmed sea, gradually moving away from me under the steam of nothing. Nothing was far away. She drifted toward it for years. It had something I could not give her. When your competition is nothingness, how do you conquer that? She got so good at it she conducted classes. She became a nothing celebrity. The big cheese of nothing from Tibet stayed at her house. What was left for me?

• • •

I TRIED A contemplative boyfriend, a New York Jew with Eastern leanings. We'd go up to his family's cabin for a romantic weekend sitting Zen. I'd get bored. I'd clean the kitchen. I'd go out and shovel the path. Maybe being younger means I'll always be a scavenger, looking for something to do. I left him perched on his *zafu*.

I need the world, I need its noisy accoutrements. I need the thin fishskin that covers the flute's key pads, and, as the skin wears through, the airy sucking sound of the fish being caught. I need the intricate architecture of perfectly ground silver screws. And the silver stick like a giant crochet hook through which you pull the handkerchief and swab the spittle, the evidence of your warm breath, out of the instrument's body. The plush blue velvet bedding that lines the case where it rests. The way it comes apart into pieces, like music when you practice the hard parts; the way it fits back together like the seamless mind of God so you can play. How it is possible to feel the immutable ongoing pattern of beats, and still play something syncopated, singular, that fits it. How it makes you bigger. How you can say anything, how you can miss a note in front of the whole audience and don't. How before they applaud not you but the luminous invisible made up of silver and hands and air, there is that moment of silence when they are still overwhelmed and cannot lift their hands to make their thunder. And then they do.

Maybe when we're young we need some genie to believe in, something in bright shining robes to augment the quotidian forms. I know we need something to follow. Somehow or somewhere there is a way to feel entitled to the mood of eternity, that beingness among beings—I know we both sensed it in the distance. I tried to follow her to it. My genie was her, and together, for a little while, our mutual genie was music. I followed the sound of her footfall, but I loved the sounds we made—her footsteps, my footsteps, half notes, scurrying quarter notes—more than the goingness, more than the pure way. But she was older, taller. Who was there for her to follow? So she followed the way itself, path of snow into dear stillness. How calm it must have been for her, when she'd gone far enough she could no longer hear my ragged half of the duet, some one-winged thing stabbing silence. She sat down, then, where she was. She seemed to have gone away.

Wherever it is now, I'd like to think the flute she donated to the *sangha*'s fund-raiser still makes a faint sound in her ears, its keys yawning open like valves of a giant heart. Light shines off the flute's silver body, and the same light shines off the Buddha's bald head. It shines off the slippery zone of choosing between noisy art and hushed religion. It shines off the hinge between one world and another, between heart and soul, between sister and sister.

Debra Spark

Last Things

MY SISTER AND I step briskly out of the greengrocer to get away from the men behind us in line who have told us, in great detail, what they'd like to do to us, where they intend to put certain parts of their bodies. The clerk, kindly, rings their purchases up slowly, so Cyndy and I have a chance to hurry across the street, almost bumping into two men who are breaking raw eggs in their hands and leaning over to slip the viscous mess into their mouths.

One of those Manhattan nights, I think.

Earlier today, as Cyndy and I were taxiing away from Grand Central to her apartment in Chelsea, we were thrilled, saying: "New York. It's so great. Look at the dirt! Look at the guy peeing in the alley! I love it!" A joke, sure, but only partially. We'd just spent a claustrophobic weekend with our parents and other two siblings in the Berkshires. The occasion, I guess, was Cyndy's mastectomy last week.

Cyndy's nerves are pretty much gone in the right side of her body, so the operation didn't hurt as much as the lumpectomy she had two years ago, when she was twenty-one. Still, I can't help thinking, Wound, especially now that we're out with the crazies. And also, I'm thinking of my own toes, which are so black-and-blue with cold (a circulatory problem I will learn later in the month) that I am having trouble walking. Indeed, at the moment, I feel more damaged than Cyndy appears to. We shuffle by the guys with the eggs, and I put my right arm around Cyndy's back—companionably, I think, because I want to restore the playful order that has reigned most of today, that was operative when we were at the New York City Opera, and I was meeting Cyndy's coworkers and admiring the Mr. Potato Head doll she had placed over her desk, presumably to supervise her efforts as rehearsals coordinator. My arm has barely touched Cyndy's black coat (the coat I will someday wear) when she says, vicious as possible, "Don't you *dare* try to protect me."

I am quiet. My throat, for a minute, as pained as my toes, and then I say, my voice strangulated, half the words swallowed, ". . . not trying . . . protect you."

CYNDY IS DEAD, of course. That is why I wear her black coat now. She died of breast cancer at age twenty-six, a fact I find unbelievable, a fact that is (virtually) statistically impossible. When she was twenty-one, she was in the shower in her dorm room at the University of Pennsylvania. She was washing under her arm when she found the lump. She was not checking for breast cancer. What college girl does monthly exams on her own breasts? Laura, my twin sister, says that I was the first person Cyndy called about the cancer. I don't think this is true, though Laura insists. I'm certain Cyndy called my father, the doctor, and that he told her to fly home to Boston. He demanded her return even though the doctors at Penn's health service pooh-poohed her concern. Finally, after a long conversation, I realize why Laura thinks Cyndy called me first and I tell her: "I think you're thinking about the rape."

"Oh, yeah," Laura says. "That's probably right."

When my father called me in Wisconsin to tell me about Cyndy, I said, "Oh, well, I'm sure, she's okay. Lots of women have fibrous breasts."

"No, Debra," my father said sternly. "That's not what this is about."

"Do you think she'll have to have a biopsy?"

He was quiet.

"A mastectomy?"

"That's the least of my concerns."

I guess I wasn't quite able to hear him right then. I hung up the phone and pulled out my copy of *Our Bodies, Ourselves,* to look at that book's photograph of a jubilant naked woman—out in the sun, with one breast gone, the stitches running up her chest like a sideway zipper. I remember wailing, literally wailing, at the image and at the prospect of my sister losing her breast.

I didn't know yet that my father had examined my sister when she came home from college. My father is an endocrinologist, a fertility specialist. He examines women every day in his office, but to feel your adult daughter's breast—breaking *that* taboo, because medical care is shoddy and you *do* love your daughter desperately and *appropriately*—and to know, right away, what it is you are feeling . . . I have to stop myself from imagining it. And I think my father has to disremember it too, because even though he knew, right then, she had cancer, he tells this story about himself. When the X ray of Cyndy's chest was up on the lightboard, my father pulled the X ray off the board and turned it over to look at the name. "Spark, C." He looked back at the picture. Turned the X ray over again to check the name. "Spark, C." He did the whole thing again. And again.

Later, two weeks before she died, I remember seeing her X ray up on a lightboard. Not something I was supposed to see, I know, but Cyndy's treatment all took place at the same hospital my father has worked in for twenty-five years. I knew my way about and I knew how to take silent advantage when I needed to. I looked, but from a distance. I was out in the hall, standing over Cyndy in her gurney, as orderlies were about to move her out of the emergency ward and up to a floor. My view was oblique and once I knew there was nothing happy to see there, I said, Don't look. Though later, all I would do was say, Look, Debra. Look, this is a person dying. Look, this is Cyndy going away.

MY MOTHER WAS always the most pessimistic of all of us, and I used to hate her for it. "She'll be okay," I'd say. And, "We can't read the future." My mother said we were lucky we *couldn't* read the future or we'd never get through it. Which is probably true. That night in Manhattan, things seemed tragic but manageable. In the past was the lumpectomy and the radiation. Now the mastectomy was completed. The chemo was to come. Cyndy had cut her hair short so the loss of it wouldn't be too upsetting. Back in Boston, she'd gone with my mother to buy a wig. Now she was trying to wear it over her hair. That was the advice she had been given: to start wearing it so it would be like a new haircut and no one would notice. I thought, Who cares who notices? I was for announcing the illness as just another fact, among many, about Cyndy. To keep it secret was to imply that it was either shameful, like a sin, or special, like a surprise gift, and it was neither.

The wig bothered Cyndy. It was itchy and, though we'd tell her otherwise, it had a dowdy look, a look that owed nothing to the haircuts Cyndy had always had—the funky asymmetrical do she'd sported when she'd gone to London for a year or the long red mane she'd had as a child. One day, while I was still visiting with her in New York, we went out to lunch with some friends of mine who had never met Cyndy. In the middle of lunch, Cyndy, impatient and in the midst of a story (she was a magnificent and voluble talker), pulled off her hair—to my friends' surprise, especially since there was another head of hair under the one she pulled off.

After all the preparation for baldness, however, Cyndy's

hair didn't fall out. At least, not that year. The first round of chemo was bad, but, again, in the realm of the get-overable. Every three or four weekends, my mother would come into New York and take Cyndy to the hospital and then out to my grandmother's house for a weekend of puking. Cyndy handled it well. The biggest long-term effect was that she wouldn't let anyone say "pot roast" when they were around her. And she couldn't stand the smell of toast for years to come.

Some time later, after Cyndy had finished up the chemo, she decided to go to business school, to get a degree in arts administration at UCLA. She loved school. She had never been too happy as an undergraduate, but UCLA was right for her. Her goal had been to make opera, which she adored, accessible to people who ordinarily wouldn't go. She had a special column in the school newspaper called "Kulture, Kulture, Kulture"; she was proud of her ability to drag business students (a surprise! stiff business students!) to the opera. I imagine Cyndy as the life of the party in those days. Cyndy going to the graduate student "beer bashes"; Cyndy leading the talk at the business school study sessions; Cyndy still earning her nickname "Symphony."

I know she slimmed down in those years, too. She had an intermittent problem with her weight, and it was probably the real clue that Cyndy—handle-everything Cyndy—sometimes had her unhealthy way of handling things. When I visited Cyndy in Chelsea, after her mastectomy, we were toying with the idea of living together. At the time, I was profoundly (read "clinically") depressed. I had left the man I had been living with for four years and had been unenthusiastically debating what I should do next. Cyndy was moving up to Inwood, and we had found a small apartment that would accommodate the two of us should I decide to move with her. I remember that one of her real enthusiasms about the two of us living together had to do with food. She was convinced that I'd have her eating large green salads for dinner, that my own good habits would rub off on her, and she would no longer find herself in the middle of secret, ruinously upsetting food binges.

Cyndy had been a chubby kid, but never really fat, even when she weighed a lot. When she was older, her figure was sensual if robust. Still her weight was an occasional issue: my father telling her, at dinner, not to be a *chazar;* my mother spinning her own anxiety about weight onto Cyndy. At Cyndy's college graduation, Cyndy said "No, thank you" to the dessert tray that a waiter was offering our table. We were all too full. My mother said, "Oh, I'm so proud of you" to Cyndy. Cyndy said, "I'll have that chocolate cake" to the waiter. And the rest of the children—Laura, David, and I—hooted with laughter. It was our turn to be proud. After all, the request for cake was her version of "Oh, stop it, Mom."

Still, toward the end of Cyndy's stay in Chelsea, I got my first glimpse of how painful the problem with food could be. Like many women, I had my own issues, and Cyndy and I would often have long talks about what all this meant. Once, she told me about how she used to have a secret way of slipping cookies silently out of the cookie jar and hiding under a dining room table to eat. This might have struck me as funny—so often our childhood stories charmed me—but I wanted to sob when she told me. I felt stricken by our—her, my, everybody's—desires. How easily they became desperate or grotesque or hateful, especially to the person who did all that desiring.

Her desires must have been met in L.A., however, because she looked so good. At the end of her first year there, she organized a student show, a big campy celebration that everyone dressed for. She brought a videotape of the show back to Boston for the rest of us to see. Now we fast-forward through the tape so we can see the intermission. Someone has filmed her—happy her—backstage exuberantly organizing things. Then we fast-forward again and there is Cyndy in a gorgeous, retro, off-the-shoulder dress. Her hair is long, just above her shoulders. She needs to flip it out of her eyes. She has long dangling earrings. She is glamorous by anyone's account and quite sexy. By this point, she's had reconstructive surgery. The new breast is lumpy and disappointing—not that anyone says this. It's just clear that when my uncle, the surgeon, said, "Sometimes they do such a good job you can't tell the difference," he wasn't 100 percent correct. Part of the problem is that Cyndy, like all the women in the family, has large breasts. They couldn't reconstruct her breast so it would be as big as the original one, so she had a smaller breast made, and she wore a partial prosthesis. The doctors had asked her if she wanted the other breast reduced—for balance's sake. But she decided no. After all, she didn't want to run the risk of not having feeling in either breast.

In the videotape, when Cyndy starts to sing, the audience is clearly amazed. And they should be: her voice is stunning. She could have had an operatic career if she had wanted it. Months before her death, a singing instructor made it clear to Cyndy that she not only could, but she had to, have a singing career. Her voice was that beautiful.

Now when I listen to the tape, I watch Cyndy's mannerisms. Each time, I am surprised by the fact that she seems a little nervous about performing. Cyndy nervous? Cyndy is never nervous, as she herself will admit. (Except about men. That's the one exception.) But she gets comfortable as she proceeds, as the audience's approval is clear. She sings, beautifully, the Carole King song "Way Over Yonder." *Way over yonder, that's where I'm bound.*

Even before she died, I knew the irony would always break my heart, once she was gone.

IN THE SUMMER after Cyndy's first two semesters in L.A., I was living in Lincoln, Nebraska. I was teaching a summer class, and late at night, I'd get tearful calls from Cyndy. Mostly about men, for I was, in many things, Cyndy's confidante. Sometimes, now, I think that I am wrong about this. I *was* Cyndy's confidante, wasn't I? She *was* the person I was closest to, wasn't she? When we were young, I always thought that Cyndy and I belonged together, and David and Laura belonged together. Laura always had a special way with David. Laura and I were close (the twins, after all), and Cyndy and David (the youngest) were playmates. Still, I felt Cyndy and I were a pair. When they met Cyndy, people used to say, "Oh, so she's your twin?" And I'd shake my head no. "Your older sister?" No, I'd say again. Cyndy loved being mistaken for my older sister. "I really am the smartest one in the family," she'd say, even when she was in her twenties. I'd have to disagree; it was a distinction I thought I deserved if by smart you meant (and Cyndy did) commonsensical.

Our closeness was somewhat competitive. We delighted in being competent—more competent than the one in the family who was spacy, the one who was overemotional. We just had things together, and we understood the world. The one fight I remember us having (I'm sure we had many when we were young, but I can't remember them) is about driving the car. She snapped at me for correcting her driving. She hated it when I played older sister.

When Cyndy first started making her tearful phone calls to me, I was proud. I took a secret pleasure in the fact that she confided in me, that she came to me first. I'd even felt a slight pleasure—mixed with my horror—when she called to tell me, and, at first, only me, that she'd been raped. It was during her first year at college. I was in my senior year at Yale. It was a date rape, I suppose, although that term doesn't fit exactly. The man was someone she met in a bar—a sailor, good God—and Cyndy got drunk and later, after some flirting, he didn't understand that no meant no. I honestly don't think he knew he raped her. I think for a while Cyndy was bewildered too. Her previous sexual encounters had not amounted to much, and, later in college, her experiences remained disappointing.

Given her history, Cyndy's tears on the phone made sense to me. I thought she was finally addressing the issue that had always so frightened her. She spoke, with uncharacteristic frustration, of the way her women friends were always talking about *their* relationships, and she didn't have any relationships and how upset it made her. With the encouragement of the family, Cyndy started talking to a therapist. I was all for this, I would tell Cyndy, as I sat late at night in my small rental in Nebraska. After all, I had been helped, enormously, by a psychiatrist. My parents agreed with my assessment, I think, although Cyndy spent less of her time on the phone with them talking about men and more time talking about her headaches, her terrible headaches, that stopped her from getting any work done.

So, it's clear where this goes, no? We hope it's not, we hope it's not—as with each test or checkup we have hoped—but it is. Cyndy has cancer in her brain. When they do the initial radiation on her brain, and later when they do an experimental treatment that *does* shrink the tumor, it becomes clear that all that crying had a physiological base. Her tumor shrunk, her headaches go away. She stops crying or talking about men.

But, of course, she does cry, though only once, when she learns about the brain tumor. When I find out, I am standing in my kitchen and kneading bread. I get the call, and then I phone MIT to tell a friend of Laura's not to let her go to lunch. I want to come get her and take her to the hospital. I feel like a rock when I do all this, like a cold rock. I throw the dough in the trash and hear the *thump-swish* of it hitting the plastic bag. Then I go and get Laura, who screams—as in bad movies, screams—and I drive to the hospital. Laura, instantly feeling everything, spins out of control with grief. She's sharp with nurses who seem to be blocking her way to Cyndy. She won't allow what my father says when he says it. She just tells him, No, no, you're wrong. She turns to me and says, Why aren't you acting like anything? And I think, because I am so very competent.

In the fall, Cyndy comes and lives with me in my big apartment in North Cambridge. This is so clearly better than staying with my parents in their suburban home. She is immensely disappointed about having to take time off from UCLA. But it is only time off, we reassure her. She will get back there. And she does. After a year with me, she goes back for a semester. But she is too sick and has to come back to live with me for good. She lives with me for two years. This is the part that I'm glad I didn't get to see when I was in my Wisconsin apartment, worrying about the possibility of my sister having a mastectomy. I think now, A mastectomy! A lousy mastectomy! Who cares? I remember once, not long after I'd moved to Cambridge and before Cyndy moved in with me, I was in bed with a temporary lover. He was an old college friend, a doctor, in town to do some work for the year. Cyndy and I had been talking, earlier that day, over the phone, about men. I was encouraging her to approach a young man she was interested in in L.A. She'd said, "But it's so complicated. Like at what point do I say, 'Hey, buddy. One of these isn't real.' " I knew she'd be gesturing, even though we were on the phone, to her chest, pointing to first one, then the other. ("I can always tell," she'd said, "when someone knows and they're trying to figure out which one it is.) That night, in bed, I'd said to my friend, "Well, if you loved someone, it wouldn't make a difference . . . say, before you were involved . . . if you found out they had a mastectomy, would it?"

He looked at me. "Yeah," he said. "I don't mean to be horrible, but of course it would."

"But," I said, as if he'd change his mind because I needed him to, "*I* said it wouldn't. That's what *I* said."

• • •

CYNDY AND I had fun in the apartment where we lived. My boyfriend Jim would come by in the evenings, and they would talk music or we'd go out for dinner. Nights when Jim was working, we'd get George, a musician friend from around the corner, to come over. Cyndy took classes at Boston University. She worked for the Boston Opera Theater. She got involved with a project involving musicians in Prague. Related to that, Vaclav Havel's press secretary and her son came to live with us for a while. And during all this, cancer would pop up in one place or another—her knees, the back of her tongue. Still, it always honestly seemed to me that we could make her better. Healthy denial, I suppose. Certainly, Cyndy had a lot of it. She was always willing to be cheered up, to imagine her future.

Some things stand out, but I can't (I won't) put them in order. Like: the number of times I would be in bed, making love with Jim, and hear Cyndy hacking away in the next room. That would be the cancer in her lungs.

Or the way she would call out to me each morning that Jim wasn't there: "Derba, Derba, Derba," she'd say, in a high-pitched silly voice. And I'd call back, "Der-ba Bird," because that was what she was, chirping out the family nickname for me. Then I'd go crawl into her bed and rub her back. There was cancer in the spine by then, and she could never get comfortable. Sometimes she'd wail at her pillows. She couldn't get them in the right position.

Or the way, one night, when I was making dinner, she said, "Oh, God," and I said, "What is it?" and she snapped, angry as could be, "You *know* what it is!"

There was an odd stretch when I felt her oncologist was trying to convince her that her symptoms were psychosomatic. Like when she couldn't get enough energy to move, and we'd spend days inside, only making an occasional trek to the back porch. Perhaps, he seemed to be suggesting, she was only depressed?

The few times Cyndy did snap at me, I felt like I would dissolve. My mother said, "Well, I guess you're getting a sense, before your time, of what it's like to have an adolescent." In truth, my mother got the brunt of it. When Cyndy was in the most pain, she would leave the apartment for a stay with my parents. When she was well enough, she would come back to stay with me. Wherever she was, though—my house, my parents' house—we were all there, all the time.

And even when she was doing relatively well, there were lots of visits back and forth. One day, in the beginning of her stay with me, Cyndy and I were driving out to our parents' house for dinner. We were talking about death, and Cyndy said, "Oh, well, you know, sometimes I think about death. And I try to force myself to imagine what it would be like but then I'm like . . . whoa . . . you know, I just can't do it."

"Yes," I said, for I knew exactly what she meant. "I'm like that too."

Now I'm even more "like that." For if a parent's job is to protect his or her child, a sister's is to identify with her sibling. Which means, of course, that the whole family gets, in the case of a terminal illness, to fail in what they most want to do for one another. So I push my imagination to death, make myself think "no consciousness." I have, regretfully, no belief in heaven, an afterlife, reincarnation. I believe in nothingness. I try not to let myself pull back, try not to say, "Whoa, that's too much." But my brain—its gift to me—is that it won't let me do what I want.

I think, in this regard, of the time ten-year-old Cyndy came home from school in a snit. She'd learned about black holes in science class. She'd stomped up to her room and flopped on her bed. As she went, she ordered the family to never talk to her about black holes. I thought she was joking. So, I opened the door to her bedroom, stuck my head in—cartoon-fashion, the accordion player poking his head through the stage curtain to get a peek at the crowd—and I said rapidly, "Black hole, black hole, black hole." Cyndy, already lying on her bed, threw herself against the mattress so that she bounced on it like a just-captured fish hitting land. She started to sob. "I'm sorry," I said. "I was kidding. I thought *you* were kidding." But why should she have been? What's more terrible than everything going out?

Once, during one of her final stays in the hospital, Cyndy said to my mother, "I'm going to be good now," as if that would make her healthy, as if a planet could blame itself for being in the wrong part of the universe.

"Oh, honey," my mother had said. "You *are* good. You are so *good.*"

One trip out to my parents that stands in my mind: Cyndy had the shingles, an enormously painful viral infection that runs along the nerve path on one side of the body. Just getting her down the staircase into my car was horrible. Cyndy was sobbing and sobbing, and ordinarily she didn't cry. I put her in the passenger's seat and cursed myself for having the kind of life that made me buy such an inexpensive and uncomfortable car. The requirement of bending was too much, and Cyndy wept and wept. I drove as fast as I could and neither of us talked. I thought, "I'll just get her home and it will be all right." My father, the doctor, would know what to do. My mother would be, as she could be, the most comforting person in the world. When we got there, I said, "It's okay, it's going to be okay," as Cyndy walked with tiny paces from the car to the front steps. My parents were at the front door and it was night. My mother brought a kitchen chair to the front hall so as soon as Cyndy got up the stairs, she could sit down. I stood behind her and my parents stood at the top of the six stairs that led to our front door: my mother (blue turtleneck and jeans), my father (stooped). Both of them had their hands out and were reaching for Cyndy but they couldn't get her up the stairs. She had to do that herself. And I thought, looking at them in the light, and Cyndy still forcing herself up through the night—*Oh, my God. All this love, all this love can't do a thing.*

But that wasn't completely true. The love did do something. It just didn't save her.

Laura, my twin sister, gave Cyndy foot rubs and Cyndy loved them. Laura would give foot rubs, literally for hours. I gave back rubs but I never liked giving them, would wait for Cyndy to say I could stop. When Cyndy told Laura she could stop if she wanted to, Laura would ask for permission to keep going—as if Cyndy were doing her a favor by putting her feet in the vicinity of Laura's hands. One day, Cyndy was lying on her bed in our apartment and Laura was on a chair at the end of the bed and she was rubbing Cyndy's feet. I was "spooning" Cyndy and occasionally rubbing up and down her spine where the cancer was. We were talking about masturbation. "I can't believe you guys," Laura was saying, telling us again about how amazing it was that, of the three of us, she had discovered masturbation first. We were giggling. This conversation wasn't unfamiliar. We'd had it before, but we could always find something new to tell each other.

"What was that bathtub thing you were talking about?" Cyndy said.

Years earlier, I'd instructed both of my sisters about the virtues of masturbating in the bathtub. Something I'd learned from my freshman year roommate at college. "Got to try it," I said now.

"Exactly how do you do it again?" asked Cyndy.

"Lie in the tub. Scoot your butt under the waterspout and put your legs up on the wall and let the water run into you. Guaranteed orgasm."

"De-bra," Cyndy said, hitting me, as if I'd gone too far in this being-open-with-sisters conversation.

"Sor-ry," I said. "Still, you've got to try it, but wait till this thing gets better." I pointed at her head. There was a new problem these days, something that caused Cyndy to get, on occasions, dizzy. She had some new medicine, so I talked as if the problem would be solved in a matter of weeks. (Aside from the dizziness, Cyndy had occasional aphasia. One night when I was on the phone, Cyndy screamed from her bedroom. I ran in. She'd forgotten a word, couldn't produce it and felt her head go weirdly blank. The word, she realized, five minutes later, was *cancer.)*

We decided to leave the topic of sex behind for something else. But not before I insisted, once again, that Cyndy try this bathtub thing. I was rubbing her back and Laura was still rubbing her feet, and I was thinking, as I stroked her skin, Yes, an orgasm. Let this body give her some pleasure.

You *do* get inappropriately intimate with a body when the body is ill. Sometimes there's something nice about it. Cyndy used to sit on the toilet in our bathroom and I'd take a soapy washcloth and wash her bald head. I'd say, "Stamp out dry scalpy skin." This struck us, for some reason, as terribly funny. We'd soak our feet in the bathtub and talk about our favorite Gogol stories. We'd walk arm in arm. Say: "This is what we'll be like when we are old ladies."

When Cyndy's symptoms were at their worst, my own body struck me, especially my legs, which stretched—it seemed amazing—from my torso to the ground. The miracle of walking. I still feel it. The air behind my legs is creepily light as I move. Who would have ever suspected that you can feel grief behind your kneecaps?

One very bad night: Cyndy was upset about everything, but especially men, relationships, never having had a boyfriend. According to her, I didn't, *couldn't* understand because I had had a boyfriend. This was a point of connection between Cyndy and a few of her intimates, an absence they could discuss and from which I was excluded. It didn't matter that I felt, for the sadness of my own relationships, included. I had had sex. Many times even—enough to have had a sexually transmitted disease which I (paranoid, irrational) thought I could pass on to Cyndy through ordinary contact. It didn't matter that I was cured of the problem. Her immune system was down. Anything I did might hurt her. My own desires might kill her.

This one night, Cyndy was crying, so I went into her room to put my arm around her, and she said, "Don't. Don't you touch me." Fierce, again. Vicious. I retreated to my bedroom. Cried softly, but still felt I had to do something. I stepped back to her bedroom, and she started to scream, waving me away, but saying, "It's just that I realize that nobody but my family or a doctor has touched me in the past five years."

It'll change, it'll change, it'll change. That was always my mantra for these relationship conversations. But it didn't. She died before it could change.

AFTER THAT TERRIBLE night when Cyndy had the shingles and had to struggle out of our apartment to the car, she spent six weeks at my parents' house. Those were miserable times. She couldn't move from her bed. We'd all climb onto the double bed, a ship in the ocean of her room, and play word games or watch TV or be quiet because a lot of the time she couldn't stand for anything to be going on. As she started to feel a bit better, she worked on the course that she was going to teach in January of 1992. It was going to be called "Opera—What's All the Screaming About?" and it was going to be for high school girls, for kids who, presumably, could care less about opera. We rented opera videos and watched them with her. Then she decided she was ready to come back to our apartment to work on her course syllabus. I cleaned the kitchen while she worked. At one point, she started to faint, but she grabbed the doorjamb, and I came in and caught her, wrapped my arms around her waist—big now, she was bloated with steroids—and set her down on the ground.

She was okay, so she started to work at her computer, and I made us some cocoa. She handed me her syllabus to proofread. She sipped while I read it, and she said, in a sort of campy voice, "Mmmm . . . this is love-ly." I laughed, still reading. She made a funny gurgling noise. I thought it was a joke but when I looked up from the syllabus, Cyndy was slipping out of her chair. I ran the few feet to her. She was crumpled on the ground. I rolled her onto her back and saw blood. There was water on the floor—her urine. "Are you okay? Are you okay?" I screamed. Her wig had rolled off her head and she looked like a gigantic toppled mannequin. She was gasping, breathing oddly. A seizure, I knew. I am, after all, a doctor's daughter. When the convulsive breathing stopped, she said, "What happened? What just happened?" She was as purely frightened as I'd ever seen her.

"Close your eyes," I said. "You just fainted. Close your eyes." I didn't want her to see her own blood. I thought that would scare her. I ran to the bathroom to get a towel and wipe her up. I tried to see where the blood was coming from.

"It's okay, you bit your tongue."

I felt—I have to say this, only because it's so horrible—a slight pleasure. It was the old thing: I would be competent, take care of this trouble. I was good in an emergency. But there was also part of me—small, I promise myself now, very small—that thought, with some relief, "It's over."

The ambulance came. We rode over to the hospital. My parents were there before us. When they rolled Cyndy away, I cried to my mother, "Oh, Mommy. I thought she was dying. I thought she was dying."

Inside, Cyndy was saying the same to my father, "I thought I was dying. I thought I was going to die."

And about two weeks later she did. But not before her body put her through enormous suffering. Not before she had a little more fun with the family. So, last things. The last thing she ever produced was a picture from a coloring book. She had asked for the book and some crayons, and we all earnestly filled in Mickey Mouse's ears and then signed our names and ages. Debra, 29. Laura, 29. David, 24. Mommy, 53. Daddy, 55. Cyndy signed hers, "The Queen." (A joke from our two years together. When she was queen, Boston drivers were not going to be allowed to be obnoxious.) Under "age," Cyndy wrote, "None of your damn business." Last meal: gray fish from the kosher kitchen, but she didn't eat it. Last thing she *did* eat: Jell-O. I know, I spooned it into her mouth. Last thing I said to her: I told her that the man she was interested in was in love with her, that I knew because of what he'd said when I called to tell him she was in the hospital. (I was making this up, but who cares?) Last thing Cyndy ever said to me: "Oh, good. Well, tell him we'll get together when I get out of here." Last thing she ever said: I didn't hear this because I wasn't in the room, but she woke up, delusional and panicked and worried because she was going on a long trip and she hadn't packed her suitcase.

As my fiction writer friends always say, You can't make this stuff up. No one would believe you if you tried.

And I have to agree: real life is just too heavy-handed.

Very last thing: her body still desiring life, she takes every third breath, though her fingers are dusky, though her kidneys have already shut down. We give the funeral director the pretty purple dress she bought for special occasions. We put her in the ground.

OUR DESIRES, I sometimes think now, as I'm walking down the street.

Today, outside a bakery, I stop myself and say, "Yes, Debra? What about them?" And I realize I don't know. "What? What?" I stand for a while feeling disgusted with the world—those horrible leering men in the greengrocers; that stupid sailor in the bar; foolish me, making love with my sister dying in the next room.

Our desires, our desires, our desires. I know what the refrain is; I just don't know what to do about it. It's a reproach for me, an always unfulfilled wish for my family, and a sad song—it's a dirge—for Cyndy. Still, since I am here, stuck among the living, I have to remind myself that the song owes nothing to the beautiful ones that Cyndy sang. So I go into the bakery and get a shortbread cookie dipped in chocolate. It is so delicious I start to cry.

Joan Wickersham

The Shadow of the Mountain

> . . . Any sense of rivalry between herself and her sister was avoided by the tacit agreement that one was to become an artist and the other a writer. But the very fact that there was such an agreement suggests an awareness of competition. . . .
>
> —FRANCES SPALDING, *Vanessa Bell*

SOME OF THE worst fights I've ever had with her have been about writing.

New York, 1985. We meet for a late dinner in a delicatessen. It happens that on this particular night we're both wildly happy. She is newly engaged and has brought her fiancé along, and they're grinning at each other and at me and tangling their fingers together on the black Formica tabletop. I've spent the afternoon with a William Morris agent who has just agreed to take on my screenplay (just so you know: nothing came of it. That's the punch line of so many writing anecdotes: Nothing came of it).

We're drinking beer, talking and joking, laughing and laughing and laughing. And she says, "I have this great idea—I'm going to write a novel about Ahma."

And I blurt out: "But *I* want to write a novel about Ahma."

Silence.

Ahma was our father's mother. Born in Germany, she rebelled against her family by becoming a dancer, rebelled again by marrying a dancer, came to America because she hated the Nazis, divorced her husband, became a physical therapist for dancers. She lived to be eighty-one, and by the time she died she was running a movement institute in New York, passing along her methods to scores of dancers and physical therapists.

"Well," says my sister, "then I guess we'll both write novels about Ahma."

"We can't both."

More silence.

I suggest that she could do a biography of Ahma and I could do a novel. (Here, you take this toy and let me play with that one . . .)

Her fiancé, who up until now has stayed out of it, says to me: "She can write about whatever she wants. It's not your birthright, you know."

His words sting, make me recoil. It's like the preliminary rattle of the snake: a warning. My sister has an advocate. It's not just me and her alone anymore, working things out in our own cryptic way. She has someone on her side, who doesn't accept the justice of my taking whatever I want and letting her take whatever's left over.

I go away from this dinner feeling shaken, and ashamed. How would I feel if someone told me what I could and couldn't write? But still there's a part of me that insists on the validity of my outburst, irrational though it was. I know I'm crazy to insist that our both wanting to be writers is a big deal, but she is crazy to insist that it's not. A few weeks later I bring it up with her again. I say:

"I've been thinking, and I had no right to say any of that to you. You should go ahead and write whatever you want to write."

"I don't want to talk about it," she says.

"No, no, listen, we should both write whatever we want, but we need to admit that this is going to be a tough thing for us." I need her to acknowledge that terrible landscape which for one instant was illuminated by lightning—it is ugly and irrational, but it's there and we both saw it.

"I don't want to talk about it," she says again.

And we never have.

I KNEW VERY EARLY on that I wanted to write. I did all the usual child-writer things: wrote books which I illustrated and bound between construction-paper covers, banged out short stories on the typewriter my parents gave me for eighth-grade graduation, edited high school literary magazines, won writing prizes. At fifteen I was overjoyed to get a "good" rejection letter from the *Atlantic*—the kind that said, Sorry, we don't want this story, but we'd like to see more of your work. (Nothing came of it.) I sent some stories to a publisher, and he wrote back that they were good student stories, but I needed to wait until I had something to say.

Fine. But what was I to do in the meantime? Most of my college friends were going on to graduate school in law, or medicine, or psychology. I believed that for me, training for a real career in something other than writing would be tantamount to accepting defeat. But neither did I want to go to a graduate fiction program—I was afraid of being told that I wasn't good enough, and afraid that a formal program might teach me writing "tricks" which I would then have to spend years trying to unlearn. So I supported myself with a series of jobs, all of which involved writing, but not the kind of writing I wanted to do. I did newsletters and press releases for a bank, alumni publications for an art school, copywriting for a series of ad agencies.

All the while I kept writing stories and sending them out and getting rejection letters. Every couple of years I would take the law boards, and then decide that no, I should hold out a little longer. Sometimes I thought of that scene in *The African Queen* when Katharine Hepburn and Humphrey Bogart get stuck in the weeds and lie down convinced they're going to die, and the camera pulls back to show what they can't see: open water just a few feet away.

But sometimes I thought of misers who hoard all their lives only to discover in old age that the currency has become worthless.

For someone who had declared herself a writer at the age of seven, I was turning out to be a very late bloomer, if in fact I bloomed at all.

MY SISTER, three years younger than I, came to writing slowly, sideways. As a child she was interested in archaeology. Then she wanted to be a teacher. Then to run a bookstore, or some other kind of business.

When she got out of college she worked at a publishing house. Then a company that produced corporate publications. Then a book club. She was dancing around the idea of writing, not yet ready to declare her true inclination, even to herself. Or maybe I'm wrong. Maybe she knew, all along, that she wanted to write, but she was hoping to find some other related occupation that would scratch the same itch. Was she afraid of what I might say? *We can't both.*

Sometimes when we were growing up she cried: I'm so tired of being your little sister! I never had to think about being *her* sister. I was free to make choices and decisions, to stride out on unmarked sands. But wherever she walked, there were my footprints; she couldn't not see them, and she was always having to decide whether to step in them or not.

But once she chose, once she knew that writing was what she wanted to do, she was fearless. Shortly after that New York deli dinner, she went to journalism school. She sent out queries, followed them up with phone calls, got assignments. Her first published piece came out in the *Nation.* She had a "Hers" column in the *New York Times.* She wrote book reviews for newspapers around the country. She published a book about the myths of motherhood versus the reality, and then another book which was a painfully honest account of three highly educated women trying to adjust to the changes motherhood had wreaked in their lives and in their marriages. Recently I got a chance to fool around with a Nexis database and I looked her up. She had forty-six articles in various publications, some of them pieces she'd written, some of them reviews of her books. What impressed me wasn't just the quantity of her writing, or the quality—it was the quiet, no-nonsense way she'd gone about making a career. She believed her experience in publishing had toughened her up; she had seen the people behind the rejection letters, and didn't have to be afraid anymore.

She tried to toughen me up, too. Rejection letters flattened me, and I would call her wanting sympathy. She gave it up to a point, but her general reaction was brisk and practical. "So that editor's a jerk," she would say. "Send it out again."

"But what if I really do stink?"

"Joan," she would say.

"But—"

"JOAN!"

She had no patience, either, for long discussions about which magazine or which editor I should try next. Her theory was: it's a crapshoot, a matter of catching the right editor in the right mood on the right day, so there's no point in agonizing about it.

Sometimes I would call complaining that I couldn't seem to finish any of my stories.

"What are you reading these days?" she would ask.

"*Anna Karenina.*"

"And what before that?"

"*Emma.*"

"Well, then."

"Well what?"

"Of course you're depressed. Why don't you do yourself a favor and read some junk?"

One Christmas she gave me a book called *Overcoming Writer's Block.*

"Did you read it yet?" she asked.

"I have a block about reading it."

Did it bother me that she, the younger one, was finding a success that had so far eluded me? If you had asked me to define my worst nightmare, in the early days when all our writing was in the future, when the tension was all about what we might want to write someday, it would have been this: she succeeds and I fail. Yet when that did turn out to be the scenario, for a few years, it wasn't as bad as I might have expected. For one thing, I could not have anticipated the pleasure I would get from reading her work; the very thing I dreaded—that her sensibility might be similar to mine—made her a writer I would have loved reading even if she hadn't been my sister. And her early success, by effectively reversing our birth order, was oddly liberating. I didn't have to feel guilty about the natural advantages of having been born first; for the first time in our lives, I was following in *her* footsteps. I didn't have to continually look over my shoulder, because there was no one behind me.

There was some friction between us because I wanted her to look at my short stories and offer criticism, and she didn't feel able to do it. Partly, she said, it was because I sometimes used people and events she recognized in my stories, and it was hard for her to be objective about them. And partly it was because she just wasn't that crazy about short stories.

"Well, damn it," I said, "you're my *sister* and you've been an *editor* and can't you overcome your aversion for half an hour and help me out?"

I wanted to be where she was, in the safe lamplit room,

instead of outside peering in. I admired her courage and wanted her to teach it to me. Now I'm ashamed at having wanted so much. Yes, she was tough and practical—but I think I denied the effort that went into her toughness. When you're trying to be brave and sensible the last thing you want is someone continually voicing fears that you'd prefer not to consider.

Yet despite the difficulties she was an important teacher for me. Patiently, repeatedly, without ever saying the words but rather by her own example, she imparted the only really worthwhile message a writing teacher can give: shut up and write.

1991. WE ARE ENTERING our thirties. She is well launched as a writer, and I am finally getting off the ground, with several published short stories and a contract for a novel. Now we spend hours on the phone talking shop: agents, editors, publicity, revisions. These days her tough irreverence about the whole publishing process, rather than making me wistful, is bracing. She makes me feel that the two of us can do anything.

The minefield is quiet; grass has grown up. But the mines are still buried, still active.

She asks to read a draft of my novel, and I send it off to her. She calls me, in tears.

"What is it?" I ask. "What *is* it?"

"It's that conversation I had with Daddy," she says. "You put it in your book. That was private."

I know the scene she means: a sister telling a brother about a disturbing talk she had with their father. "But I changed it."

"Well, you need to take it out."

"But it's not like I wrote a scene where the father and daughter are actually *having* that conversation. I was writing about what happened between you and me, when you told me about your talk with Daddy and it made me realize we saw him differently."

"I told it to you because I trusted you."

I am silent for a moment. Our father died only a few months before, with brutal suddenness; we are both dazed and raw, and we've told each other a lot of very personal stuff. This is a fight about betrayal. But is the betrayal personal or literary? Is it that I've broken a confidence, or that I've stolen her material? It's both. It doesn't matter. If she's this upset, I'm taking the scene out.

I tell her I'll take it out, but she's too distraught for the concession to make any difference. "I just don't know if I can trust you anymore," she is saying.

Rage. What a ridiculous overreaction. Of course she can trust me. I'll never do it again.

But maybe she can't trust me, since I'm still not entirely sure what it is I've done.

WRITERLY ETIQUETTE: you never steal a story from another writer.

But what if the other writer is your sister, the story is about your family, and the two of you have talked so much you're no longer sure where your perspective ends and hers begins?

That is where the tension is between us. That is the green field where the explosions happen. It is not competition, precisely. It's not wanting to do better than she, or get more recognition. It's a struggle over territory. It's: Who does this belong to? Who has a right to this material?

You have to share, says the wise inner voice. There's more than enough to go around.

But no, there isn't. There never is.

That's why, I think, so many horrible arguments seem to erupt over wills. I know of three different families where the siblings have stopped speaking to each other, and all the rifts have to do with inheritance: either the parents left the property evenly and the poorer children resented it, or the parents tried to equalize things by leaving the poorer kids more, and the richer siblings felt neglected.

In a family with two writers, the legacy comes down to material. There are family stories I want to tell, and I assume she wants to tell them too. So in a sense, although it's unspoken, we're engaged in a race. Those stories will belong to whoever tells them first.

But I don't want to be forever locked with her in some mad battle for the Pole. (If Scott and Amundsen had been brothers, would the wise voice have said to them, Now, now, boys, the South Pole isn't going anywhere and there's enough of it to go around, what difference does it make who gets there first?)

The exploration metaphor isn't as facetious as it sounds, because that, after all, is what writing is: a process of exploration. When you begin working on a piece you know something of what you want to say, but you can't know everything. It's the sense of venturing into new territory that keeps you going. You must feel that the place is open and unexplored. You have to be free to surprise yourself.

When Edward Whymper was attempting to scale the Matterhorn in 1865, an Italian party was assaulting the mountain by a different route. They were just beneath the summit, perhaps a few hours' climb away, when they looked up and saw that the Swiss had already reached the top. So although they had been planning for years, climbing for days, the Italians turned back.

A mountain doesn't belong to anyone. It's nobody's birthright. But the people who grow up in its shadow dream of climbing it. And it happens that my sister and I grew up in the shadow of the same mountain.

And I know, I know: We're not talking about the South Pole here. We're not talking about the Matterhorn. The struggle for territory always looks silly and self-important to those not engaged in it. I watch my cat crouched in the driveway furiously staring down another cat who has dared to venture onto the asphalt, and I think, My God, you guys, get a grip on yourselves, it's only a *driveway.*

THERE IS SOMETHING shameful in these reflections. They deny the infinite variety of human experience. As my sister has so often reminded me, I am not her and she is not me. We see the world differently, and we are not the same writer.

Here is an example: She and I both spent the two years before high school in the same bizarre and fascinating place, as girl day students at a boarding school for dyslexic boys. There was one other girl in the school when I went there; when she was there it was slightly more coeducational, with five girls. I've always wanted to write about this experience, but as it happened, she got there first. There's a long section about the school in her most recent book. She told about being called upon in class to give "the female point of view"; she told of the humiliation of being asked by boys whether she wore a bra or used tampons. For her the experience was political; being at that school made her, at the age of twelve, a feminist. I was fascinated to read what she'd written; we had never really talked about the school, and I admired the clarity of her thinking. She had taken raw experience and made it mean something. Seeing it in print, though, made me realize that what it meant to her was different from what it had meant to me. When I think back on that school, I remember the loneliness of it, the other girl who was my friend only because neither of us had another choice, the teachers who were remote and stern and called us by our last names, the dark spruce trees, the frozen pond, the mournful Victorian air of the place. My memories are anecdotal, emotional; I'd like to write about them someday, and her having written her version does not close off the territory.

For a moment I can see quite clearly that there's plenty of South Pole to go around.

1993. MY FIRST NOVEL has just come out. I call my sister almost every day and she counsels patience: reviews will come, people will read it, readers will "get" it. It's a good book; why am I such a wreck?

I bristle at her cool tone. Doesn't she understand that I need my hand held? And we have another fight: I am holding your hand, she says impatiently, but you want me to hold it your way. You can't make up a script in your head and expect me to follow it.

Well. She arranges for me to do a reading at the Chicago bookstore where she works part-time. I fly out there still feeling miffed and haughty. When I arrive I find out that she's been sending notes to book review editors all over the country, telling them about my book.

"Why didn't you tell me?" I cry.

She shrugs.

The night of the reading, she stands up at the podium and introduces me. She makes extravagant comparisons to books and authors she loves; the things she says about my book are better than the dream reviews I compose in my head when I'm falling asleep at night. I stand up, and before I start to read she smiles at me, a huge, happy, holding-nothing-back kind of smile.

It's one of those moments of perfect reconciliation that happen all the time in novels but too seldom in real life.

WHAT REMAINS between us, the last fence dividing my garden from hers, is the question of genre. That is how we've split the territory: I've written fiction, and she's written nonfiction. So far.

But lately the boundaries have begun to blur. I'm writing this essay. And a few days ago she called me to broach, in an offhand, self-deprecating way, the idea for a novel she might want to write. "What do you think?" she wanted to know—asking for my opinion, but perhaps, also, for my permission.

"I think it sounds great," I said. "Exactly like the kind of book I'd want to read."

Somewhat to my surprise, I meant it.

Writing this essay, turning these thoughts over and exposing them to the light, has been tremendously calming. And that's the other reason I've come to feel so strongly that we both have to write whatever we want: writing is catharsis. You're trying to find the universal chords in anecdotal experience, but you're also working out what's bothering you, and neither of us can do it honestly with someone else breathing down our necks.

On the other hand, because we love each other, she and I will always be yoked together. As egregious as it is to have to keep asking permission, it's more important for me not to do anything that might hurt her.

So that's where we are. Writing is an anxious, greedy, furtive, solitary undertaking. It is jealous. It is competitive.

And we are both in it. We're in it together.

Donna Gordon

Temporary Shelter

IT'S 3 A.M. I'm sitting in a chair next to my older sister's bed in the emergency psych ward of Boston's Massachusetts General Hospital, waiting for a decision which will determine the next phase of her life. Not just tonight but the days that follow. Next to us, separated by only a thin partition, a man tied down at the ankles with leather restraints plays with his floppy penis under the sheet and shouts obscenities into the night. At the other end of the hall, an Asian woman whose face floats blankly upward into the whiteness of the ceiling, lies in coma after an overdose of barbiturates. I know these things because I've been here for several hours now, listening to the doctors jargoning back and forth, watching the repeat recording of vital signs. This is the waiting room for abandoned souls, for those temporarily dispossessed of their better judgment. You can almost feel the presence of the devil lying in wait for a chance to bid on their worst moment.

This endless waiting doesn't seem to phase my sister, whose longtime schizophrenia—untreated for the past twenty years—has already placed her life in a kind of parentheses. Financially dependent on meager monthly Social Security checks—and with the look and lifestyle of a bag lady—she barely gets by.

At forty—nearly two and a half years older than me—with her shorn hair and boyish physique, she looks like an aged Joan of Arc. She's sitting up in bed in one of those paper-thin white johnnies decorated with faint blue stars, her thin body folded in half at the waist, barely holding on to wakefulness.

Thirty-six hours ago, when fire struck her downtown rooming house—a dingy Beacon Hill establishment tucked invisibly into the elite row of brownstones owned by Boston's wealthiest Brahmins—she lost the small sanctuary that was all she had. Her tiny room was neat but filthy, with its stained bed and one small window taped over with layers of newspaper. Later, I learned from one of the Red Cross workers that the fire had begun at 5 A.M. in the room next door to hers, how she was screaming for help and had to be led down three flights of stairs like a child.

After spending that first night in an emergency Red Cross shelter, the following morning she was shown rooms that were more expensive than she could afford. It was then she wandered off and disappeared. Later that night we found her standing in front of her charred building, her thin silhouette nearly invisible in the winter dark, except for the flicker of cigarette ashes, somehow under the delusion that she could go back in.

She stayed with me and my husband and our eighteen-month-old son in Cambridge that night. I made a bed for her in the study with pillows and a blanket and kissed her good night like a child. The next morning I could see the sunken impression her body left on top of the covers where she had slept fully clothed. I invited her to stay with us through the weekend so that we could begin to look for a new room on Monday. But after breakfast, still disoriented and confused, she insisted on going back out on the street. Despite the fact that her things were gone, destroyed by the fire, and the building boarded up, she had all intentions of going back in.

I spent most of the day stalling, trying to distract her. I knew that even if she tried to leave, she wouldn't be able to find her way back downtown. It was early February in a season of unprecedented snowfalls, and we were expecting a major storm that night. She had been sitting in the same kitchen chair since ten o' clock that morning, one eye on the failing vertical hold of the TV screen showing *Brady Bunch* reruns and cartoons, and the other on the door. I had told her I would take her downtown, but was careful to keep it vague, not specify a time. Her ability to sit in one place for most of the day both comforted and disturbed me. Finally, after breakfast, lunch, and dinner had passed and it was growing dark, she stood up, went to the door, and insisted on a ride downtown, her seeming calm giving way to sudden anger. I agreed to drive her, provided she first go with me to the hospital to have someone make sure she was okay. "I want to make sure you're all right after the fire," I said. "You've been through a lot even though you don't think so." And though neither of us really believed she would willingly enter the hospital, we each needed a pretense to set things in motion, to get us out the door.

During the ride from Cambridge to Boston I was trying to think how I might talk her into actually going inside the hospital. When we pulled up in front, it was almost nine o'clock and dark. The emergency entrance was lit up brightly with orange lights, and a police cruiser sat parked next to an ambulance, its doors ajar. The air was cold and snow was just beginning to fall. My sister opened the car door and stepped out onto the curb, cupped her hands, and lit up a cigarette. She nodded to me, simply, almost sweetly. "See ya," she said, and then turned away and started crossing the street. For a few seconds I did nothing. I watched her cross the street and begin the slow climb up Beacon Hill on a wobbly diagonal, her huge clothes drowning her emaciated body in a wash of colorless gray. All along Cambridge Street cars were abandoned in the road on jagged snowbanks, and the walking space on the icy sidewalks had shrunken to a mere few inches. The snow swirled above us, and began to come down heavier, salting the sky.

In those few moments I had to ask myself who I was. Who

was I to reel her into what I believed was safety, and who was I to let her go? Then I just acted. I ran to catch up with her. In all the years between us, I had always been afraid to say *I love you.* I thought the words might hurt if I said them aloud. No one in my family had ever said them to me. But someone needed to say it to Linda finally. Suddenly I felt if she walked away into the night I might never have another chance.

I caught up with her. "Linda," I said, and she turned around. "I'm afraid I'll never see you again. I love you," I said, and I was crying. "Linda, I love you. Please come with me. You have no place to go."

She had tears in her eyes then. "You don't need to worry about me," she said. She stood still for a second, then took a drag on her cigarette. Her eyes seemed inhumanly large, the prettiest shade of blue surrounded by two floating islands of white. Her face was glazed, luminous. She turned and then quickly looked back, gave a small wave, and started walking up the hill toward the boarded-up rooming house.

HOSPITALIZING HER AGAINST her will involved bringing in the police. After she started walking away, I went into the emergency entrance and spoke to the doctor on call, who agreed, when I described the recent fire and her general disposition, that we should bring her in. I knew in some ways I was going against her privacy, her freedom. After all, how much had I successfully intervened on her behalf before? How much had I really been there for her? But it was painfully clear that she couldn't make decisions in her best interest that night.

I rode with two policemen in the back of the car and directed them up Hancock Street to where she had lived. Though fifteen minutes had already passed, she walked slowly, and from a distance I could make out the ghostly shape of her body wandering up the hill. The car pulled over and I called out to her. She turned around briefly and then continued walking. Then I ran to catch up to her. By now, the two policemen had gotten out of the car and were standing next to me, keeping a slight distance. They had a typewritten form I think they called a Section 8 that demanded she come with us. "Linda, if you don't come voluntarily, they'll make you," I said. Suddenly she seemed small, disarmed, in her oversize leather jacket and wool cap, a child wanting to cooperate, to be a good girl.

Checking into the hospital and changing her clothes, she was annoyed and made me turn away. I caught a glimpse of her curved emaciated torso in the mirror, the countable ribs and vanished breasts, usually hidden under several layers of clothes.

In her teens, my sister had been beautiful. She had a kind of softness added to her extraordinary beauty that stopped people on the street. She had voluptuous curves and a sensuality. And perhaps, worst of all, she believed in the power of these surfaces, she believed that her looks could bend someone's will. The result was a naive waiting game for happiness based on fairy-tale myths —marriage to someone both handsome and rich—that never came true.

In her early twenties, after dropping out of college from too much depression and too many drugs, she tried a handful of suicide attempts, so many that she was on a first-name basis with many of the doctors in Boston's best-known emergency rooms. The last attempt was nearly fatal. She was twenty-two and desperately seeking release from life. The doctor in the emergency room of Boston City Hospital phoned my mother in New Jersey and told her that my sister wasn't going to make it. But miraculously, she pulled through. She's been like this ever since—emotionless, eccentric, with something irrevocably broken inside.

While the nurse is taking my sister's vital signs, I call my mother in California to tell her about Linda's condition. I tell her that she will probably be hospitalized. "Don't do it," says my eighty-year-old stepfather in the background. "They'll throw away the key." But my mother understands. Nearly twenty years ago, when my sister was visiting my mother in New Jersey and shooting heroin into her veins, she got out of control and tried to attack my stepfather with a hammer. My mother had to call the police and have her hospitalized for ten days. It was a state institution and from what I gathered, pretty horrific.

Before agreeing to have the police pick her up, I spoke to the psychiatrist on call, a young woman, who assured me the hospitalization would only last until my sister had a place to stay. Besides, these days, at $1,000 a day, they don't put people like my sister in the hospital and throw away the key because the insurance companies won't pay for it. The best I can hope for is that she'll be off the street long enough for me to find her another place to live.

The doctor has come to interview my sister for several minutes. She calls her questions a test. Linda turns her back to me as if to say, this is none of your business. Then she is asked a series of detailed questions that have to do with her age, the date, who the president is, etc. "Where will you sleep tonight?" the doctor asks her again. "I'm concerned about your welfare," she says. My sister groggily mutters back: "I'm okay, I'm okay. It's not your concern." The doctor is kind but persistent. She asks several more factual questions, has my sister spell a word I can't hear backward, and then has her write down a random question. She thinks for a second and writes: *The floor is green.* My sister does surprisingly well on some things on this test, but overall, she unequivocally fails. The doctor takes me aside and tells me she is trying to get my sister into MacLean Hospital in Belmont tonight, the best mental hospital in the city. One of the goals of the hospitalization is to try to help my sister—who like so many others has slipped through the cracks—to get hooked up with mental health services again. But after two more hours and a handful of other emergencies, I am disappointed when she comes back and tells me that my sister's insurance has been turned down. Her Medicaid marks her as virtually untouchable, destitute, one of society's invisible breed. The hope for serious care that came with the possibility of her going to MacLean is gone. Instead, she'll be sent to a hospital called the Arbour in Jamaica Plain.

As the hours pass, and the paperwork is completed, all that's left to do is get her out the door. The doctor periodically comes back to try to talk my sister into willingly going into a hospital for the night, so that she won't have to force her into a straitjacket. Despite exhaustion, my sister holds her ground, refusing to fall asleep. "I'm all right," she says, "I'm all right. It's none of your affair."

FOR SEVERAL YEARS NOW, we've lived in almost the same city, she in Boston, me in Cambridge, separated only by the thin blue ribbon of the Charles River. As long as she lives here, I can never think of leaving. My mother and half sister live three thousand miles away in California. When I am in my sister's company, I feel a certain braveness, a sense of doing battle on her behalf with the rest of the world, the world that takes one look at her and either laughs or turns mean. When we're apart, and my life is almost normal, running its course with all of the responsibilities of home and family, I feel in some ways that despite all this, it is still a masquerade. I will never be myself, I will never be whole, I am still walking around with some part of me invisibly broken, longing for her return.

The daily world she depends on is small, encompassing Boston's downtown neighborhood of fast-food restaurants and five-and-dimes: Dunkin' Donuts, McDonald's, Woolworth's, the CVS. She doesn't know the time, fashions a calendar from notebook paper. Her toilet articles are always neatly laid out: comb, washcloth, soap. For years her letters have talked repeatedly about the nature of the planet and of God. Her reading materials are both impulsive and obscure, covering everything from heavy-metal music to antique dolls. She favors horror movies, laughs at the bloodiest parts when the heads are hacked off at the neck or when spikes are driven through the heart.

The tragedy of the fire was compounded by the tragedy of ignorance, of not knowing how to make her way in the tangible economic world. One of the reasons she wandered off was that the rooms Red Cross workers tried to show her at sixty and eighty dollars a week were too expensive compared to the thirty a week she had been paying for the past twelve years.

My sister is both stubborn and proud. There is no bargaining with her. Despite her illness, she almost always calls the shots. Once, several years ago when her rent had been increased by five dollars, she grew indignant, packed her few belongings in a shopping bag, and walked out into the street. Slow moving in huge clothes and oversize men's construction shoes that give her a lumbering dinosaur gait, my sister is an easy target, not just for lack of awareness but for lack of speed. As she walked the streets, searching for a new less expensive room, two teenage boys beat her up and stole all her things, then slashed her arm with a knife. The next day she returned to the old rooming house with her arm in a sling. The landlord felt sorry for her, reinstated her old rent, and never raised it again.

She literally has *no one,* no friends to say hello to, no one to call on the telephone. Her life is made up of a loneliness I couldn't imagine. Every once in a while my mind plays tricks on me, and I believe what I secretly want to: that she's really an actress perfecting her greatest role, a lifelong job which calls for a mixture of intelligence and absolute vacancy. Sometimes I look at her and think how we shared our mother's body, how we grew up so entirely close but separate. Now I wonder what secrets she might have left behind in her room that she wants so desperately to get back in. What could she possibly value?

Over the years we've gotten together about once every

month or two months, communicating by mail. We go to Legal Seafood for lunch, where she orders wine and something grand like lobster or filet mignon, and then eats with her fingers, keeping one glove on. When I got married two years ago I felt in a sense I was leaving my sister behind. When I had my son eighteen months ago, I felt, too, that I was abandoning my sister for a second time. Being with her is a study in patience, in everything we do: in ordering from a restaurant menu, in looking in stores in which every bag of jelly beans must be handled and examined. The holidays are her friends, all of the crass Hallmark paraphernalia: the Easter Bunnies and chocolate eggs, the Christmas Santas, the Valentine hearts. They have enormous appeal, as if they are the center of what's meaningful in life.

MY SISTER'S schizophrenia probably began in the early seventies when she was in high school. We lived in an Orthodox Jewish neighborhood, in an industrial town about forty-five minutes south of New York City, where we were among the small handful of nonreligious. My father had his own used-car business and my mother kept house. My father was your typical father of the period, silent and moody, with a defective heart that kept us quiet and kept him on medication. My mother was striving for perfection like so many other housewives of the time. She was the kind of mother who made green Jell-O and Shake 'n Bake chicken in the afternoon, while underneath it all, prepared and ready, she was wearing leopard print underwear to please my father later at night.

Our father died when my sister and I were nine and twelve. He had been through heart surgery in Bethesda and was recovering at home when my mother went to wake him one morning and found him dead. Three years later, my brother David, born during the year between the birth of my sister and of myself, died of pneumonia at fifteen. We woke one morning to find him splayed out on the bathroom floor, pale, in rigor mortis, his lungs exploded in hemorrhage.

Within weeks after the death of my brother, my sister's usual hypochondria intensified, and she insisted on being hospitalized. She believed that she had contracted both mononucleosis and hepatitis at once. Her eyes were yellow and jaundiced, and she was extremely depressed, but the diagnostic tests all came back negative and she was sent home.

The three of us—my mother, my sister, and myself—spent the years that followed as phantoms in our own house. I don't remember ever hearing any explanations about what had happened to the men in our family. I don't remember any explanations of loss. The darkness of my thoughts was all-consuming. I remember feeling responsible, relied upon, in a sense being asked to take my mother by the hand. I was her confidante and cheerleader; I sensed in myself endless emotional depths from which I could dig deep and administer comfort. I was my mother's fashion consultant and chef, I helped her cook dinner and pay the bills. Looking back, I feel sure I did some of these things out of concern and even need, but behind it all I realize suddenly that through all my scurrying to heal the wounds, to keep new wounds from happening, all the while that I was doing what I thought was helpful, in the back of my mind I was doing all those things in the simple hopes that I, too, would be loved.

During those early teenage years, the world suddenly went from round to flat. Because lives came and went around us, because we were offered no absolute explanation of reality, my sister and I were free to make up our own version. I think that this life of enforced illusions, of giving and taking away without explanation, led us to believe we could do anything without consequence, led us to believe that it didn't matter if we hurt ourselves, because on many levels we lived but didn't feel.

From the time we were in fifth and seventh grades, my sister and I stopped going to school. Somehow we learned early on that we could legally be absent forty-five days a year before being held back. The truant officer came to our house while our mother was at work, but we sent our huge German shepherd dog downstairs to bark, and never answered the door. Upstairs, in the vague rooms of our family house, that to me now resembles the house of ghosts, after my mother would leave for work, my sister focused on beauty rituals and on cleaning her room. I took the bus into New York City from our northern New Jersey town and walked the streets, meeting strangers on street corners and in Central Park, going to art museums, wasting time.

My mother seemed to grow youthful overnight. She abandoned her frumpy oxford shoes for heels and dyed her hair blond. She joined a social group called Parents Without Partners, and on Wednesday nights and weekends went out on dates. She was a good dancer and had silver and gold gowns with matching metallic shoes. She was pretty and youthful with her girlish ambitions intact.

As young women, my sister and I were taught to follow our mother's example—an example which she inherited from her mother—to believe that if we were pretty enough, our respective princes would come. Only years later did I come to understand that this belief in our beauty was a belief in our powerlessness. I wish I had known then what I know now. Instead, we tragically convinced ourselves that we would be unworthy of love if we weren't saved suddenly and completely in a fairy-tale way. Even now, as I read my son the story of *Snow White*—which I think he loves more for the characters of Grumpy and the Wicked Queen than for anything else—I rewrite it aloud and throw the old version away. I don't tell him about jealousy or hatred, or about how beauty can sweep us away. Instead, we talk about love, how Snow White loves the animals in the woods, how the dwarfs come to love her, how when people help one another there is always a way. In the end, he still wants the Wicked Queen to give Snow White the poison apple so that she can fall asleep and he can pretend to be the prince and wake her up. But he doesn't think he is saving her. It is just a game.

I think my mother viewed my sister's early strangeness as a kind of supernatural mysticism, a superiority that extreme beauty somehow grants. Beauty like that somehow strikes us as immutable. I think my mother was afraid of looking too hard, for fear of finding something she wouldn't be able to comprehend. She had grown up close to an older sister who had tormented her from childhood into her late teens, until it became clear—after she threw money in the garbage and did an assortment of other seemingly abnormal things—that something was terribly wrong.

The devices that were supposed to be in place to help, failed. My sister's high school teachers let her slide, trying their best to push her through the system. Her therapist in college seduced her. Countless men used her. She used to say you could judge a man's character by his shoes, by the style and how he wore them in.

As a child and teenager, it was easy to overlook my sister's illness because I didn't really know it existed. When we were young children she was sharp-tongued and mean, puritanical, giving orders. She insisted I play the obedient student while she was the proper schoolmarm. It was my job to be the responsive child while she played a severe mother administering castor oil and aspirins.

As I grew older, my sister was increasingly guarded and refused to admit any disturbance to the family. When she left home for college in Boston, where she attended Boston University and then dropped out after little more than a year, she insisted on living in an apartment alone, rather than in a dormitory on campus. I visited her there once and saw that she kept a Doberman pinscher and a boa constrictor in her tiny room, sinister animals bred to protect and destroy. But as far as she was concerned, everything was fine. As the years passed, she was so abrasive and angry if we inquired after her health or finances that we stopped believing we could help or make a difference. My mother's way of demonstrating her concern was to become a faithful correspondent, writing letters and sending her extra money, and making the trip from California once a year for ten days.

I grew up with only a shadowy definition of "family." Soon after I got married and my husband began to talk about the idea of having children, I could only haltingly respond. I often wondered to myself why it was I didn't want to have children of my own, why it never really occurred to me. And then slowly after I decided to go ahead and have my son, I realized that I had already twice felt the responsibility of being a parent, first with my mother and later with my sister, whose illness, however vague and undefined, had infiltrated my soul when we were much younger children. Now that I have had a child of my own, I'm beginning to understand the enormous capacity that women keep in reserve. It takes far more than I ever realized to give birth, to mother a child, and to reinstate one's self back into life with a new, far more complex identity.

WHEN I KNEW that my sister would have to be forcibly taken to the hospital in a straitjacket, the doctor gave me the option to leave. I couldn't bear to have that memory of her being taken against her will left to replay itself in my mind. By 5 A.M. everything was in place to take her to another hospital. I felt cowardly abandoning her at her worst moment. I walked out of the hospital in a daze and watched a private ambulance pull up in front. Four huge men the size of bodyguards got out. When I realized they were there to take my sister, I cried in the cab all the way home.

She was in the hospital for fourteen days. I visited her every other day and called her on the days I couldn't come. The morning after she was hospitalized, there was a huge snowstorm in Boston, a foot high, paralyzing the roads. I felt a little relieved that I had made the right decision because in this weather out on the street alone she never would have survived.

When I went to see her the next day at the hospital I brought her coffee and cigarettes. She was angry and determined to stay isolated. None of the staff people, except for those involved in admitting her, had even bothered to ask her her name. All she could say was that she didn't belong there and that it was a court case, meaning she thought she had grounds to sue someone. She repeatedly said: "I'm waiting for them to close my case."

"Linda," I said, "in order for them to close your case, we have to find a new place for you to live."

"It's none of your affair," she said to me, and grew silent again. I changed the subject and asked her about her room and she said she hadn't been in it. She didn't seem to know where anything was. I spoke with one of the mental health workers at the desk and he said that she had been sitting in that same chair since she arrived and had refused to talk to anyone.

Lunch was being served: chicken chow mein with egg rolls. She was so weak she couldn't lift the tray of food off the cart. I sat with her in the dining room that doubled as a crafts and TV room while she had lunch. The huge windows overlooked the newly fallen snow. "What do you think of the snowstorm?" I said. "Oh, did it snow?" she said blankly. I introduced myself to people who worked there during that shift, the nurses and social workers, so that despite what they might have thought, I made sure they knew that someone was looking out for her. I thought that my normalcy might help buy her decent care.

As I visited with her over the next few days, two more snowstorms followed in a hush of whiteness that covered the earth. As I watched her interact with this society of people similar to herself and worse, keeping track of their moves out of the corner of her eye, steering clear of outbursts and merging with the shadows, I saw how she moved in and out of their world like a veteran. And I realized how she had, unbeknownst to me, learned to cope in this world, one that despite its odd layers of frailty involved degrees of cunning and self-protection.

The patients on one of the hospital's locked wards, were a little scary as they walked the halls licking their tongues, muttering the same word repeatedly, drawing ominously close to strangers, using foul language. Each time I visited, the same young man with long dark hair and black eyes accosted me and called me by what he believed was my name: Mary Magdalene. It was an ominous environment, understaffed, a place in which time could literally stop and it wouldn't matter. The social worker assigned to my sister's case confided that though she had taken some of the medication prescribed, there was little hope of improvement. She was, as he described it, a burned-out schizophrenic. This seemed to me a subtle means of telling me that her value to society was zero.

At first, my sister didn't want me to get involved in helping her find a new place to live. She kept saying it was none of my affair. The social worker was interested in moving her through the system and out. In order to close her case, I needed to find her another place to live. If I couldn't find a place before she was discharged, she would find herself back on the street.

Through the Red Cross, I obtained a list of rooming houses and started calling them one by one. Single rooms were not easy to come by. Unlike apartments, they're primarily taken up by the sick and transient, those without money and those without long to live. Many of the phone numbers I had gotten for rooming houses were already obsolete. Finally, I located a building on the same street where my sister had lived, a clean building with an expected vacancy in about a week. I went to look at it that afternoon and put down a deposit. The rent was higher, more than three times what she had been paying, but somehow we would work it out.

Two days later, about halfway through my sister's stay, I arrived at the hospital and my sister's hair was clean and combed for what was probably the first time in several months, and her clothes had been washed. She looked more vibrant. We had gotten a pass from her doctor to go downtown and show her the room. After several minutes of paperwork and some confusion, we were ready to go. All the patients in her locked ward had items of clothing considered personally dangerous taken away. Both my sister's shoelaces and her belt had disappeared from the locked cabinet. One of the nurses located the lost-and-found box and we got some other shoelaces. My sister used two safety pins to hoist up her pants.

The sun was shining on the snow and the sky was blue for the first time in days as we drove along the Jamaicaway past the icy pond. Downtown, we parked and went across the street to take a look at the room. It was much nicer than her old place with a twin bed and a desk and chair. She agreed to take it right away. When she asked how much the rent was, I told her it was the same as the old place, thirty a week, though it was really a hundred. It was worth the extra money just to know she was in a safe place.

Our agreement with the social worker at the hospital was that she was to stay there five more days until the room was ready. Then later that day I unexpectedly got a phone call telling me they were going to release my sister to a shelter, the Pine Street Inn, the next day. I was angry and argued with the social worker, telling him that they couldn't do that, she had nowhere to go. "All the time she spent in the hospital will be a waste if you send her back out on the street now," I said. "We don't have a choice," the social worker said. "Her insurance won't cover her any longer."

I insisted on speaking with her doctor, who had never returned any of my phone calls in the past two weeks. He finally called me late that night and was both coldhearted and rude. "Why do you bother to get involved now?" he said. "The time to do something was twenty years ago. You could of course pay the thousand dollars a day yourself."

Because his opinion was that she was neither suicidal nor in danger of hurting anyone else, they had no grounds for holding her and threw her out on her ear.

Furthermore, and the thing that really bothered me, was that she had insisted that she was okay, she had insisted on going to the shelter rather than staying where she was. I called her the following morning to make sure she understood that she was being discharged to the Pine Street Inn that day. As usual she was emotionless, monosyllabic. "Make sure you call me over the next few days so I know where you'll be," I said, and she agreed.

I was devastated to see that after all this time spent trying to get her back on her feet, she was choosing to put herself right back out on the street. So a few hours later, when I got a call from the Pine Street Inn asking me to pick her up, I was surprised. Her timing was bad. I couldn't bring her back home. Her presence made my son hysterical because she refused to acknowledge he existed. Not only was my husband going through an intensely stressful period at work, but it was a very stressful time in our marriage. I agreed to pick her up and take her to an inn, a bed-and-breakfast nearby, which I had discovered early on in the process of making phone calls and looking for a room.

The Pine Street Inn, to which the hospital had discharged her in a cab, was big and overcrowded. It struck me as a holding pen for the ominous. The place was a little frightening, filled with homeless men and women with filthy clothes and surprisingly new-looking sneakers donated by the city's Good Samaritans. It struck me almost as death's halfway house, a near last stop. Situated at the end of the Mass Pike and the entrance to

Route 93, it dead-ends in a gray place of intersecting ramps that looks a little like the end of the world.

Linda was waiting for me at the door, somehow poised above it all, almost as if she were Audrey Hepburn hailing a cab. We drove to Cambridge over the Charles River. The lights of the city made me feel the world was alive though I felt a little dead inside. I looked over at her and she was relaxed, breathing deeply, her freedom intact. I took her to the Irving House, an old New England inn just a few blocks away from me where she would be safe and independent for the next several days while we waited to move into her new room. It was a bed-and-breakfast, much like a youth hostel, with affordable rates and filled with students. I pointed out the stores in the neighborhood and helped her set the bedside clock. She was worried about whether the plug alone could keep it running on time.

Five days passed quickly. I visited with her every day, gradually replacing some of the things she had lost. She never left the room by herself. I think she felt safe in the small room with its white bedspread and two small prints of Paris streets. She tried my patience in various ways—for instance, by taking a good hour to try on every single belt in the men's department of DeCelle's.

The day we checked into her new room, we walked in carrying only one small bag. Later, we took a walk up the hill to the old house. It was still boarded up, now with a For Sale sign in front, proof finally that part of her past was gone.

Now we're trying to put her life back together by replacing the simple things she had lost: a belt, a new pair of shoelaces, a radio, a watch, a new pair of pants, a sheet and blanket for her bed. I offer to buy her a green plant, a living thing, but even this is too much responsibility.

Most of all I wonder how she can live with such loneliness. I close my eyes and try to imagine the workings of her mind. I imagine myself deaf, dumb, blind, perhaps with some fragmented memories of childhood. Every once in a while she'll remember something, some small kindness or connection to the natural world. But mostly she draws a blank. What we share in common now is this: we've been through something together and we both know it. I've seen some of the danger she faces, and she's seen how I will try to help her in any way I can. Maybe that experience has created some kind of foothold for each of us, something we can look at inside ourselves and say we understand. I know that one day I will probably get another phone call with news like this or worse. But in the meantime, we've reestablished what we had perhaps too quickly forgotten: our sense of trust and family. Despite the fact that the world takes one look at her and keeps going, for a while now at least, she's found a place from which she doesn't have to hurry and move on.

Lucy Grealy

The Other Half

1.

MY SISTER SARAH is ten minutes younger than I am, making me the older sister, something I lorded over her for years. Until we were about nine, it seemed perfectly logical to me that when I died, Sarah would automatically die ten minutes after me. After convincing her of this obvious truth, we tried to come up with complex plans about how she could be notified immediately upon my death, walkie-talkies perhaps?, and so know that she had exactly ten minutes left. I was very jealous of this: I wanted to be the one to have my life filled with such sudden, however brief, urgency. At night, I used to lie in the bed next to hers and imagine such a momentous gift. When I became seriously, possibly fatally ill at the age of nine, we forgot all about this plan. Not because it suddenly seemed indecorous or even too close to the bone, but my life suddenly gained that urgency I'd been up until that moment living out through her.

My illness offered to me the self-definition and self-knowledge that previously I'd sought out, through the negative, from being a twin. Paradoxically, it was just as the myth of the twin began to crumble for me that it became most intriguing to others. How could having a twin and such a serious problem affecting one's appearance not affect me? Had Sarah been my identical twin, things would have been different, I'm sure, but because she isn't, it's the myth of the twin itself which rises to the surface, exposes itself. People simply cannot let it alone, simply cannot believe that, armed with a twin yet blighted with a singular disfigurement, I am neither advantaged nor disadvantaged (it is interesting that people cannot decide which it is) to know my own self and fate in greater depth. There is something rather moving, ultimately, in this need to know who we are, in the extremes of meaning we are willing to go in order to believe that it is possible to know who we are.

If we are not lucky enough to have a twin, then we are lucky enough to have an imagination that can ponder the twin. If we do not see who we are in the flesh, there are still those uncertain dreams we wake from at night, that almost-seen face which faded just before we could make out whose it was. There are all those songs about strangers on the dark ends of streets, all those startling moments when we are rushing down the street and see someone beside us and turn, only to recognize our own selves in the storefront glass. All those moments of love when we say, "You're just like me in that way," those moments of fear when we feel we are losing sight of ourselves. Even if we have to invent our twin either in the form of a myth or experience her in the realm of intense longing, our twin winks at us from across the room to tell us "You're over here."

People are always surprised I have a twin. "Really?" they ask, almost suspiciously. "You never told me that before." They eye me as if I've just accidentally slipped and revealed some clandestine past, displayed for them at last the tip of that mysterious iceberg heretofore known as me. "A-ha," they might actually say, and I can see them mentally rubbing their hands together, certain they have uncovered the missing clue, are about to glimpse the bottom of my essential nature.

If they had a twin, people assume they would understand something better about themselves. They would have a flesh-and-blood mirror to look in and see themselves. They would never be lonely. They would know what Plato was talking about when he spoke of "the missing half" of ourselves. They would finally get to the bottom of all this "nature versus nurture" business. They would know what it was to look into the eyes of the Other. There would always be someone who remembered their birthday; they'd possess a reasonable idea of what they looked like from behind. Everything that is missing would come together. Everything would be whole.

The difference in mine and Sarah's twinhood from that of other twinhoods has not so much to do with what happened to me when I was nine, when I got jaw cancer, but with the story I told about it afterward, the book I wrote about growing up with a face different from everyone else's. My publisher sent me from bookstore to bookstore to give readings, and after each reading came a question and answer period. Soon I learned to expect the question:

"You say so little about your twin sister, why is that?"

This could be asked with a tone of concern—obviously I am not in touch with an important aspect of my psyche. Or it could be asked with something approaching accusation: I am withholding obviously critical information.

I could never, or at least not in the arena of the podium of a crowded bookstore, get across to my inquisitor that the real story is that there is no story, at least not the one they're looking for, the simple story of parts that click together and create a pleasing, distinguishable form. I can't blame them. Who wouldn't want such a story?

2.

FROM THE BEGINNING I knew I would write about how my sister did not mean for me the things other people told me she should. The essay, then, wanted to be about this lack, about how meaning resists the molds we want to pour it into. But that was what the essay wanted; what I wanted was something different. Without even knowing it, I wanted the essay to be about how I *do* want my sister to mean something extraordinary, something difficult and beautiful to me. Even now, as I type, this essay wants my yearning to enable me to render my sister in precise terms, wants my desire to take on the shape of something that vaguely resembles me. But what I know, and what the world and even this essay do not know, is that really this essay is about *not* having a twin, about how there can't possibly be a correlation between me and my twin because if there were, how could the world leave me to experience moments of such intense loneliness? How could such a thing happen? How could the world, my sister, this essay, leave me high and dry like that?

And yet we do have a history, a childhood together.

My mother and father, who already had three well-grown children by the time Sarah and I arrived, always introduced us with "and this is Sarah and Lucy." When we were instructed to do things, it was "Sarah and Lucy come here, Sarah and Lucy go to bed, Sarah and Lucy, time to eat your dinner." Accustomed to distinguishing themselves from others, familiar with separation both in label and, often all too painfully, in life, this was a natural and convenient way for adults to speak to and about us. No one thought much about it until one day, I don't know how young I was, someone asked me while alone what was my name. I responded, so I am told, that my name was Sarah and Lucy.

Sarah and I took baths together when we were small. She was afraid of the end with the drain, afraid she was going to get sucked down it and into the netherworld of her nightmares below. My brothers encouraged her in this, teasing her by pursing their lips together and making deep sucking sounds. At that sound, I could see the fear come into her face, I could hear the sounds of self-congratulatory delight in my brothers' shrieks, and if I'd been just a bit older, my external social choices would have been clear: side with her and tell them to stop, or side with them and tease her even more. But I had my own watery abyss nightmares to deal with, and my actual choice was this: be Just Like Her, or not. I took a deep breath and slid my naked body over toward that fascinating hole.

From the very start, Sarah and I were opposites. Even at birth, she weighed a full pound more than I did: the nurses at the hospital called us Laurel and Hardy. I try to explain this contrariness to my bookstore questioners in the hopes they will settle for an answer of two people so perfectly opposite that these differences themselves are perfectly balanced and symmetrical. My choices against Sarah continued throughout childhood. We chose separate friends, preferred different games, aspired toward different states of being, she always seeking accordance and outward displays of affection, while I picked fights and became known as a loner.

I knew all along I was developing as my own person while at the same time I was acutely aware that my choices were informed, however negatively, by Sarah's. Our family was not a particularly open one to begin with, so Sarah and I's estrangement not only went unnoticed by the rest of the family, it seemed perfectly normal. When I got cancer, this was merely the final straw, not the ultimate chasm. People who read my book and notice Sarah's absence think my illness was the great divide between us, but in truth it was the great metaphor.

3.

ONE THING THAT intrigues both scientists and sensationalists alike is the idea that twins are sometimes known to form their own secret languages. There is a story in my family about Susie and the Spider. Susie is our older sister and for a short while, when we were only two and Susie was eight, the three of us shared a room together.

The point of the family story is that a spider was crawling on the wall near Susie's head while she was still asleep. Sarah and I woke her and pointed it out to her, and, much to our entertainment, she started screaming so loud my mother had to run in and capture it in a pair of Susie's underwear, which in her panic she then threw out the window.

Another part of the story, though, is that Sarah and I clearly remember being awake in our cribs next to each other for a long time before we woke Susie, discussing the various options at our disposal. It was a complex discussion, involving many conjectures and much reasoning, and, in retrospect, was far more subtle and thorough than our English language abilities at the time could possibly have allowed. We remember that discussion very clearly, but we have no memory of what tongue we actually spoke it in. If we did not have each other to verify that this conversation actually took place, if would be easy to ascribe various tricks of memory as an explanation for believing something that otherwise couldn't possibly be true.

I never tell people this part of the story, the part of our conversation. I never tell it because I don't know what it means, I don't know what *really* happened, and I know that other people, not just people who aren't twins but people who just simply aren't me, would immediately assume that they did.

4.

MY FACE, the lower half of it anyway, is a made thing. A partial mandiblectomy and years of reconstructive surgery have completely shorn from me an image of what my face was "supposed" to look like. It's taken me this long into the writing of this essay to bring this up as an issue because I don't want people to think that what my twin sister represents for me is the alternate version of the person I'd have become, or at least looked like, had I never had cancer. I don't want this to be part of my story, her story, our story. Partly, this is denial that something tragic happened to me, but mostly it is my innate knowledge that the story (the story of my having a twin) is really about something very different from what other people think it is about. I cannot articulate exactly what it is about, at least not with the language I have, not with the process of thinking about it which I employ at this moment, but I don't want people to step into this perceived gap and fill it with their own ideas and theories.

I remember once walking to elementary school with Sarah. We did this every day for years, until I stopped going to school because of my illness. One day we walked in the leaves of a late autumn, wet leaves because it had rained all night, kicking them along, me looking for an earthworm or bug I could shake at Sarah. The sky was growing darker, it looked like it might rain again within the next hour. Why we are suddenly moved to do these things I don't know, but there was something about the sky darkening over our heads, something about the way the birch trees looked whiter against this sky than usual, something about how the usual neighborhood sounds were muffled, but suddenly I was moved to look at Sarah and realize that I did not know who she was. At the time, I annoyed her by repeating to her over and over, "You're my sister, you're my sister." I did not really know what I was feeling, though I did know that it was not unpleasant, I did know that it was something important. It was a profound sense of distance from her, a keen unknowing of who this person walking beside me was, how we two, by pure chance it seemed, fit into the world together.

• • •

5.

WHEN WE WERE about ten my father bought me a stuffed gorilla while I was in the hospital and told me not to tell Sarah because she might get jealous. Not long after I got home, I just couldn't keep it to myself anymore.

"You see this gorilla? Daddy gave this to me and he told me not to tell you because he wasn't giving you one."

We were in the middle of some gathering fight which had not yet erupted, but the tension was there. This bit of gorilla information seemed like the perfect weapon against, or, actually, for, the display of anger I knew was coming. Sarah has big, obvious buttons which are easy to press and I loved to press them, to see the sparks fly. Temperamentally, we've always been eerily dissimilar to each other. I am calm and slow to anger; Sarah is the proverbial firecracker. I am brave; Sarah is a scaredy-cat. I like to be alone; Sarah is very social. I am very quiet; Sarah is talkative.

I threw this gorilla grenade at her and, to my surprise, rather than yelling at me, hitting me, storming out of the room, she was quiet. She looked at me with her big open blue eyes, eyes almost, but not just like, mine, and I watched them start to fill with tears. She looked at me as if she had never seen me before, and, in doing so, offered an image of herself, and of myself, that I had never seen before. For most of my life I'd been trying to hurt Sarah, get back at Sarah, provoke Sarah, and for most of her life she'd been trying to do the same to me. Now, for the first time, I saw that I affected Sarah. The curtains were yellow and I noticed they were blowing in the window, and the usual clutter on the floor was the usual clutter, but somehow I recognized it as being part of the scene, part of the room I was in, part of the life I was living. Sarah was part of this life too, part of my life, but for the first time I consciously registered her as having her own life, her own version of herself, her own version of me. The room was quiet except for the gentle rasping sound the curtains made against the windowsill and the obnoxious snorting the dog was making as she suddenly felt the need to chew on her leg. Something had just happened, but neither one of us knew what. We sat there and stared at each other until the next everyday thing happened and drew us back yet again into our lives.

Jesse Lee Kercheval

Earth

1972

MY SISTER KAY and I were on the roof waiting for a moon rocket to blast off. This is not a science fiction story. We were waiting up to see the last Apollo mission, the only one to leave the earth at night.

It was supposed to go up at ten, then around eleven, but the countdown kept getting stopped, the launch time delayed. At first, most of the mothers and kids in the neighborhood were on top of their houses. The fathers were at the Cape, trying to get the rocket up. But by the third time the countdown was stopped, the mothers were gone, sure the whole thing was going to get scrubbed.

On this night, I was fourteen and Kay was sixteen. We had lived in Cocoa, Florida, five years, about a third of our lives. Our house was only a block from the Indian River, and on the other side of the river was Cape Kennedy. The Cape was such a big tourist attraction that the Rocket Motel once put up a sign that announced: "Secret Spy Satellite Launch, 6 pm today." But for us, the day shots, with their skinny trails of vapor stretching across the blue playground sky, weren't much anymore. Not unless, like the fifty-million-dollar Mars probe, the rocket went up and up and then started down and down, and they had to blow it up, all those monkeys and mice gone in an instant.

At least that's what we heard. Kay and I didn't know as

much about this as a lot of kids because their fathers all worked at the Cape while ours was the vice-president of the local junior college. Our car didn't have a back window obscured by Saturn, Gemini, and Apollo stickers, and our mother didn't have hysterics when she heard that Gus Grissom had burned up on the pad.

But this was not just any shot. Anyway to me it seemed like a good excuse to stay up all night while our mother slept right under our butts. My father was still at the office, working late on some interminable important report. He never came home unless he had to. He even kept an extra electric shaver in his desk. I closed my eyes and imagined my parents' dark cherry wood bed, my mother completely unnaturally still. When we were little, she used to yell out in her sleep—*No no no!* But by this night, she was on twenty milligrams of Valium a day, was mixing it with bourbon, and so didn't do that or much else anymore.

Up on the roof, the countdown resumed. The mosquitoes were bad so I turned off my flashlight, and we sat without talking in the humid dark. Kay turned up the radio and we squirmed on the warm asphalt tiles. Below us, though it was too dark to see, was a grove of old orange trees, half choked with Spanish moss, where I used to climb and get chiggers before I had better things to do, and beyond that the warm shallow water of the Indian River. It stank. Even for someone who was used to the way it smelled, tonight it stank.

My biology teacher had explained it was not really a river, with a current down the middle, but a tidal estuary, a wide shallow puddle of brackish water. The current, such as it was, was around the sides, just where the Army Corps of Engineers had built the causeway to the Cape. There, algae and weeds sank and rotted, sending up fat sulfurous bubbles.

Sometime after twelve, Kay said she was giving up. She had never been able to stay up late. Not at Girl Scout camp, not even at slumber parties where the penalty for falling asleep was having your face painted green with eye shadow or your bra frozen in a solid block of ice. But I begged her to stay, afraid I would have to go in too. She was only twenty-one months older than I was, but she worried about me. She thought she was my mother. Or at least, she thought somebody should be.

Kay opened her mouth to say something—*Yes, I will stay? No, I won't?* But in the same instant that I realized that I could see her mouth, pink lips, white teeth, and thought to wonder where the light was coming from, I knew. The rocket was blasting off. It was like the sun, it was so bright. The red spread out across the river, into the sky. All around me, I could see colors, the green leaves of the orange trees, the white of their blossoms, the yellow of the oranges themselves, mottled with sooty black mildew. Above the flame, the sky turned blue. Birds began to sing in the trees. Somewhere, a dog barked.

Then the sound hit us, an ungodly roar, a sound so loud it made my bones itch, louder and more total than any rock concert I had yet been allowed to go to. Kay and I were on our feet, hugging each other, spinning dangerously on the sloped roof, our blond heads bright in the night. Kay was shouting and I was shouting, although we couldn't hear our own voices. As the red and gold trail burned through the sky, heading downrange, we tracked it with our eyes. Our bodies leaned forward, longing to follow.

Then, in the fading light, we saw who was on the next roof, Gary Heck and the Mize boys, one my age, two older than Kay. And over them a cloud of smoke. They were smiling and waving a bottle at us, and they were obviously stoned. All over Brevard County people were either stoned or selling or sorting or smuggling pot. It was at that moment the drug capital of the United States. But somehow, this had left my life untouched. Partly that was Kay's doing. Or maybe all her doing.

"Oh, it's just Julie Watts," I heard one of them say my

name, mocking me for not being with them. I had already made it through my first two years of high school without ever being allowed in the rest room, dealer central. Among other things, it was going to ruin my bladder for life. But they didn't mock Kay. Somehow, they respected the fierceness of her convictions. She did not drink, smoke, take drugs, or chew gum, because they were all bad for your voice, and she was serious about her voice. But that night, for just one second Kay started to lift her hand, wave back, but then, as the roar faded, she didn't. The light died.

Then we were off the roof and inside the air-conditioned silence of the house where our mother was sleeping. Kay was shaking her head, her fine arched nose a study in determination. I thought her nose was beautiful. I thought she was beautiful and strong. She was the one who demanded that we act like a family, put up a Christmas tree, eat in the dining room on Thanksgiving, when my father would rather stay at his office, I in my room, my mother in her bed. I loved her more than anything in the world. "Remember," she said, "a Watts doesn't do things like that."

THE NEXT NIGHT was the opening of the Cocoa High School production of *Oklahoma!* Kay was singing lead alto. This was not a named part. She had been going to try out for the female lead, but Mr. Bright, her chorus teacher whom she loved with all the fierce loyalty of which she was capable, told her he needed her in the chorus. Where would he be, he said, without his lead alto? Probably he said this looking into her eyes, maybe with one hand on her shoulder, thumb resting at the base of her neck. He touched when he talked and kissed people hello and goodbye. I imagined Kay nodding, agreeing with whatever he said.

Because of rehearsals, Kay had been gone at night for weeks and weeks. She'd wandered around the house singing the alto parts to "Surrey with the Fringe on Top" until the soprano parts, which carry the melody, sounded weird to me. She'd gotten my father to pay for a pink gingham dress and white petticoat. Mr. Bright had also declared everyone had to wear boots, lest the production lack authenticity. Kay had very narrow feet (7AAAA) and so had had to mail-order boots. They arrived, finally. Too late for the dress rehearsal, too late for even me to see them, but in time for this, the opening night.

My father came home at five for the first time in months to get ready. My mother got up and after some prompting got dressed. *Oklahoma!* was being staged in the Multitorium of my father's junior college. It was a Multitorium, my father had explained, because the Baptists in the legislature up in Tallahassee had forbidden the use of state money to build theaters. But it had red plush theater seats, even an orchestra pit, and orange, pink, and green carpet my father had picked because he figured it would never show stains or wear.

An usherette, a girl from the junior chorus, showed us our seats. My father, my mother, me, and Kay's boyfriend Jeff. It was the first time Jeff had ever done anything with our family. Kay had arranged this, making my father buy the extra ticket. It felt very significant, also odd. I sat there hoping people who didn't know better would think Jeff was my date. He had light brown hair and was thought cute, although what Kay seemed to like best about him was that he was diabetic and had to shoot himself up with insulin twice a day. She found this tragic and appealing.

The school band began the overture. The curtain went up to reveal hay bales, a front porch that was not attached to any house. Tonti Treppler, our future homecoming queen, sang tenderly of the absent Bill Larson, our class president. Bill danced up behind her in cowboy boots. Tonti turned, swinging her skirt. They were playing at being in love. But since elementary school Tonti and Bill had heartily disliked each other, a fact that everyone but Mr. Bright knew, so it was not good casting. I yawned, waiting for Kay. Jeff stirred restlessly beside me and my mother was asleep, slumped discreetly in her seat. Something I hoped Jeff didn't notice. Where was Kay?

Finally, the chorus started singing, low, offstage. I heard Kay's voice. I could always hear her voice. I told her this once, after her first chorus concert back in junior high, thinking it was a compliment, but she was furious. "You did not," she said. "The mark of a good alto is that it *blends.*" Still, I heard her. Each note clear and strong as across the back of the stage, behind the hay bales, the chorus came trooping. Then I saw her and my heart stopped.

Someone, in a hurry to make up the whole cast, had sprayed her long blond hair a sticky gray to kill the shine and drawn a single dark eyebrow across her forehead above her long nose. The pink calico dress looked fine, was just Kay's color or would have been if her hair were its usual blond. The real problem was her boots. Big, mud brown, they looked more like waders than cowboy boots. The chorus hoedowned across the stage, arms swinging, deep in song, but all anyone could hear were Kay's boots. *Clump, thud, clump, thud.* Beside me, Jeff froze in his seat. I felt my face turning red. *Clump.*

Kay had made a terrible mistake. I watched, sweating with a sympathy so strong it was if we were twins, or even the same person. Then I remembered stepping off the bus on my first day of junior high wearing ankle socks instead of little invisible tan footies, people staring, and I felt a flash of anger toward Kay. She was my older sister. She had certain responsibilities. She should have warned me about wearing footies. And she shouldn't have worn those ugly, ugly boots. She had been my only protection, and now I could feel her social standing dropping like a thermometer in an ice bath. All around me, people were laughing.

Thud. Behind Kay in line was Lulu Felton, a fat, legally

blind girl in thick tinted glasses who was obviously moving her mouth without singing, a clear proof of what the standards for being part of this chorus were. Lulu and Kay passed with lowered eyes behind the beautiful Tonti. *Clump.* I shook my head, unbelieving. Kay trusted Mr. Bright, adored and adoring teacher, and he had done this to her. Lulu stepped on Kay's heels.

The chorus crossed into the wings, disappeared. The boots echoed back: *Thud.*

A SOUND AT my window woke me. Someone was knocking on one of the jalousies as if it were the door. "Julie!" I cranked open the window, almost catching whoever was there in the head. It was Jeff. He was standing with a flashlight in one hand. When he and Kay had left for the opening-night party, he'd looked faintly embarrassed to be seen with her. Now it was late and he just looked worried.

"Um, hi," he said. "Your sister isn't feeling very well." I stood there for a moment, warm air pouring in through the window. I considered that I might be dreaming. Then I heard the central air cut on.

"Give me a minute," I said.

He told me Kay was down on our dock. He turned on his flashlight and I followed him. Actually the dock was not our dock. It belonged to the neighborhood civic association. That was to say, to all the people who lived in our subdivision who kept up with their annual dues. One summer, the fathers (but not my father) had gotten together and built it out of pilings that Mr. Heck, who worked for the phone company, stole. A long flight of stairs led down a steep overgrown bank to the stinking water.

I found Kay hanging off the end of the dock, throwing up. Jeff's flashlight flickered over an amazing array of empty bottles. I caught sight of a couple of labels—Strawberry Ripple, vodka. He kicked one of the bottles into the water. "It was quite a party." He sounded proud of Kay.

"Yeah," Kay said, her voice echoing from under the dock. It sounded remarkably cheerful. Then she gagged and was sick again. I knelt and took one of Kay's ankles. Jeff took the other. We sat looking down into the water. After a while Jeff told me a math puzzle he had been working on. I was hopeless in math. I couldn't understand a word he was saying, but that didn't seem to matter. The puzzle was from a book of mathematical puzzles. He told me another.

The river was so dark, the stars reflected in it looked like they were hung in some second black sky. Looking down was so much like looking up that only the warmth of Kay's ankle in my hand gave me any sense of direction. I had no idea what time it was. Jeff was on his fourth puzzle when the cops pulled up, shined a spotlight out over the water. Jeff's voice died in midword. One of the cops called out, "Who's there?" I opened my mouth, but it was Kay who answered, her voice clear and strong.

"Members of the Sunset Heights Civic Association, Officer." A pause. The cop didn't answer. "We appreciate your concern." The spotlight snapped off, and the cruiser moved on. Jeff and I pulled Kay up.

"Can you make it up to the house?" I asked. She nodded, then regretted it. We did get there eventually. Down the dock, up the stairs, the hill, our driveway, the steps to the front door. There Jeff left us.

"I'm going to catch hell," he said, sounding both proud of himself and genuinely worried. "I'll call," he said to Kay.

Kay and I made it down the hall to her bedroom with one stop at the bathroom. Her sweat smelled like Ripple, but by now she only had the dry heaves. And now that she seemed mostly okay, I was mad at her. I couldn't believe after all she had said about what it meant to be a Watts, she had gone and gotten drunk. Suddenly she seemed no different than Sergeant Nichols, the cop who lectured us on bicycle safety in elementary school and in high school on drugs. He would hold up this tiny glass vial and announce that it contained enough LSD to turn on the whole state of Florida. *Liars.*

"Thanks," Kay said when she was at last in bed, the covers up to her chin.

"I'm not sure I'm speaking to you," I said.

The next day Kay was still sick, and the next. She had always had the kind of stomach that once she threw up, she had a hard time stopping. She told my mother she had the stomach flu. She had me call Mr. Bright and tell him that *Oklahoma!* would have to go on without her. He didn't sound too upset. Jeff called but Kay was too sick to go to the phone.

After three days, my father called our doctor, the one who was giving my mother the Valium, and he called in a prescription for an antinausea drug for Kay. The blue station wagon brought it from Peebles Drugs with my mother's weekly refill. But after the medicine came, Kay complained more, not less—now her legs kept cramping, her tongue felt funny. I thought she was overdoing it, afraid of getting declared well before the last performance of *Oklahoma!* But also I thought she was trying to get my attention. But I didn't want to forgive her just yet. I wanted to get even.

So I went to see Mark Lish. Mark had been my best friend in sixth grade. He and I and Joanna Fossbleck were inseparable. Another case of the blindness of love. I used to think Joanna Fossbleck was the most beautiful name in the world. How it rolled off the tongue. Jo-ANN-a Foss-BLECK. She moved away at the end of sixth grade. Only Mark and I went on to junior high. But on the morning of the ankle socks, I turned and saw Mark with new eyes. He was fat and his voice was still childishly high. I left a note in his locker saying maybe it would be better if we didn't see each other for a while. Though I knew it was a shitty thing to do, I felt I had no choice.

But Mark had become popular in his own way. By this time, he was widely reputed to be the biggest dealer in the school. Actually, he wasn't. His little brother Dana was, but it was a family business. Mark's house was in the next subdivision over, an older, slightly less desirable one where most of the houses didn't have central air. I walked there, crossed his yard, brown and full of sand spurs.

His mother was just coming out. She was a short dark woman who worked at the public library. "Julie," she said, stopping in the doorway, looking at me. "We haven't seen you in a while." I nodded, not sure whether she meant since she had seen me at the library or with Mark. Both were true. "Go on in," she said, holding the screen door for me. "Mark's in the family room."

Mark was tall now, without an ounce of fat. He was sitting on the couch with his feet up on the coffee table, watching *Star Trek* and drinking from a quart bottle of Tab. He looked up. All the way over I had been rehearsing my apologies—also trying to think of how to get around to what I wanted. But Mark did not act surprised to see me. "Hey, kiddo," he said.

"Hey," I said back, and sat down. He handed me a bowl of potato sticks.

After a while, while Kirk and a landing party beamed down to yet another planet with an odd-colored sky, Mark got a box from under the couch and rolled a couple of joints. He lit one. I watched as he seemed to swallow the smoke, hold it. He handed me the roach clip and I tried to do the same. But I coughed and some of the smoke came out my nose. It was surprisingly hot. Mark handed me his Tab. He took another hit and then I tried again. We passed the joint back and forth, until it was no more than a hot, red point of light. Mark finished it. At first, I felt nothing. Then I realized I had been breaking a single salty potato stick into smaller and smaller and smaller pieces for I didn't know how long. I ate it. Then stick by stick, I ate the whole bowl.

I looked up to see Captain Kirk standing, legs spread, hands on his hips under an especially purple sky. "Humans are not happy living in comfort," he said or something like that. "We *must* suffer. We like it." I nodded. It seemed obvious.

"Come on." Mark took me by the hand. He put a motorcycle helmet on my head, pulled the strap under my chin. Outside, he got on his bike.

I had never been on a motorcycle before. I was the kind of kid who when I saw a ball coming, instead of trying to catch it, covered my face. But I got on. Mark told me to put my arms around his waist and hold on, so I did. Then we were off, and I closed my eyes against the wind. I felt the warmth of Mark's body through his T-shirt on my arms, my cheek. I felt the vibration of the bike. The way the cool air flowed out of the shade when we rode past a clump of trees. I knew, even with my eyes shut, we were on the River Road. Narrow, curving, dangerous. We flew down it, the wheels leaving the ground when we hit a bump. I smelled car exhaust and the river and the detergent Mark's mother used, and I had never, never, been so happy. I felt paralyzed with joy.

We left the River Road, headed up into Empire Heights, an unfinished subdivision. Up empty paved streets, past half-dead orange trees. This was our playground when we were friends. Mark tore right up the tallest hill, the knobby tires of his bike spraying sand. At the top, he laid the bike on its side, warning me in advance to lift my leg. We rolled off and found ourselves in a hollow, all that was left of our old sand fort. We lay side by side, but not touching. My body missed his warmth, but Mark made no move to touch me and I felt incapable of moving, numb. We smoked another joint.

I was happy again. Mark said he had decided to become a nuclear physicist. It took hard work and years of study, but would be worth it. Then he told me that his father had been laid off at the Cape. We both knew that this was the beginning of the end. Soon, whole companies would be shutting down. The race for the moon was over. We had won. Mark's father, who had his own secretary and thick memo pads with his name engraved on them, had taken what he hoped would be a temporary job as a toll taker on the Bee Line Highway. Looked at in this light, it seemed like a good thing Mark was on his way to being independently wealthy.

We got back on the bike. After too short a time, Mark pulled up in front of my house. I got off, my legs unsteady. I took off the helmet and he strapped it on the back. Mark looked at me and I thought he was going to say something like—"If you need me, you know where to find me." But he didn't say anything, and then he was gone. I stood in the hot sun on my driveway, my hair in my eyes. I tried to run my hand through it, but the hair was so tangled, my fingers got nowhere. Now I was ready to talk to Kay. I brushed the sand off my legs and went inside.

It was dark and cool, as always, but not quiet this time. My parents were in the kitchen arguing.

"I don't want to call Dr. Bach's service again!" my mother was saying. "You don't know what it's like—I call and I call. He ignores me."

"But this isn't for you. Didn't you say it was about Kay?" I slammed the front door, coughed.

"Julie!" I heard Kay calling, but her voice sounded strange, like her head was under the covers. "Jul, please." I walked down the hall, opened her door. But what I saw was so strange that I thought it couldn't be real, thought I was still stoned. I blinked and shook my head. It didn't go away. Kay was lying on her bed, but her back was impossibly arched, her face twisted. Only the tip of her head and her heels were touching the mattress. Even from across the room, I could smell her sweat and her fear. She was having some kind of convulsion.

"God," I said, running to her. I tried to push her down on the bed. How could I have doubted her when she told me how bad she felt?

"Please," she hissed between clenched teeth. "Get me out of here." *Get me out of here.* Out of this house, this family. I felt ashamed. Even Kay had given up on us.

I ran to the phone, called an ambulance, using a number from the orange emergency sticker on the receiver. My parents were still arguing. *You call. No, you call.* Like children. I wanted to scream at them. Instead, I just told them what I had done. By the time the ambulance attendants arrived, they were grown-up again. They acted like parents, asked questions. The attendant said it was an allergic reaction to the antinausea drug. A pretty common one. "Is she going to die?" I asked. I wanted them to say, *heavens no.*

Instead one of them said, "It's best not to think about that right now." They put an oxygen mask on Kay, shot something into her arm. She relaxed a little and turned her head away from my parents. She looked at me. I leaned closer and she said something I couldn't quite catch.

"Mmmm . . . nnn . . . mad at you," was what it sounded like. *Am* mad at you? Am *not* mad at you? Either way I was sure she knew everything, knew where I had been all afternoon.

My parents climbed into the back of the ambulance with Kay. Serious, adult, my mother clutching her purse. The last thing I saw before they closed the ambulance doors was Kay's toes. It was not until the ambulance started down the driveway that I realized I had no way to get to the hospital. I ran after it, hoping one of the attendants would see me, let me sit between them on the front seat. Instead the driver hit the siren and was gone. I stopped at the end of the drive, breathing hard.

Just then a sheriff's car passed, stopped, backed up, and a

deputy got out, hitching his belt. I was suddenly aware of my matted hair, my sandy clothes, which might or might not smell like pot.

"So," he said. "Somebody here ODed?" He said the ambulance crew had called in a drug-related incident.

At first, I was so furious I couldn't say anything. Then I did. In a torrent. *My mother's doctor. A prescription drug.* The deputy nodded patiently, and it occurred to me that he had heard this before. That my mother could have been unconscious in that ambulance, full of bourbon and Valium. Or Mark. Or me. To him, it was all the same.

He offered me a ride to the hospital. But I didn't shut up. I couldn't. I told him how when we were little, Kay would get so mad at me for reading all the time that she would tear the book from my hands. How I would just pick up another book, then another, until she would fall on me, punching me, pulling my hair. "She wanted me to play with her," I said. He nodded, without taking his eyes from the traffic. " 'Look at me,' she used to say," I told him. "She wants people to *be* there when they're there."

"Yeah," he said, "well." He shrugged.

He dropped me off at the emergency entrance. I saw my parents on the far side of the waiting room, standing closer together than I could ever remember seeing them. I was walking toward them when the double doors swung open and a doctor in green surgical scrubs stepped out. My parents turned their backs to me, their faces to him. I strained to hear what he was saying, but he was too far away. But I knew. I knew.

He had to be saying that Kay was dead.

The doctor's inaudible words seemed to roll like a wave across the room, washing over first my mother, then my father. I saw my mother's hands rise, my father's head snap back. Tonight, I thought, my mother will throw her Valium down the garbage disposal, grind even the plastic bottle to bits. From now on, my father will come home every day at five. We will take up gardening or decoupage or Chinese cooking—a hobby we all can share. We will eat every meal together. It is not too late. For Kay, we will be a family.

I braced myself, waiting for the wave to hit me. But it didn't. Instead I heard my father's voice, irritated. "I told you she would be fine," he said to my mother.

Kay was not dead.

I took a deep breath, prepared to feel joy, or at least profound relief. But what I felt mostly was strange. Like I didn't know these people. Like this wasn't my family at all.

Lori Hope Lefkovitz

Leah Behind the Veil:

Sex with Sisters from the Bible to Woody Allen

Sister Love

THEY TEACH THIS story to us as children: A young man falls in love with a beautiful girl and works seven years to earn her. When he wakes up on the morning after his wedding, he finds that he has been tricked: at his side is not his beloved but her "weak-eyed" older sister. Promising to labor for seven more years, he is permitted to marry the sister of his heart's desire as well.

How deeply familiar this story is. The hero is the biblical Jacob, and the sisters are Rachel and Leah. I connected to it early because my Hebrew name is Leah, and my sister, seven years younger than I am, has the middle name Rachel. Yet as early as childhood, I found this Bible story particularly troubling and incomplete, and while other readers were interested in the love story between Jacob and Rachel and in the motif of the trickster tricked, *I* wondered about the sisters in the story: What was Leah thinking when she was at the altar in her sister's place? Did Rachel know about the rule that elder sisters must marry first, and did she approve the plan? Was Rachel sad, bitter, resigned, or is it possible to imagine that she was pleased? Did Leah feel resentful, used, happy, smug, or ambivalent? Did the father discuss the substitution plan with his daughters, and did Rachel and Leah talk it over between themselves? Loving my sister as I did, I wondered if these sisters loved one another? Why, in the narrative of the sisters as mothers, is envy the only expressed emotion between them? Most urgently of all I wondered why neither the Bible nor other readers seemed to care, why no one was moved by my concerns.

I felt the force of these questions long after my first encounter with Leah and Rachel when I walked out of a movie theater, as it happens, with my own sister and my husband, having just seen Woody Allen's *Hannah and Her Sisters.* The film had been praised by friends and reviewers, but I disliked it; it was tiresome, and it offended me. My sister disliked it too, and our conversation, back in 1986, anticipated the public scandal years later about Woody Allen's personal life when he was accused in 1993 of sexual involvement with the teenage daughter of Mia Farrow, Allen's own longtime partner. What my sister and I decided is that in this plot the successful seduction of a wife's sister (and I see now that the observation applies as well to a wife's daughter) responds to a subconscious resentment of women's intimacy with one another. The story reassures the hero, whose masculinity is weak by the standards of his own self-representation, that his virility is indeed adequate; he is the world's center, more necessary to the potentially closest of women than they are to each other.

Perhaps hearing the biblical resonances of Hannah's name, my sister and I were driven back to the story of Jacob and Leah and Rachel, conscious of the accident of our own names and a Jewish literary heritage that offers almost no other examples of sisters besides Leah and Rachel. I remembered that the Victorians loved this sin in particular, and Charles Dickens and Sigmund Freud were each imagined (probably falsely) to have had an affair with his wife's sister. *sex, lies and videotape, Like Water for Chocolate,* many cheap novels, and several other movies play with twists on this time-honored plot. Our culture likes this story. It is everywhere, a fantasy in many variations, a pornographic doubling of the woman in her sister, that has a calming effect on a culture (or an individual who presumes to speak for his culture) that is particularly anxious about patriarchal potency and the political threat that might be posed by women's intimacy. This story says, "relax; women are easily seduced away from one another; they compete for you and envy each other, and you may have them both, at no cost." My reflections here on the theme and variations of "Leah and Rachel," Hannah and her sisters, and the male fantasy of sex with a sister-in-law, is grounded in sister-sister love and in the conviction that so-called realistic representations of sisters rarely do justice to that love.

Flipping through for sisters in my mental card catalog, I see patterns: Cinderella stories, Antigone/Ismene stories, Rachel and Leah stories, Procne and Philomela stories. Over and over again, I see these patterns animated by fear that a mortal threat is posed by women's intimacy. Myth and later stories by men often divide sisters and render attractive only women who are independent of their sisters.

It is an old wisdom about Cinderella: the girl who deserves to be princess is a free agent, independent of the selfish bond between stepmother and sisters. As the Brothers Grimm tell this story, in its less sanitized version, the wicked stepmother encourages her daughters to amputate parts of their feet (a toe, a heel) that each may squeeze into the "fur" slipper. (In its early versions, until the French *ver* was mistaken for *verre,* the slipper is fur.) The fetishizing prince, who evidently has dim memory of his beloved's face, is in each case deceived until his attention is drawn to the bloody fur. So, the mother, like generations of Chinese women who dutifully bound their daughters' feet to make them marriageable, initiates her daughters into women's rites of passage, into woman's blood and self-mutilation. In both Chinese lore and Freudian explanations of foot fetishism, the foot substitutes, of course, for female genitalia. The unnatural sister with the tiny (fur) foot that does not bleed (is she still a child?) is rewarded for her childhood loneliness among sisters with the glory (perhaps a lonely glory) of becoming Princess.

The myth in Ovid's *Metamorphoses* of Procne and Philomela, in which these sisters triumph over Tereus's cruel efforts to keep them apart, offers the lesson that a fierce loyalty lends unnatural power to the conspiracies of sisterhood: in a gesture by which sister love is made at once greater than mother love and infinitely brutal, Procne and Philomela punish Tereus for raping and silencing his wife's sister by killing his son and serving the cooked child to Tereus for supper. This story presents the other side of the coin: if the Bible promises that sisters would choose a man over each other principally because women (as Freud insisted) want sons above all, then the Ovidian myth expresses the anxiety that requires this reassurance, the deep fear that a woman would kill her son for the sake of her sister.

In the Beginning

MY EARLY DIFFICULTIES with the Bible's portrait of Leah and Rachel, my feeling that something important was missing, seemed to be about the absence of complexity in the relationship between the sisters. As co-wives, Rachel envies Leah's fertility, and in the events that lead up to their marriage to the same man, their relationship is elided entirely. This omission is made starker and more startling in the context of a betrayal theme that surrounds Jacob's marriages: Jacob once betrayed his brother Esau; his Uncle Laban (father of Leah and Rachel) now betrays Jacob. Ultimately the men reconcile through trade, business negotiations, and deals.

The story is as old as Oedipus and retold tirelessly in every generation. Male competition for a woman is the stuff out of which the family, the male adult, and ultimately civilization are born. Jacob and his Uncle Laban enact the Oedipal drama in its second phase, an adult working-through of the young boy's conflict of envying the father for possession of the mother. Every erotic triangle in countless stories of men vying for a heroine repeats the same drama; and in the end one man wins and the other may go on with his life, ready to find a woman of his own and strengthened by the struggle between men.

So, Eve Kosofsky Sedgwick reminds us in *Between Men* that rivalry between men creates a social bond stronger than the love of the men for the woman who is objectified by them, "the object of desire." Citing Gayle Rubin's anthropological work, Sedgwick observes that "patriarchal heterosexuality can be discussed in terms of one or another form of the traffic in women: it is the use of women as exchangeable, perhaps symbolic property for the primary purpose of cementing the bonds of men with men" (pp. 25–26). And so it is for Jacob and his brother Esau, and Jacob and his Uncle Laban in patterns of rivalry, betrayal, and reconciliation.

The sisters, by contrast, are not capable of betraying one another because there must first be trust for a betrayal to occur, and Leah and Rachel, shadow sisters, are deprived of the intimacy that is requisite for betrayal. Neither are the women reconciled to one another in the manner of male rivals who ultimately compromise or struggle to a conclusion. In the Bible story, Leah and Rachel are forever trapped in their erotic triangle, polarized by Jacob's permanent position between them.

I once lamented the slight to the sisters, the love that might have been but whose voice fell on deaf ears. But more than a careless neglect of sister love I now suspect a violent stifling of the possibility of a choral sororal voice. I think now that with the deliberateness and power of subconscious logic, this story's purpose is to keep the matriarchy's sisters forever divided.

Why, after all, is Jacob tricked? What is Leah doing there in his bed? The story offers the sound historical explanation that elder sisters had to marry first. Also Laban is greedy and uses the excuse to squeeze his nephew for more labor. But the larger narrative context provides the most compelling explanation. In the preceding chapters, Jacob, younger twin to Esau, twice "cheats" his brother of the birthright due Esau by rules of primogeniture. Just as Jacob deceived his blind father by wearing fur skins and answering to Esau's name to gain the coveted blessing of the firstborn, so, in an act of narrative justice, will Jacob be deceived, given the elder sister when he wanted the younger.

Compare the brothers. Jacob, the younger son, is gentle and smooth-skinned, the favorite of his mother, the domestic boy. Esau, the elder twin, is hairy, is a hunter, and is favored by the father. Jacob, at his mother's insistence, tricks his brother out of the birthright by leading his blind father to believe that he is his more masculine older brother.

So it is that the second matriarch, Rebecca, and the feminine boy inherit the narrative. And so it was too when Sarah, the first matriarch, banished the wilder older boy Ishmael, against Abraham's wishes, that he might not threaten the young Isaac's inheritance. The pattern metaphorically recuperates the apparent effeminacy of a younger people less physically powerful than the surrounding tribes. At the same time, these are anxious stories. The rule is that femininity prevails, and always in a way that challenges patriarchal power. Always subtle and behind the scenes, we see evidence that mothers and wives are the agents of God's plans and that masculinity is at grave risk. Always in these stories, the more obvious deception between father and son, the usual totemic rivalry, entails an implicit victory of wife over husband. Through the favored son, the mother acquires power of place over the husband and father. The stories choose the younger, physically weaker man, and the subtext postulates a maternal source; the hero's effeminacy and maternal control combine in the textual subconscious to suggest a male fear of inadequacy.

The story of the final matriarchs, Leah and Rachel, is compensatory. Jacob's eventual acquisition of sisters puts the matriarchy firmly under patriarchal control; Jacob must really be something, virile, desirable if he is loved by sisters who become rivals for his seed. Esau, for all of his hair and hunting ability, does not compete. He is deprived of a marriage story, and his posterity fades out of this narrative history, while Jacob gets a double marriage story, marriage to sisters. The brothers reconcile; the sisters are forever divided. The story goes on: Leah is fertile and has many sons; Rachel is called "barren" until she bears Joseph, who is younger than Leah's sons and who will accordingly inherit the narrative future. Joseph is young, vain, hated by his brothers, effeminate, and sold into slavery. Poignantly, Rachel dies in childbirth with her next son.

Midrash and Thomas Mann

ALTHOUGH THE BIBLE does not seem to care about Leah and Rachel, I loved them. I was glad when I learned that rabbinic midrashim, medieval stories that fill in the gaps in biblical narrative, do imagine a relationship between Leah and Rachel. In some of these stories, Leah is the more beautiful and pious sister; the sisters love one another dearly, and Rachel coaches Leah on how to deceive Jacob. In one story Rachel hides under the bed that first night so that Jacob may recognize his lover's voice. At the same time, Esau is rendered evil and is made Leah's betrothed from birth. The deception that wins Jacob both sisters works to save Leah from Esau. The midrash demands justice, and romantically, in fairy-tale style, it eliminates the unpleasantness of sister rivals or a hero whose triumph is undeserved and comes unfairly at Esau's expense. These midrashim allow us to imagine that Rachel and Leah enjoyed a friendship as co-wives.

And so it seems does Thomas Mann when he returns to

this plot early in our century. In the sixth chapter of *Joseph and His Brothers* (titled "The Sisters"), at first Rachel and Leah do love each other. But jealousy ultimately overwhelms them because envy is natural to women. Initially, Rachel inwardly disapproves of Jacob for his utter rejection of her beloved sister Leah. At the same time Rachel "could not quite put out of her heart all feminine satisfaction in his preference" (p. 316). For all of her virtue, Rachel gloats. Leah is also ambivalent: she visits Rachel before the wedding, and in a symbolic foreshadowing, she tries on Rachel's veil. The women seem to be tender and intimate, but Mann tells us that when "they caressed each other with tears . . . they had different reasons" (p. 323). Over time, the envy between the sisters deepens. Rachel hangs about Leah's son's cradle, and her helping with the baby is not what it seems. Leah's consoling words on Rachel's barrenness are similarly double-edged.

For all of his psychological insight into the sisters, Mann too takes for granted that Jacob was necessarily more important to them than they were to each other, and for all of his elaboration of the story, Mann does not worry over the details of the trick, does not ask what Leah was thinking when she took her sister's place. Finally, the narrator explains the degenerating of Rachel's character and her once loving relationship with Leah by appeal to "woman's nature": "She was friendliness itself, but it was more than a woman's nature could bear and not feel jealous of her sister." At last: "thus, sisterly tenderness was at an end, and Jacob stood embarrassed between the two" (p. 351).

I talk about the Rachel-Leah story; I draw attention to its pervasiveness, and I ask: How often does this really happen, a guy sleeping with his wife's sister? Why does it happen so often in the movies? One friend confesses, yes, her sister slept with her first husband, and the sisters then left him in the dust and walked off into the sunset together. Another confesses, if *my* sister did such a thing I would be unforgiving. And after a thoughtful pause: my brother-in-law envies our closeness; he'd love to get me in bed, just to get between us.

Leah Behind the Veil

I REMEMBER THAT before my wedding ceremony there was another smaller ceremony in which my soon-to-be husband covered my face with my veil. In a traditional Jewish wedding the groom may veil the bride, a ritual that effaces the woman but is designed to assure the groom that he is about to be married to Rachel and not Leah. According to Levitical incest laws, a man may marry his deceased brother's childless wife, but Jewish law forbids marriage to one's wife's sister (in her lifetime). Freudian theory teaches us that the taboo is greatest where the desire is strongest.

Writing about incest taboos, Freud himself puts the sister-in-law under erasure. *Totem and Taboo* addresses in close detail the temptation to the young boy of his mother and sisters. Freud then goes on, omitting any mention of sisters-in-law—often fixtures in Victorian homes, including his own—to talk about how the early incest temptation shows up in the relation of sons-in-law to mothers-in-law. Following an impressive list of evidence from "primitives" that literally keep this pair apart, Freud says that indeed one reason for the mother/son-in-law antagonism is the possibility of an excluding closeness between the mother and daughter. (Here one recalls Freud's own jealousy of Martha's relationship to her mother.) But Freud is more confident in a second explanation that displaces the envy: mothers, because they live through their daughters, can fall enviously in love with their sons-in-law. For the man's part, his mother-in-law "actually represents an incest temptation" because she reminds him of his own mother. The ambivalence comes of a likeness to his wife but as the older, less lovely woman he fears she could become.

Since Freud's discussion of the incest taboo includes sisters as equal to mothers, it is surprising that he has nothing to say about sisters-in-law, who also may remind a man of his wife without the "matronly" qualities that the biographers of our eminent Victorians find so unattractive.

What I see in Freud's emphases and omissions in *Totem and Taboo* is a powerful but overlooked temptation, one codified in texts as venerable as the Bible and as recent as Woody Allen's *Hannah and Her Sisters.* Freud omits this taboo, though rumors about Freud and his sister-in-law circulated in his lifetime. I think that the temptation of the sister-in-law exists less because she may remind a man of his wife and his own sister than because the wife and sister together threaten the man's potency, his patriarchal power; having both women undermines their intimacy as it reassures the man of his exclusive and excluding desirability.

Hannah and Her Sisters

THE FILM'S TITLE suggests that this is a movie about women, but it opens with an on-screen chapter title, "God she's beautiful," articulated in a voice-over by Elliot (Michael Caine), Hannah's husband, going on about *her* (we wonder whose) pretty eyes and sexy sweater, wishing he could get her alone, wishing he could tell her he loves her, and most emphatically wishing he could take care of her. Then: "Stop it, you idiot, she's your wife's sister," he tells himself. We learn that he has been consumed with Lee (Barbara Hershey) for months and that he thinks it is "disgusting." We soon hear Elliot compliment his wife's sister's catering, and we come to realize that he means Holly (Dianne Wiest), Hannah's other sister. Only then do we see the three sisters together in the kitchen, chatting about Thanksgiving and their parents; Lee, we learn, would like to work with children;

Hannah's first husband, Mickey (Woody Allen) is mentioned ("crazy as ever"). The viewer cannot see this scene comfortable in the sisters' evident intimacy. Hannah's husband, in his absence, governs our reading of the sisters together. We already know about Elliot's obsession, and we wonder how the man's lust for his wife's sister will affect the relationships within this family enjoying Thanksgiving. A man is the absent center that controls our reading of the sisters' relationships.

When Hannah (Mia Farrow) is complimented for her successful performance as Nora in *A Doll's House,* the allusion suggests that the film functions within a tradition of narratives about women who assert themselves. Hannah then gives a stereotypical speech about how the role tempted her back to the stage, but she is glad to be back doing what she loves, caring for her husband and children. Allen's film celebrates these nostalgic values even as we appreciate the ironies; after all, this husband to whom Hannah is devoted lusts after her sister.

Meanwhile Hannah's first husband, Mickey, becomes a character in his own right, a typical Woody Allen "nerd" in contrast to his handsome and successful former partner. Mickey visits Hannah and their twin sons, and he observes that he likes and identifies with Hannah's new husband: "he is awkward and clumsy and under-confident—a loser like me." Both of these men, both Hannah's husbands, are characterized as losers, yet not only will these losers win the very attractive Hannah but Elliot will seduce Lee, and Mickey will end up married to the talented Holly, whom we learn he always had a crush on, clearly implying that he lusted after Holly even while he was married to her sister Hannah.

Because of the doublings in this plot, Hannah has two sisters, one for each husband. The husbands are Jacob types, mama's boys, but the story will make them virile first by giving them sisters and then by recovering their potency. We discover that Mickey's sons with Hannah are technically not his. His dubious virility is initially epitomized by a low sperm count. The twins (a product of the patriarchal virility that generated Jacob and Esau) were conceived by artificial insemination; the donor was Mickey's manly former partner.

Hannah's new husband, Elliot, intends to seduce her sister Lee, and a parallel plot develops in which Holly and her best friend, April (Carrie Fisher), begin dating the same man. When we are in Holly's consciousness for the first time, she is conflating her sister and her friend, comparing herself first to Hannah and then to April. As she listens to April joke with David, Holly regrets that she cannot tell jokes as Hannah can. She thinks, "I hate April. She's pushy. I really like him a lot." April replaces Holly's older sister as an object of envy, and we hear the ease with which envy becomes hate when a man enters the arena. April and Holly are best friends and business partners; they have known David for less than an evening.

Elliot begins his seduction. He directs Lee to a sexy e. e. cummings poem, and he offers to accompany her to an A.A. meeting. It is a cheap and silly seduction, but it works. Referring to Elliot's lies about his marriage, Lee muses, "Hannah never said anything. We are very close. Poor Hannah." She repeats that she and Hannah are close, and in the next scene, that closeness is ironically reiterated when we see Hannah caring for their drunken mother, and the mother tells Hannah that her sister Lee worships her. Immediately, we see Elliot and Lee in bed; the sex was "perfect." In Allen's film, this betrayal is the price of the sisterly worship so often emphasized by the characters.

Competition and rivalry—sexual and professional—underlie the sororal intimacies that are betrayed by Hannah's sisters in conversations with her husband and ex-husband. Lee says to Elliot, "I was so worried that I wouldn't compare to Hannah," and she confesses to having such thoughts all the time. She imagines that her sister is passionate. Elliot admits that Hannah is warm but not needy enough. Lee reassures him, saying, "I want you to take care of me."

Mickey's memory of his love for Hannah triggers a memory of his first date with Holly after his divorce. On that occasion Holly shouted like a child in the throes of sibling rivalry: "I am my own person." Hannah, like Leah, the eldest and the fertile sister, wants more children. She already has four. Her sisters, women loved by her husbands, are childless. Elliot kindly thinks he would prefer to hurt Lee a little than to destroy Hannah, and Hannah tells Elliot that she would be destroyed if he were in love with someone else. Elliot is acquiring destructive power.

The three sisters go out to lunch. When Hannah agrees to loan Holly money, Holly accuses Hannah of condescension. Lee rushes to Hannah's defense. For the viewer, Elliot is the absent presence at the table. We are encouraged to see Lee's former alcohol dependence and Holly's former cocaine dependence as symptoms of Hannah's success and sisterly rivalry.

In Woody Allen's version of the family romance, sexual taboos are twice violated, as three men prove that they know what women want, managing to win sisters and best friends with no consequence to themselves. One Thanksgiving later, Holly has written a play in which Hannah sees her marriage represented, and she says to Holly, "You make it sound like I have no needs." Confronting Elliot, Hannah says, "I have enormous needs." Elliot yells back, "I can't see them and neither can Lee or Holly." In the married couple's next lovemaking scene, Hannah begins weakly, "I feel lost." Elliot becomes reassuring, and the viewer knows that because Hannah showed vulnerability (reversing Nora's progress in *A Doll's House),* the sex will be as satisfying as that which her husband Elliot enjoyed with her sister Lee.

Hannah's flaw is that she appears too self-contained. Her sisters (for whom she provides) resent her, as does her husband.

The message is that to be loved, by husband or sisters, a

woman should show no strength. A husband needs to be generous; other women are maliciously jealous. Hannah, like the fertile Leah of Scriptures, is unloved. For all of her children and successes, both men, husband and ex-husband, turn to her childless sisters for satisfaction. Her sisters, to calm their envy, jump at the merest offer.

As the plot signals closure, Lee has a new boyfriend, and we are led to believe that this relationship will succeed because with him she can become a mother. Mickey and Holly date, and Holly produces some wonderful scripts. Coda: One Thanksgiving later, the fairy tale is complete. Hannah, perfectly happy with Elliot, has a new role as Desdemona. Lee is married to Doug. A sign of the conservatism of the script, in the background the black maid dims the lights in the dining room. Holly, who has arrived late, is looking at her beautiful face in the mirror as Mickey, whom we now discover has become her husband, kisses her neck and thinks that "it would make a great story, a man married to one sister, it doesn't work out, and years later, he marries the other." Holly speaks: "Mickey, I'm pregnant." They kiss. Like Rachel late in life, both "barren" sisters will now have the satisfaction of children, as the film ends with this biblical miracle.

Hannah and Her Sisters repeats the same story three times, and yet reviewers barely noticed this scheme. Three neurotic and essentially unworthy men succeed in bedding down with two women each, two women who, in each case, we have reason to believe, should be more loyal to each other then to the men who succeed, with precious little effort, in seducing them. Thus, the "schlep" is made patriarchal. Allen succeeds because we are conditioned to accept gender stereotypes in which men desire, and women are seduced. How to make the nebbishy Jewish boy virile is the subject of many Woody Allen films. It is also the story of Isaac and Ishmael and of Jacob and Esau. Who pays the price?

The film is touted as a great comedy, and it is a comedy in the classic sense. Ending with the sisters' father playing "Isn't It

Romantic" on the piano, all four women (the three sisters and April) have found their appropriate mates, and all will live happily ever after. No guilt, recriminations, or retributions. The reconciliation among the sisters seems genuinely grounded in their intimacy. Thanksgiving, the dust settled, everyone has something to be thankful for. A funny allegory complete with miracles.

The principal gain is virility. Once more Allen succeeds in making a man of the inadequate male self. Even Mickey—the Allen alter ego with a low sperm count—can impregnate a woman if she is the right woman. No loss? Only if we accept the movie's assumptions, part of the subconscious of the culture, about women, their relationships, their loyalties, their needs, their priorities. These assumptions are rearticulated in this popular form at this particular historical juncture because they provide the soothing voice of tradition to those worried about, rather than encouraged by, the new "sisterhood" that feminism heralded.

The message hides behind the plot's familiarity so that viewers regard this as Allen's feminist film. In the *New York Times* review of *Hannah and Her Sisters,* Vincent Canby cannot contain his praise. He concludes from this movie that Allen "is our only authentic auteur," and introduces the film as a "beneficent, funny, psychologically complex family chronicle" (February 9, 1986). Although he will later point out that Mickey, the character played by Allen, is the movie's "lodestar," Canby's paraphrase of the plot implies that the movie is essentially about the sisters of the title; it is, Canby writes, "about three Central Park West–bred sisters and their emotional entanglements with their husbands, their lovers and their mother and father. . . ." In this review, Canby promotes the film by implying that its values are feminist: "It is as if Mr. Allen had liberated . . . the three sisters of *Interiors,* to allow them to become their own women in this new work."

I see it differently. From Genesis to *Hannah and Her Sisters* women are inexplicably, but necessarily, silenced in their relationships to one another. Allen's seemingly weak and dominated men, like the victimized and relatively effeminate biblical Jacob, become patriarchal through a plot that divides the matriarchy. *Hannah and Her Sisters* represents itself as a film about attractive, urban, contemporary American women: a comic, touching inquiry into the lives and relationships of three sisters. Reviewers have, by and large, accepted this self-presentation. But it is the same old fantasy: a relatively weak hero overcomes his self-doubts and becomes potent by triumphantly sleeping with his wife's sister. This fantasy repeats itself within the film, and it works to empower the hero by undermining the relationship among sisters who, by all rights and by the logic of the story, should be more loyal to one another than to the men who succeed with little effort and with no averse consequences in seducing them.

Steven Soderbergh's 1989 film *sex, lies and videotape* challenges precisely these gender stereotypes by playing with the roles in the sleeping-with-sisters plot. In this story the sisters are complementary and antithetical: the one fully restrained, the other uninhibited. The younger sister, Cindy ("Sin," played by Laura San Giacomo), is sexual, desired by and in bed with her elder sister's husband, John (Peter Gallagher). Enter the feminine "brother" Graham (James Spader), John's aimless sweet, impotent frat brother who videotapes women talking about sex and who has grown distant from his mightily successful friend John. The sisters compete for Graham. Dramatically reversing the gender positions in the mythic plot, here John, the man who betrayed his wife by screwing her kid sister, loses everything: his fancy job, both women. The elder, inhibited sister, Ann (Andie MacDowell), triumphs, apparently cures Graham of his inability to have unmediated intimacy with women, and the sisters move toward one another, each more like the other and with the viewer hopeful of a developing connection between them.

Here, uniquely, the betrayal *is* between sisters, is discovered and is consequential. *sex, lies and videotape* thereby challenges a "truth" rooted in Scriptures and biography. The traditional plot of the hero who sleeps with his wife's sister allays an anxiety about female intimacies as the plot reasserts male control over female relationships. As such, we may read the success of this story in contemporary America as a conscious or unconscious response to feminist ideology, consoling to those made anxious by the sisterhood that feminism (in the academy, criticism, and the arts) promised.

The question is an ethical one: why is it that in stories, whether biographical or fictional, in which a husband desires his wife's sister, the regard in which the sisters hold one another is elided? The question becomes increasingly pressing: the omission is odd when it occurs in the biblical narrative about Leah and Rachel.

The contemporary American interest in Allen's movie and in movies since then suggest a reaching back to a story so pervasive that its meaning is obscured, a story which justifies the speculation that women, no matter how close, principally feel envy for one another, and that this envy may be sexually exploited to ensure male mastery over sorority.

In these stories with meaningful variations, sisters are deprived of textual relation with one another as they enter the bed of a shared man. Weakening the bonds among women, they reassure the insecure hero of his potency and his connections to the social world: his potency shows up in the female belly, perversely, in a woman's conception of her brother-in-law's child. The ostensible theme of these stories is betrayal—that variety of deception that assumes intimacy—and while uncle betrays nephew, wife betrays husband, mother betrays son, and husbands betray wives, sisters are not represented as betraying one another because, in one way or another, they are deprived of the requisite intimacy. If this plot betrays a fear of women's intimacies, then among the reassurances that the plot provides is that male communication is what woman wants and male seed is what she needs. As such, the womb occupies a central place. The feared relation of woman to woman (exemplified in what psychology and the metaphor of sisterhood alike tell us is an especially intimate female relationship: that of sister to sister) is rendered unfulfilling and fruitless.

The story of the hero who sleeps with his wife's sister, like the Cinderella story, is often told, sister rivals, sister meanness. The other story is more rarely developed, but it is the story behind this story: Jacob is off center, not so important; Leah and Rachel love each other and each other's children. Their feelings are complex and strong and various, and they do not worry about Jacob nearly as much as he worries about them.

Works Cited or Consulted

Canby, Vincent. Review of *Hannah and Her Sisters. New York Times,* February 7, 1986, C4.

Canby, Vincent. "Woody Allen Tops Himself—Again." *New York Times,* February 9, 1986, Arts & Leisure section, pp. 23, 40.

Freedman, H., and Maurice Simon, eds. *The Midrash Rabbah: Genesis, Vol. 1.* New York: The Soncino Press, 1977.

Freud, Sigmund. *The Basic Writings of Sigmund Freud.* Translated and edited by A. A. Brill. New York: Modern Library, 1958.

Ginzberg, Louis. *The Legends of the Jews.* Vol. 1. Philadelphia: Jewish Publication Society, 1974.

Lefkovitz, Lori. "Coats and Tales: Joseph Stories and Myths of Jewish Masculinity." In *A Mensch Among Men,* edited by Harry Brod. Los Angeles: The Crossing Press, 1988.

Mann, Thomas. *Joseph and His Brothers.* Translated by H. T. Lowe-Porter. New York: Alfred A. Knopf, 1936.

Sedgwick, Eve Kosofsky. *Between Men: English Literature and Male Homosocial Desire.* New York: Columbia Univ. Press, 1985.

Kathleen Norris

Borderline

SINCE MY BOOK *Dakota* became a surprise best-seller in 1993, I've received thousands of letters responding to it. Along with the reviews, these responses have been, for the most part, positive, and often so enthusiastic that I wonder if the person has read the same book that I wrote. I was enormously relieved, then, to receive the following from my sister Becky: "How are you? Everyone here talks about you and your book. I feel left out. I tried to read it, but it was boring."

Now for the first time in our forty-two-year relationship, my sister Becky had acted as a kind of *amma* for me, a desert mother who challenges my complacency, and allows me to see the world (and myself) in a new light. I was reminded of a saying by Amma Synclectica, a desert monastic of fourth-century Egypt: "Just as it is impossible to be at the same moment a plant and a seed, so it is impossible for us to be surrounded by worldly honor and at the same time to bear heavenly fruit."

Synclectica sums up, I believe, the difficulty writers have in America in surviving success: to keep bearing fruit, one must keep returning, humbly, to the blank page, to the uncertainty of the writing process, and not pay much heed to the "noted author" the world wants you to be. Becky's letter was a godsend. Reading it over, I laughed myself silly, and found myself released from much of the tension induced by sudden notoriety, the rigors of a book tour stretched out over three years: too much travel, too much literary hoo-ha.

Becky's life has been a kind of desert. When she was born, the doctors at Bethesda Naval Hospital gave my mother too strong a dose of sedative. Having already given birth to two children, she knew something was wrong when she couldn't push enough to release Becky from the birth canal. Precious oxygen was lost. My mother recalls one doctor saying to another, "You got yourself into this mess; let's see you get yourself out." While the doctors squabbled, my sister's brain was irreversibly damaged.

Becky is diagnosed as "borderline." She is intelligent enough to comprehend what happened to her when she was born. She is not intelligent enough to do mathematical computation. A tutor my parents hired when Becky was about ten years old told us that Becky could grasp a concept long enough to work out several problems in the course of an hour-long session, but that by the next week she'd have forgotten what she'd learned and have to start from scratch. Her elementary schools were just passing her along; there were no "special ed" programs then, and no one knew what to do with her, where she belonged. Becky's life has been lonely in ways that most of us could not comprehend.

Yet our family ties are strong, and for years we've acted as Becky's advocates within the educational and medical establishment, sometimes taking consolation in the fact that Becky is a good enough judge of human nature to wrap psychiatrists round her little finger. Several times, when she's been given a tranquilizer or some other drug she didn't like, she's learned enough about the contraindications to fabricate symptoms so that the doctor would be forced to change her prescription. When she realized that alcoholic families were fashionable—at least "in" with therapists—she convinced one psychologist that her mother was an alcoholic. (My mother is the sort of person who, on a big night out, once or twice a year, drinks a tiny bit of crème de menthe.) In order to survive in her desert, my sister has often resorted to being a con artist: you get what you want by telling people what they want to hear.

She learned all of this, of course, in the bosom of our family. Our parents decided when Becky was very young that she didn't belong in an institution, but with us. I believe that being raised with myself and a brother, both older, and one younger sister, was good for Becky; I know it was good for me. Very early on, I had to learn to respect Becky's intelligence, although it was very different from mine. I also came to respect her tenacity. When she was two years old, and learning to walk was still beyond her capabilities, she became adept at scooting around the house, always with a security blanket in hand. I also had to learn to discern the difference between what Becky was truly incapable of knowing, and what she was simply trying to get by with. When she destroyed my first lipstick by writing with it on a brick wall, I took off after her. She yelled, "You can't hit me, I'm retarded." She learned that she was wrong.

When I was in high school I began to discover how much my sister and I had in common. We were both in difficult situations—I was a shy, ungainly newcomer at a prep school where many of the students had been together since kindergarten, and Becky had a particularly unsympathetic teacher. On coming home from school, she'd immediately go to her room and play mindless rock music—"Monster Mash" is one that I recall—while she danced around her room (and sometimes on her bed). She talked to herself, incessantly and loudly. The family accepted all this as something Becky needed to do.

One day, as Becky carried on her usual "conversations," with her teacher, with other girls in her class, with a boy who'd made fun of her, I was doing homework in the room next door and realized that I, too, needed release from daily tensions, a way to daydream through the failed encounters and make them come out right. Usually, I lost myself in reading or practicing the flute, but sometimes I listened to music—the Beach Boys, Verdi, Bob Dylan, Frank Sinatra—and imagined great careers for myself, great travels, great loves. I didn't have the nerve to stomp around my room and yell, as my sister was doing, but our needs were the same.

We were both struggling with our otherness, although I suspect I did not know this then. Now that I'm a writer, it's clear to me. Rejection comes to everyone, of course, but for those who are markedly different from their peers, it is a daily reminder of that difference. To most people, my sister and I didn't seem to have much in common; but I knew from that day on that we were remarkably alike.

If nothing else, this insight helped me to survive the intensely competitive atmosphere of my prep school. I knew that getting a C on a test was not the worst thing in the world. And when I got an A, when my writing got praised by my English teacher, as it often did, I could put it in perspective. I knew there were other kinds of intelligence that were just as valuable; needs that could not be satisfied in school.

OUR PARENTS ARE nearing eighty years of age and, while they often seem to have more energy as the years go by, the fact of their mortality looms large for their children. Becky, God bless her, is incapable of hiding her fears. We went for a walk one Christmas Eve not long ago, and she said, out of the blue: "I don't want Mom and Dad to die. I worry about what will happen to me."

"It scares me too," I replied. "But *everyone* is scared to think about their parents dying." I'm not sure I convinced Becky on this point—she tends to think that she's alone in her suffering, and all too often in her life, that has been the case. But I believe I did manage to reassure her that her brother and sisters would not abandon her.

As we walked through a light Honolulu rain—bright sunlight, prickles of moisture on bare skin—I remembered the two little girls who used to hide in their rooms every afternoon after school. How good it is to have those difficult years behind us. Becky will tell you that she's "slow." I guess I've always been fast by comparison. What does it matter, on the borderline? We're middle-aged women now, and our parents are old. As for the future, human maturity being what it is, the slow process of the heart's awakening, I sometimes wonder if Becky is better equipped for it than I.

Bonnie Friedman

My Gertrude Stein

SHE SLEPT THREE FEET AWAY. From across the ocean between us she described the glories she witnessed, the spectacle of a life worth living. She could look straight into the apartments across the street.

She saw an unmade bed, a man and a woman drinking out of cocktail glasses in a small gold kitchen, the silhouette of a cat poised in the window like a vase, and a woman in a poofy plastic shower cap pulling on panty hose and then throwing perfume between her legs. Anita narrated for me. I saw just a corner of cabinet and a piece of distant wall. Once I saw a door shut, but I could never see who shut it, even though I stared until even in my dreams I was seeing that shut door. From my view, everything across the street seemed molded of dust, inconsequential. If only I had Anita's bed!

"Star position's what I call this," she said. "It's how to sleep when the weather's hot." Arms splayed, legs far as they'd divide, she looked voluminous, voluptuous.

Beyond her, the door to the terrace hung open on its chain. It was a humid night. The streetlight held a dusty smudge around it, an agglutination of air as if we were breathing chalk. Anita sighed. "What a breeze," she murmured.

"I didn't feel anything."

"No? There, *that*. Did you feel that?"

"No." I twisted in my sheets.

"Wait," she said. "Okay, now nothing. Nothing. Now *there.* It's—oh. It's exquisite. Like a cat brushing past. Like, like—no, now it's over."

"But I didn't feel *anything,*" I moaned.

She stretched, more starlike.

"Let me have your bed. Just one night," I said.

"You chose your bed."

"Ages ago!"

"So what?"

When we first moved to Riverdale, the street had frightened me. In our old apartment the windows were far away, and a big blue tree guarded us like a risen moon. Here the city pressed close. The streetlight was an inquisition, and people walked under our window, jangling the change in their pockets. I wanted to be toward the room's inside, toward the hallways, the narrow ventricles winding to the kitchen, to my parents. I'd begged Anita to take that bed.

But now beside the open door I imagined she heard the tidal music of the street. I heard it too, but like the ocean in a shell: miniaturized. She heard the real thing, car whoosh, laughter, the far-off haul of the 100 bus curving around the Henry Hudson Parkway, and the whispery road itself, an asphalt arrow pointing away. Anita's whole body pointed away, legs, arms, and even stomach, which rose to meet the world, and which had lots of the world inside it. She ate what she pleased. Jelly donuts, Godiva chocolates, tender slabs of farmer cheese, lavender wafers that tasted like soap, that tasted like churches, but which came in a beautiful package, all silver and purple. Anita was like an iguana or a baby, learning the world through her mouth. She advanced one tongue's length at a time. By now she was deep into Manhattan shops and mail-order catalogs, which she read with biblical attention, staring at the pictures in Lillian Vernon, ordering the stamp-thin ginger crisps and the sacks of undyed pistachios, the Jordan almonds colored like sun-bleached gum balls and just as hard, the Danish cookies that crumbled to sugar at the first bite, spending her baby-sitting money with a wild hand.

I imagined grand futures for Anita. She had the aura of someone on TV. She often spoke in such capacious sentences, with so many passionately expressed opinions and odd facts built in, that while she spoke I felt undeserving. Others should hear her, too. She should be a Personality like Julia Child or a special on the *Hallmark Hall of Fame.* She could tell the plot of a Mannix episode in more time than it took to watch it and yet she kept it interesting. She could describe what she'd seen on the street so that you felt you'd seen it, too. Above her flame-blue eyes, her bangs lay straight as a level. Anita cut them herself. But she let her ponytail bush out in a thicket behind her, as if what was over her shoulder did not exist. It was a snare, a rat's nest, a clotted glory. My grandmother threatened to snip it off; my mother whispered in a loud and mournful voice what a shame it was that such a pretty girl should have such a wild head. Anita smiled. She sat in an orange flower-power muumuu sipping Swee-Touch-Nee and eating candied fruit slices with my friend's mothers, and giving her opinion about a daughter who ran off to get married or a son who needed the name of an excellent dermatologist. She was fifteen. It was just a matter of time before she lived beside the Seine.

Yet for all Anita's aplomb and appetite, it was I who left. I went off to find a place where I didn't envy someone else, a place where I didn't covet someone else's bed or chair, where I was who I wanted to be. In fact, I wanted to be Anita. The real Anita stayed in the Bronx. She stayed more and more in her body. Her arms weakened; her legs stiffened into marble sculpture she needed to be balanced over, or collapse. She had multiple sclerosis.

How to match the girls we were to the women we became?

A sister's life interrogates yours, saying, Why do you live this way? Are you doing what's right? And when the sister has a disease, she has it for you, so you don't have to have it, just the way she picked up heavy knapsacks when she was stronger than you, or took the bed beneath the windows when you begged, so you could feel safe.

"I weigh as much as the street Yankee Stadium is on," she told me from the hospital where she now lives. This is the hospital in the movie *Awakenings*, and there are yellowed clippings on many patients' walls showing Robin Williams here. Anita's roommate, Kathleen, was an extra. Kathleen has cerebral palsy, and a sign taped to the back of her chair: "Leave me the hell alone" below a picture of Edward Munch's "The Scream."

"You weigh as much as the street Yankee Stadium is on?" I said. "How much is that?"

"One hundred sixty-eight."

"Oh."

"And now they're going to put Yankee Stadium in New Jersey. I think it's a shame. The Bronx has so many problems right now, it needs Yankee Stadium. Besides, what would Yankee Stadium do in New Jersey? It wouldn't be the same thing at all. It would be meaningless."

"You're right," I said. Anita came to Beth Abraham when she could hardly walk, and every day she's more static, while I keep traveling farther and farther from home.

"I heard you were going on vacation to Mexico," she says. "Send me a postcard."

"Okay. Hey, do you remember the postcard you sent me from Israel? It was an airplane, Anita! A Pan Am jet."

"I call that a good postcard," she responded. "You wanted to see travel, and travel is what I sent."

"Oooh, you're a smart one!"

"Jane Lilly is always telling me to join MENSA," she said. "She thinks I'm wasting myself."

"You are not wasting yourself. You are providing wonderful conversation to everyone around you."

"I'm glad you think so," she said.

I did.

WHEN I BEGAN PSYCHOTHERAPY, Anita was the one topic I refused to talk about. I was working on a novel about her, and I was afraid if I told my story I wouldn't need to write it.

"Have you had the experience of things you shared being appropriated?" my therapist, Harriet, said.

"No."

"You haven't had the experience of things you told about being taken away?"

"Not in particular."

Occasionally Harriet's chin looked fleshy and stubborn, like Anita's. Occasionally I heard the ball of her palm rubbing callously against the page as she took notes. This reminded me of Anita, too: an insensitive body pursuing its own course.

"Tell me more about why you don't want to tell me about Anita," said Harriet.

"Because then it won't be mine," I said. "It will become yours. Whatever I tell you I won't want anymore. I've noticed this happening already with things I've told you. I have no feeling about them anymore. Sometimes I miss them."

"You miss these things you've told me about," she inquired in a way that struck me as controlling. She shifted her skirt under her bottom in a way that seemed smug to me, Anita-ish.

"Yes."

How much she was writing! Her palm scraped along, murmuring, "Shush. Shush."

"You send double messages," I said.

"Do I?"

"Your hand is saying to be quiet. But your mouth keeps urging me to talk. Which should I trust?"

"You think I am divided?"

"Yes."

"Tell me about that. Anything at all."

"Well, I feel like you try to say the right thing. You try to be a very nice person. But underneath, though, on an unconscious level—I feel that perhaps there is all this aggression. That underneath there is a punitive person, like the bogeyman with a wolf's snout. You might be like the wolf that's eaten Grandma. You look like Grandma, but maybe you are the wolf."

"Why would I be angry?"

"Hmmm. Maybe you wish you were lying on the couch, and I was paying attention to you!"

I glanced over to share a smile with her. How beautiful she seemed!

"You envy me," she remarked.

"Ha!"

"Go on."

"Why would I envy you?" I asked her. "I've never wanted to be a therapist. Maybe you wish I *would* envy you. Because in fact *you* envy *me.* I teach at Dartmouth. I am a writer. I get to be on this couch right now and tell you all the stories I see and think."

Her hand was moving fast against the page.

"Sometimes you remind me of Anita," I said. "Sometimes you seem very bossy to me—"

I stopped.

"Yes?"

"Anita wasn't bossy. I don't know why I said that."

"She wasn't bossy?"

I shook my head. "I don't know. No, she was good. I loved her."

Harriet nodded. "Why are you quiet now, Bonnie?"

"I'm confused. I don't remember Anita being bossy. I feel like that was something you suggested to me. I wish I could remember. In my book about her, she isn't bossy. She's wonderful. You see, this is why I don't want to talk to you about Anita. You change things."

"Do I?" she said, a smile curving beneath her snout.

ANITA SEWED LITTLE BOOKS. Palm-sized, they were cheap typing paper stitched up the binding with three bold strokes. Into these books she set fabulous stories about sisters and fireworks and pounding drums. You opened the book and stepped in.

I copied her books and called them mine. "By Bonita Friedman," I wrote. I folded and snipped the same kind of paper, then sewed it the way Anita taught, with a long needle that hurt my thumb when I shoved it through the wadded sheets. I drew the fireworks she drew, and the two sisters walking, their held hands like five-pronged forks entwined, their skirts like little bells, and their hair a flip. Crayon smell filled the room, or else the besotting scent of markers—you had to use orange with such care: it soaked everything.

Some days Anita drew her stories on endless spools of adding-machine paper she bought for thirty-five cents at the Temple bazaar, and those days I drew scroll stories too, persuaded by watching Anita that really these were better than folded books, these tales taped to a pencil at one end and rolling around and around in a cocoon of imagination, girls following fireworks following pigeons and Johnny pumps and cats and drums and fire escapes and more girls still holding hands until they all lived in a realm you could enter anywhere, a great big padded bolster of a realm like a thicker and thicker epithelium made of a tissue of stories. In fact, lacking adding-machine paper, we actually used toilet paper, which required an agony of tenderness and much precise administering of that free-flowing orange, which bled like methiolate. The result was a pudgy column, a sort of saturated snowball of color that to the uninitiated might look like a collapsed mess, but which, to Anita and me, was visual shorthand for stories themselves, better than even *Harriet the Spy.* Once finished, the tissue scrolls were too fragile to open: they nested like eggs in Anita's drawer. Glimpsing one imparted an instant's delirium, my first contact high.

While we worked, Anita sat on the scabby yellow Windsor chair. I sat at her elbow on an overturned wastebasket that pictured Bohack-brand vegetables. Where did Anita's stories come from? I wondered. How did she know how to draw? Somehow she saw that fireworks were airborne spiders, and that curtains hung in windows like a central part in a chunky girl's hair. She had a visual alphabet that encompassed a million things: garbage pails were webbed tubes, flowerpots were cups with a cuff out of which poked a circular serrated flower, hats were flying saucers squashed on round heads, money was an oblong with a dollar sign in someone's hand. Anything you asked, Anita could draw in this simplified, charming way. It was all like entering a doll house.

Similarly, her handwriting, always print, was unstoppably expressive, a parade of characters tumbling across the page, her plump lowercase *a*'s Winston Churchills propped by a cane, her *m*'s the top of the Ten Commandments. I watched the letters appear out the tip of her pen. What fun to be her, I imagined. Collections assembled around her. In her big white Formica desk stood sky-blue letters from pen pals, each marked "Answered," pamphlets from Weight Watchers shaped like loan coupon books, bright "god's eyes" woven in Girl Scouts on crossed sticks, clinky gold-plated charms for a charm bracelet. There was even an envelope holding phosphorescent pollen, the most finely shimmery yellow-green earth dust possible, an exhalation of the trees, which Anita had swept from a certain porch floor. I'd seen Anita's heels glowing like night-lights. "Anita!" I'd said. She looked and laughed. "Pine tree pollen," she announced, and swept it up in one of the little envelopes she carried in her pocket as nature counselor. That envelope now lay in a coil, bound by a rubber band, in her top drawer. I seldom saw it. Anita forbade me to investigate her desk without permission, which she rarely gave. The insides of her desk were private. A feminine scent of bath powder sifted up when you opened a drawer, and I once discovered a fascinating lumpy package that looked like it should unfold but wouldn't: it was a sanitary napkin, Anita later explained.

I knew the inside of Anita was like the inside of all these things, of the desk, the books, her sprightly alphabet. The inside of her was like the night sky on Independence Day, lit with the fireworks she loved, or the black-crayoned drawings she taught me to scratch with a pin, revealing rainbows of nighttime carnival underneath. She was the first person I met who had an actual internal life. How I wished I were she!

What is it to grow up wanting someone else's eyes and fingers and mouth and mind? I erased so much of what I wrote in second grade, my teacher cracked the tops off my pencils. In third, the teacher, Mrs. Claw, gave me a silvery-blue change purse shaped like a heart that she herself wove with lanyard when she was sick in the hospital. I was amazed: I believed I was invisible! Similarly, when my mother came home from Open School night I was always astonished by the reports. I didn't believe that the teachers *saw* me. When they glanced, calling attendance, I thought they saw something erased, like the gray clouds after they erased the blackboard, or like the neighbors in the apartments across the street, composed of dust.

My girlfriends in those days were decisive: In Follow the Leader, they enjoyed being the Leader. In Mother May I, they were Mother. "Bonnie, you may take one giant step. Ah-hah! You didn't say, 'Mother, may I?'!" How did you get to feel comfortable being Mother? I liked being in the sea of girls doing umbrella steps, doing two bunny hops. Sitting on my Bohack wastebasket, I liked sewing Anita's books and hoped my handwriting resembled hers. It was such good, round handwriting! I sat very close to Anita. I thought if I copied long enough, I would learn how to create.

Anita seemed to copy no one. She went off to Israel and came back with a tingle in her elbow that wouldn't go away. This tingle was the beginning of her body erasing herself, although this took a while to find out. I was there the day the doctor stuck a needle in Anita's palm and she felt nothing. I saw the needle jab, and Anita, with her eyes closed, waiting for a sensation to start.

"Do you feel anything now?" asked the doctor.

"No. Not yet," Anita said.

The doctor pushed the needle against another part of her hand. "And now?"

"I don't feel a thing. Are you touching me? I don't feel anything at all. I can't feel a thing."

I also saw Anita, with her eyes closed and her arms out, attempt to walk straight across the examining room. She took one baby step and then another, and the more she walked, the more she diverged.

"Anita," I said, and she opened her eyes.

She was in the wrong part of the room.

"Here is your pocketbook," I said. "I want to go home."

WHERE ANITA LIVES NOW, men and women loll in wheelchairs. Pieces of them are missing. Some have a bandaged stump where a leg should be. Others are too skinny, and remain collapsed sideways in their wheelchairs. Their eyes follow you down the linoleum, past the café where angels—volunteers—serve weak coffee and day-old chocolate chip cookies, and where many wheelchairs are lined up in late autumn, so that people can gaze out at the treeless courtyard, the peeling white gazebo, the two patchy street cats, black-and-white, climbing the wood like squirrels, and then dashing across the pavement. "Look! Look at that cat! She's so fast!" a few patients murmur admiringly. After the cats are gone, they continue to gaze into the stark yard.

People here are friendly. If you ask one patient where the elevator is, three or four will answer. They all point you down the hallway, elaborate what you will pass on the way, and many smile encouragingly and, like parents, watch your progress. To each other they don't say much, though. They seem to find their own company stale, as if they have become half-furniture. Maybe this is always the way with people together from dawn to dusk to dawn.

The home has a compelling, miraculous atmosphere. The heat is amniotic. You're on the verge of a sweat. A urinous antiseptic fatigue enfolds you. The granules in an hourglass are floating up and down throughout the corridors. Time has assumed a gauzy detachment, a free-floating deep-space granular air—as if a field of dandelion seeds is drifting, as if all the Jean Naté Anita ever powdered is rising in a gust and subsiding, as if you are seeing the very molecules of the earth recombining, decaying, recombining again. "Dr. Hall, report to the third floor, please. Security, pick up line two." The building makes announcements to itself. No place is private. Even in the bathrooms, broadcasts permeate. One feels that in here no doors really matter. Nurses and TVs and PA systems can enter even one's dreams.

During Anita's birthday party her new roommate, Rhea, left her TV tuned to Sunday afternoon football, although she didn't watch. A woman in her late seventies, Rhea sat in a pink robe and slippers, an old *Newsweek* lying in her lap. "Thank you, darling," she said when I gave her a piece of cake, and "No thank you, darling," when I offered coffee. Mostly, she daydreamed. Meanwhile, the rapid, monotone male voice on the set announced plays, cheers erupted like static, and there were flickering shots of lowered men running, charging, poising themselves in configuration. We licked our frosting and Anita opened her cards bathed by the sportscaster's excited, distant voice.

The hospital, as I mentioned, blares with announcements. When my phone rings at home, and the stranger at the other end firmly advises what to add to my guacamole or what's coming up on *Entertainment Tonight,* I know it's Anita calling. "And now the latest on President Clinton's summit trip," I hear, and Anita materializes in the foreground: "Bon? How are you?" It's as if she's reporting live from the scene, as if the events of the day are clamoring for Anita's attention, but she's decided for the moment to ignore them. The very impersonality of the voices behind her imparts a sense of futility, as if she's calling from a loveless place.

Anita asks me to take home Mishka, the Olympic teddy bear I brought her. She didn't ask me to bring him, she says, and wishes I hadn't. This is a hospital, and ought to look like one. She's leaving as soon as she's strong enough, she says. Twice a week she has physical therapy.

Twice a week seems very little to me, I think, almost a token amount. But wouldn't it be wonderful if she could get stronger? Who's to say it won't happen? Who's to say it out loud? Maybe a miracle will happen. Maybe a doctor will discover how to make nerves grow back.

"I'll take Mishka next time I come," I say.

"Good. I want him home, next to the piano. And take home the poster of orange groves, too. The more you bring now, the less we'll have to occupy our arms with later."

"You don't want it there to cheer you up?"

"It does not cheer me up to have it here."

When the elevator door opens on the sixth floor of Beth Abraham, I usually find Anita sitting outside her bedroom door. She wears cherry-red or navy-blue cotton housedresses with snaps down the front, which my mother buys at Kress's, and reads *Ellery Queen's Mystery Magazine,* holding the magazine close.

"Let's get your coat," I announce.

"Bonnie!"

"Where's your hat? Do you want your purse?"

"I had no idea you were coming today! I want a kiss." She tilts her face to the side, and I kiss her.

"Now, where's your other glove?" I say. "I've signed you out. I've sprung you! Let's get some fresh air."

"Slow down!"

"Oh, it's not cold out. You don't need your other glove. Let's go."

Nothing feels as good as taking Anita out of here.

I DON'T LIKE what's happened in therapy. I feel as if I'm scraping the bottom of the pot, as if a pot of milky coffee got scalded, and when I scrape, a big brown piece floats up. I pluck it out and chew on it. Bitterness fills my mouth. I fought with my best friends. I'm estranged from my parents, from my husband, and even from my own self. I feel as if paper has been inserted between the layers of me. I feel detached, deadened, and anxious.

"You always felt detached and deadened," Harriet claims. "These are your earliest experiences."

"I miss joy," I say. "I used to feel joy."

"You are taking your happiness away from your own self. Don't you see? It's intrapsychic."

I laugh. "Paul says, 'Intrapsychic's just another way of saying, It's in yo' own head!' "

Harriet remains silent.

I don't like what's happened to my feelings about Anita, either. I used to think of her with wild affection and pity. She was overweight in adolescence, and I recall watching from the bedroom window as she toiled up the street in her oatmeal-cloth coat, moving like a fifty-year-old woman although she was seventeen. How that sight contracted my heart!

Now, though, my view of her has flattened. Was she domineering, or is this simply a puny, resentful, younger-sister way of seeing her? I can perceive her as either magical or mean. When I feel she was mean, I hate her, and have no access to her magic; the world drains of color. When I see her as magical, gratitude floods me. I love you, Anita, I want to proclaim. Yet some part of me is left out. Some part of me is banished into the hall, sent wandering down school corridors. And the part of me left inside, left hugging Anita, feels hollow, ersatz. Where is my real heart?, I wonder while Anita slowly turns her majestic face to give me what I craved so long—her smile, that enchanting smile which in the old days imbued me with joy. At last I would receive her smile! But not deserve it.

In fact, I realize, Harriet has become the magic person. But I resent having to drive many hours to receive one exorbitant contact every other week. Ninety-five dollars for the three minutes of euphoric peace I achieve at the very end of a session. Could cocaine be more expensive? More addictive? I don't like the granular gray heartless way I mostly feel these days. Like the beach after the tide is gone: grim and cutting. Like Anita, in fact, now that her magic has migrated.

"I miss my old view of Anita," I say.

"Yes?"

"Now I feel just a dead feeling toward her. A gritty, wood-shavings, statue-like dead feeling. As if you've taken someone alive and made her into an inert icon."

"Who made her into an icon? Did I?" Harriet asks.

"You've taken away my good feelings toward her. You have appropriated them for yourself. I'm angry at you. And I'm angry that I'm angry at you!" I say, knowing how childish I sound. "It deprives me of the happiness I feel when we're close."

Harriet smiles happily. I am silent for a long while, and still her pen keeps scratching, long past how much I've said. For an instant I imagine it is her very writing behind my back that has given her so much disproportionate power. She has scratched her way into me. What is she writing?

"What's in that white bowl?" I point to her Matisse print. "It looks like it's either arsenic or milk."

"Which do you think it is?"

"Well, poison. Unless it's milk. It's like you. Sometimes you seem extremely beautiful. The thought of you fills me with good feelings. Other times, though, I feel like you are cruel and greedy, that you are using me for your own purposes. But then I look over and see you, and I'm ashamed of my thoughts. It makes me want to not think at all. I can't stand all the distortions."

"The distortions are transference. They're a sign that the therapy is working."

"The difference between us is that you think the distortions accurately portray what's inside me."

"And you?"

"I think they're distortions!"

"There must have been other people in your life before me about whom you felt ambivalent, who you felt oppressed by and yet loved."

"I would like to know the truth about *you,*" I say.

"Ah."

"I would like to know the truth about that white bowl." I've done this therapy long enough to know that the truth of something lurks in its proxy. Anita, I occasionally even see, is a proxy for me. Anita was the angry, bullying daughter I wasn't. We fit together like the two candlesticks and the vase. The two bright candlesticks create the dark vase in the middle; the sides of the looming vase define the candlesticks.

"What do you imagine that white bowl contains?" she asks.

"Chalky powder," I say immediately. "I imagine if you drink it, it would seal your insides up. You would need someone else to crack into you, to break open the statue you'd become and release you. It's like the apple the envious queen gives Snow White . . . I wish I could release Anita."

"Yes?"

"I wish I could free her from her rigid body. And I would like to crack open my own rigid sense of her and let the love out. I can't feel it. When I was a child, I used to tell Anita, 'I can't feel anything from here!' " I smile.

"Why couldn't you feel anything?"

"I was too far from the door."

"What door?"

"The door away from my parents. Anita was right next to it. She felt the most ineffable breezes. Breezes that somehow seemed more wonderful than any I'd ever felt."

"In those days did you feel like a statue?"

"I tried very hard to be good."

She nods.

"You know, Harriet, I sometimes feel as if *you* have broken into me," I say. "But the way someone breaks into a house. I feel invaded. I would love to get rid of you."

"Maybe you've never been close to someone who would tolerate your desire to leave. You had to stay and do what the other wanted in order to feel safe. But you felt rigid."

I laugh. "Yes! Keep talking! When you were speaking I felt —oh, such joy! Such wild joy!"

We are silent. I am trying to savor the moment. The sun flings a golden carpet across the floor. It swirls with dust, like a sparkling scrim curtain rising. For an instant my cheek is cooled by a delicious breeze, and I'm sure she feels it.

ANITA FELL, and I became the star. What sort of joy can there be in this? My handwriting looks like what hers used to. Her handwriting looks like a child's now. I found her once in the hospital's empty dining room, writing a postcard against the paper tablecloth. She was writing to Jane Lilly. Nine or ten of her arduously shaped words would fit on the whole card. She laid her pen down in midsentence. It took so long to write each word, she would finish the card later.

Just going to the bathroom is an expedition now. Anita has become mindful of small pleasures. "Mom brought me a basket of strawberries and two cans of Coca-Cola when she came yesterday," she tells me. "When I'm done drinking them, I'll rinse out the cans and save them for Mark." Mark is her husband. She collects empties for Mark to redeem. Anita had suspected an orderly had taken some of her cans. Now she keeps them locked in her cabinet.

"Her horizons have narrowed to a pinpoint," my mother once said.

Mine have expanded. I have a bed by the road, a night view of stories. The black field of my computer screen kindles with tangerine letters, like the art Anita taught me, black crayon scratched to rainbows underneath. But these glories don't feel entirely mine. I had wanted to become Anita, but I'm me, sitting in her place. How can I help but feel fraudulent? In her sleep, Anita can still walk. In my sleep, I am still on the Bohack garbage can.

"My body is attacking itself," Anita said over the phone recently.

I nodded, twisting the cord between my fingers.

"When people ask me how come you're here," she said, "I tell them, 'Because I donated my blood to the floor.' The first time was on my birthday. The insurance company came, picked me up, and took me to E.R. They stitched up this part of my head so the blood would stop. After the second time, I was brought here. Two days ago I saw the neurologist. He said, 'I haven't seen you in a year.' 'You haven't cured me in a year, either,' I told him. We talked. What doctors generally do is ask questions. You give them answers."

"I've noticed that, too," I said.

"Well, there are a lot of things they still don't know. Speaking of which, did I tell you there's a man here that wants to feel me up? I told him no. You are my boyfriend but Mark is my husband."

"Anita, don't let him! Unless you want him to."

"I don't want him to. But, you know, we all get old at the same rate. One day at a time."

"Meaning?"

"I'm happy for the attention, I suppose."

Once upon a time I wanted Anita's attention. I craved to see the world from her perspective. When she went to Israel after college, all her furniture became mine. The bed had a trough. The desk was stuffy. Steam pumped from behind it in a way that gave me a headache. I studied for long hours into the night, wanting to succeed, wanting to live up to the promise of the Windsor chair. Sometimes a motion reflected in the night glass jolted me. Was the door opening? Was it Anita come back early, by surprise?

I kneeled like an acolyte before her desk, sitting on my ankles, bending my head beneath the halo of her Lightolier lamp, studying for longer hours than Anita ever studied, desperate to forge a mind for myself. I discovered that I learned best by copying. I must have copied my entire history book three or four times. I'd take a fresh pad, close my eyes, and write down everything that I could remember from the chapter, then compare it to the book. My mind grew bigger by the day. I'd wake up thinking. My eyes teared from the glare of the lamp. I felt as if I was pushing books into my head. I wanted to shove a whole library in my head, and was disappointed by my memory. Certain facts I'd known in October had vanished by April. I had to put them back in again. Summer came, and I spent it exiled among pine trees at a Jewish sleep-away camp. I sat on a big rock and ate fizzy candy and fake-vanilla ice cream bars bought from the canteen, and by September my head was empty again. I gazed at the apartments across the street. They still seemed uninhabited.

Anita, meanwhile, was walking in orange groves, sipping ginger in her coffee, cutting purple cabbage into salads heaped with fresh feta cheese she served her new friends, speaking Hebrew at the Ulpan and practicing Italian to sing arias at the Ruben Academy. She wrote home on the translucent blue paper I'd always admired, the paper that was a layer of sky you could hold in your hand. Anita plucked some sky, covered it with her adventures, and sealed it all around with a lick of her tongue. The return address was in hieroglyphs more expressive than anything I'd ever imagined. Her *beth* was an eye lurking in a cave. Her *aleph* an upright person who could also bend. "Answered," I wrote on her envelope before tucking it in her drawer. Wherever I sat, I would never be the person sitting in the desirable place.

I once house-sat for a man in New Hampshire whose house turned out to be full of guns. Every book on his shelves was about war, as were the videotapes and magazines. In the barn, beside the Ford Taurus, was a genuine World War I jeep. "He trained to go to Korea, but never went," his son explained. "He was too young, and the hostilities were over by the time he was prepared." He's been fixated on fighting ever since.

I didn't train for war. Nor did I really train for achievement. My training was in appreciation. Like Alice Toklas, that's what I felt I did best. I was good at admiring the other's art—Anita's illustrations, the beautiful light blue and dark blue afghan which, before she went to Israel, flowed from her needles in opulent woolen waves. I loved to hold my hands apart while she spooled a hank of fresh wool into a ball. I loved to gaze at the tips of her needles, which made a soft rubbing clacking sound and turned like the mouth of an origami fortune-ball, opening with unconscious assurance in this direction and that. More than anything, it was that assurance I craved. "Anita, in Hebrew, means 'He answered,' " Anita once told me. "Ah. Nee-ta." She seemed the answer to me.

What if your job were to describe what it is like to eat a kiwi? Well, watching someone else eat a kiwi, I can imagine the lush strawberry-mangoish flavor in their mouth. I can imagine it so vividly that my own mouth waters with the sweet green taste. I can also imagine sitting alone behind the living room curtain of my childhood and savoring a kiwi by myself. But to stand up front and eat that kiwi! To describe that taste for others!—to think the way that kiwi tastes to my mouth is significant, and to trust the way I knit language can do it justice—there I falter. There I murmur, "You taste it, Anita. See what you think. You tell it, Anita. You are good at telling."

I carry her in my mind as the real one, the original, the *aleph* to my *beth,* the word to which I am the rhyme, the person whose vision is clear while mine blurs with distortion. The fact that she fell when as a child I must have craved her falling—only makes my ancient fantasies more frightening.

I sat in Anita's chair and slept in Anita's bed. Goldilocks broke all the family furniture except what fit her. Yet I wanted Anita to persist. This is the dream that goes unfulfilled: that I can break her and she'll remain, that I can topple her and she'll still be triumphant, that I can rip and punch and bite her and she'll know this is the demon me, the puny me, not the me who loves her, who really loves her—not politely, not for show, but savagely.

I want to tell Anita, my secret desire was that you could be even stronger than you were. I wanted to reveal everything to you. I wanted to bring in the exiled me, the pariah me, from where it was banished under my bed, in the farthest corners of my terrifying closet, in the door that stayed shut even in my dreams because I could not imagine it opening, because even my drowsing self knew I could not keep sleeping if that door opened. I wanted to bring in the part of me that hated you and have you see it and still let me bask in your smile. Your smile! It lit me like a bulb in a lampshade. If only I could harvest that smile, and dry it, and put it in a box! Oh, a little box like a matchbox, and from time to time when I'm sad and desolate, when the sky is all grainy ash, slide open that little box and take a pinch of you, and have my whole being blossom.

Or did you already know my heart when I didn't? Was it bitter as cyanide? Was it sweet as the apple the envious queen sent? Was the knowledge that apple held so appalling you went rigid? Do we always hate those we love? Hate them because we can never leave them? Hate them because they have so much power over us? Hate them because their heels glow like night-lights and their eyes are boxes of sun? It felt like your life or mine, and mine won. You fell and fell, and now you can't keep from falling. If only I were far away! Then I wouldn't see you lean against a walker, having your heavy feet lifted for you.

You once told me that you console yourself with the thought that because you have this disease I probably won't ever get it; the chances seem diminished. This way your life is of some use. I'm in your prayers. When the nurse leaves, and your door is swung open to the hospital corridor, you ask God to keep me safe. Mark, our parents, our brothers and their families, me. Could I ever really have hated you? Wasn't it you who taught me to scratch through love's darkness to find the carnival colors pulsing underneath? You knew they were there all along. Orange as methiolate, red as an open gash, white as arsenic. You walked this jungle constantly. It glowed inside you, the blaze in the jack-o'-lantern, the glare in the fireworks, the night apartments where phosphorescent strangers shone with loneliness, the sense of personal bizarreness, the wild, wild desire to run away from here.

• • •

I TRY TO REMEMBER ways Anita was mean. Surely she must have been mean, otherwise why would I be so attracted to grumpy women, to college girlfriends with furious faces, to demanding landladies and housemates with peroxide hair and an unpleasable manner, to older students in white big-pocketed blouses who declare that their problems are unsolvable?

Such women compel me; I rush to placate them. I bring them valentines, chocolate cakes, compliments on a blue wool coat or scarf, sincere reveries on the talents they display and to which they seem callous—mistaking their happiness for my happiness, thinking if only they could be happy with me, then we both could be happy. They seem to have devoured my happiness with their unhappiness. With what vigor they insist on their dissatisfaction! If I could give them their own joy, then we could each have ours, like each person having her own chicken pot pie, her own dinner plate, and nobody being Helen Keller before she met Anne, wild, grabbing with her fingers the food on someone else's plate. The fat women, the clench-faced women, the stubborn women, the scary women—all draw me. I think, Oh, I know how to make her happy, and try what worked with Anita: the Bohack wastebasket, the oddly pleasurable groveling, the acknowledgment of strengths, the reflection of what, in fact, *is* spectacular in this woman. How safe I feel! When the lion is smiling, she is not eating you. When the lion is letting you pull the splinter from her paw, she is not slashing. Yet I can come up with just one memory of Anita's being nasty to me. It is an almost inconsequential moment.

One childhood summer morning she tripped on the bungalow's concrete steps and went sprawling.

"Are you hurt?" I asked, anxious.

"Of course, you idiot."

Finis.

Although I recall, too, the shamed way I trailed after her like a kicked dog, wondering why I was such a jerk, why, why, I hadn't thought of something intelligent and helpful to say.

"Anita was trouble," a friend of mine remarked.

"How do you know?" I asked, excited.

"But it's what you say all the time!"

ANITA CRACKED big sticks across her knee to stoke a campfire. She banked the logs until the fire tipped back its head and roared. She suspected our mother disliked her, that everyone else was her favorite. She suspected our father thwarted her, preferring to satisfy our brothers' ambitions. She was deposed, and deposed again by a torrent of siblings.

I thought of her with her thicket hair, her pilot-light eyes, her enraged impulsiveness, her pointed tactlessness. She was asking for something with her mouth and hands and stomach and stomping, tantrumming feet—but what was it? The wilder she got, the more my mother shunned her. She saw in her first daughter her tyrannical mother. What she couldn't confront in her mother, she left unanswered in her daughter. Scalding tears, doors flung shut, hungers that no quantities of food could satisfy, something avid and wanting worked its way through Anita, and her way of reaching out was pushing away.

I walked around the bungalow colony with her when she returned from months of camp—my heroine, suntanned, reeking of woodsmoke and pine sap, the muscles in her legs like bowling balls, her hair a warren, and what she was saying was, "How could she do this to me? Look how fat I got! It was her—I was doing so well, I'd lost so much weight on Weight Watchers, but she said I had to go. And look at me now. All they feed you are starches! There's a loaf of bread at every meal. They pass it around, they keep filling the basket. Yellow margarine as soft as mayonnaise. Spaghetti, white ice cream, sloppy joes on hamburger buns, Kool-Aid in a tin pitcher. It tastes good in that pitcher! And I was thirsty. Empty calories. Empty, empty, stupid calories. She did this to me," she said, punching her leg.

I skipped alongside to keep up, marveling at her words, struck by her beauty.

"What are you doing a little jig about?" she said. "What's the matter with you?"

"But Anita—you look, you look great."

She snorted. "If everyone were as blind as you."

"No, Anita. You do. I'm so happy you're home!"

She laughed. "You're her favorite child. That's always been obvious."

"But that's just not true! We both are. That's what she always says."

"Blind, blind, blind," Anita replied, but she grabbed my hand nonetheless, and swung it while she sang a new song:

"High in the heavens are clouds floating free.
If I could fly away . . .

"When I worked for the State," Anita says often, "I went to the bathroom one day. As I was leaving it, I slipped on a wet floor. I fell down backward flat on my back. Then I had a dream. I was at a party where all the walls were green. We were laughing and having fun. But then people started to leave. I heard a voice say, 'The party's over.' I woke up. I was lying on my back. Nobody had come to help me. They just continued to do their jobs. Later, X rays were performed on my hand. It was determined that the very tips of my fingers were gone."

"What do you mean, gone?" I ask.

"They were gone."

"Were you bleeding?"

"No, it happened inside me. In my fingers. The bone was sheared off."

"Ah."

People are leaving. She can't quite reach what she needs.

I try to reconcile the strong Anita to the weak one, the adored Anita to the despised one, the Anita who really lives and the one I seem to be forever inventing. Nothing matches. Always I feel I'm lying. Everything is too absolute, but I don't believe the truth lies somewhere in the middle. The truth rarely lies somewhere in the middle. Is it true I wanted her to fall? As often as I say it, I take it back. As often as I say she wasn't oppressive, I disbelieve. She is a thimble and Twin Towers, vague as a photo of a photo of a photo, and clear as lightning—a forty-two-year-old woman who told me on Friday she painted a jewelry box in occupational therapy. "I painted one side of it pink, and then on another side I used yellow," she said. I would like to kiss her too hard, a kiss that lets me feel her teeth underneath.

Somehow we are forever sitting side by side and caressing one another in the bodies we once had. This is the scroll-story constantly uncoiling, the truth as it persists. Anita stretches her arm out to expose the silken bruised-blue of her inner elbow, where the vein leaps toward the surface and the body is most sensitive. "Right there," she murmurs. "Ah. Nice. Good, Bonnie."

Or else it is New Year's Eve, and I am still trying to untangle the briar patch of Anita's hair. I dip my comb in water and work as carefully as I can. The knots are hungry spiders with hard centers. Anita's eyes are tearing. "Shhh," she says, as if I'm being loud, not rough. "Shhh."

"Okay," I say, dipping my comb. There's more knots than hair. I sink the comb's teeth into the edge of a knot and pull, holding the top of her hair with my other hand. "Just think—by next year, your hair will be smooth. Anita, this time don't let the knots grow back."

"Shhh," she says.

"No, listen, Anita. You don't have to go through this again. Don't let the knots come back. They always want to come back, but this time, don't let them."

"I can't help it," says Anita.

"Of course you can. Just remember to brush behind you. Just remember people can see that, too."

"I don't want to think about people seeing me all the time. That's their business. I can't live like that."

"Of course you can. It's so easy. Just—"

"How do you know? You don't know anything, Bon! You live in this world like a blind person. You can't even see what's in front of your own nose."

I see your knots, I think, but remain silent.

"Ouch! That's exactly what I mean!" she says. "Look at what you're doing! Try to see it. Look inside each knot."

Her hair floods reddish brown in the lamplight and swarms with knots. For a moment, it is an impossible task: untangle this by midnight. But then I take a breath. The comb's long teeth plunge slowly.

"That's better," Anita murmurs.

I work as kindly as I can, and Anita knows it's always an accident when my hand slips.

bell hooks

GIRLS TOGETHER:

Sustained Sisterhood

GROWING UP, I was not close to my five sisters. For most of our lives together we shared two bedrooms. Ours was a patriarchal household and both in the world outside that home and from inside we learned to be suspicious of females together. While men gathering in groups, whether on the basketball court or hanging out on the corner, were seen as positive examples of bonding and closeness, female groups were seen as sinister, as necessarily an occasion for concern. When we shared with strangers that there were six of us girls, they would often "freak," express concern for our dad and brother, show sympathy for Mama, since it was assumed that it was her job to keep all this unruly female energy in check, conveying again and again the message that there was something dangerous—threatening even—about females in groups together.

No wonder, then, that within the space of our household, we too internalized the sexist socialization that encouraged us to look at one another with suspicion, to be fearful and watchful. Mama came from a family of many sisters. And she preached to us endlessly about the necessity of living in harmony with one another. Constantly alluding to the danger of strife between sisters without ever sharing the reasons for her concern, she believed in sisterhood. Despite her many allegiances to patriarchal thinking, when it came to the politics of female bonding in our household, Mama asserted "feminist" values. She repudiated competition, encouraged us to respect one another's individuality and autonomy. We were admonished to stay out of one another's private stuff—friends, including boyfriends, were among those things that could not be shared. Mama would tell us that she had seen too many households where sisters had grown up hating one another, doing evil to one another, and that she was not raising us to be each other's enemy.

Her "feminist" concerns for sisterhood were constantly pitted against the sexist socialization that was all around us. Even though she did not allow us to engage in hostile exchanges or fights with one another, when her back was turned every now and then, all that she preached against was expressed. If she found out, the culprits were severely punished. Overall, there was not much overt sibling rivalry in our household. Even so, sexist thinking about females—about the nature of us coming together in groups—shaped our interactions with one another.

In this female-dominated world we did not revere the black female body. It was subjected to constant ridicule and mockery. We poked fun at each other's big butts, skinny legs, flat chests, skin color, or large feet. When looking at each other's bodies, we could always find something wrong. No wonder, then, that we offered each other a legacy of shame handed down from older siblings to younger. Undressing and dressing so that no nakedness would be revealed, we learned to look at one another's bodies with the same fear that the rest of the world expressed of women in groups. We taught each other bodily shame.

We policed each other's sexuality in ways that were terrorizing. I can still remember S., my older sister, the intruder, who came from Mama's first previous marriage to live with us, catching my hands in my panties masturbating, threatening to tell, and telling. She was truly the spy in our "house of love." Oddly enough, I did not realize the intensity of her collusion with the older world until I grew up. As a child I merely thought Mama had these magical ways of knowing—that she understood our bodies and knew what they were going through. When in fact my older sister was constantly reading diaries and journals, reporting back. A major issue around sexuality in our household was the issue of pregnancy. We were constantly told by Mama's raging didactic voice "not to bring any babies into this house for me to take care of." Our mother had been pregnant as a teenager. She wanted us to do life differently. Yet that was never what she said. Instead she made us see our bodies as this site of shame and betrayal. Any day now those feeling, sensual, sexual bodies could lead us away from ourselves into a shame so powerful we could not come home. This threat of expulsion from the household of our mother, from her attentive eye and care, was enough to keep all longing for sex or babies away. I can remember only our sister T., who was growing up, the perfect mother caretaker, longing to have children. The rest of us were always more uncertain. T. was also the one who lied to be with men, who dared to be sexual.

I remember the night she did not come home on time, the night our parents "caught her in a lie." That night as we gathered in our pink rooms, wondering about her fate, the atmosphere was thick with the combined tension of pleasure and danger. I no longer ponder why our father waited until she climbed the stairs to those pink rooms, until she undressed, waited until she felt safe, before he climbed the stairs—something he never did. His heavy footsteps were the sound of danger. And he beat her. And he beat her. And he beat her. And he kept repeating, "Don't you ever lie to me." We betrayed our sister that night. Instead of hating him, we hated her for bringing this dark brutal wrath into the sanctuary of our pink rooms. We were violated. We thought then that she was the cause, that she had ripped and torn the veiled space of our secret longings to reveal our shame. We thought that she had seductively courted violation by lying and longing. We could not accept then that he was the violent, violating one who would never have heard our truths even had we the courage to speak them.

Once again our older sister had been the spy, the double agent, encouraging and betraying. Later I would understand that this public humiliation, this violent beating of T. in front of the rest of us, in the face of our undressed vulnerability, was an object lesson beating back into silence our sexual feelings. Sexuality and shame, so intimately connected in our mama's life, was the legacy she passed on to us. Long after the pill and other modern means of birth control were available, our sexuality was kept in check by terror, fear of our bodies, fear of the male other, fear of punishment, fear of shame. Not one of us brought babies into our mother's house growing up. To this day, I do not know if any of us even allowed ourselves a space of sexual abandon. Whenever my body was touched by any hand save my own, I could see lurking behind a raised hand the cries of my sister, the fear of the body's betrayal. It was enough to beat back desire. It was enough to kill sexual longing.

The terrorism of our father was rare. It was our mother who policed the female bodies in her household with a vengeance. She who inspected underwear. She who stood by our side at the doctor's office to find out about discharges, vaginal odor, and all other pain. She counted pads and noticed missed periods. She who wanted no babies in her house, no little bodies, no sexuality. Mama desired an end to desire, for herself, for her daughters. We were to have fuller, deeper, more meaningful lives. We were not to be trapped by desire.

In our pink rooms desire was hidden, so secret as not to be seen. The only visible reminder of the possibility of desire was adornment, the freedom to be alluring, to dress up. We grew up with old-style vanity tables with low stools for seats, small drawers, and a huge round mirror, where we could stare at ourselves all day long. We could not look upon the naked body but we could dress ourselves and each other as though we were dolls. That seductive space of dress-up was the space of female bonding. There we nurtured one another. Helped each other choose an outfit, do makeup, comb hair. My sisters loved to comb my hair.

The ritual of sitting around waiting to have our hair combed was the fun female time. We all washed our hair on the same day. And it was "plaited" then as always. Mostly Mama and T. did hair. The rest of us sat around reading magazines, talking, showing the latest dance. When we left the stage of braiding hair, an art I was never to learn because my sisters did it better, we went to the kitchen for the ritual of straightening our hair. This was another time of communal talk and play, another female-only time. The times I remember most are those Saturday days, when the smell of fish frying (caught at the creek by Baba, Mama's mother) mingled with the scent of burning hair grease. While one of us sat in the chair with her back to the stove, getting her hair pressed, the rest of us gathered at the table to drench white bread in hot sauce and pick tiny bones from the bodies of fried fish, to eat homemade french fries and drink ice-cold pop. Such moments of shared female ecstasy haunt me—linger in the shadows of a grown-up world where there are no Saturday mornings where we women gather.

Mama had created a hierarchy of responsibility among her girls, with my older sister S. being second-in-command, then authority rested with T., who was the gentle caretaker. S. was the fascist. We hated it when she was left in charge. When it was my turn, I was never given authority over my younger sisters because I had been labeled the "crazy" rebellious one—the outsider. I was the sister who cried at night, whom the other sisters often hated, complaining always to Mama, "Make her stop crying." No one cared about the reasons I cried. In this female world, crying was a sign of weakness, worthy only of contempt. No one talked to me. My sisters paired off in buddy systems, I had no family buddy. Later in womanhood when I asked my sister G. why no one talked to me, she shared that our parents had told them not to talk to me, that I was crazy, that if I spoke to them they were "not to believe" anything I said. All those years I had thought there was something inherently wrong with me, something that made the group shun and punish me only to find they had just been following orders. None of us remember what truths I might have spoken that they wanted so badly to silence.

My one brother always talked to me. In the patriarchal world of our family he had greater rights and privileges. Just as our mother catered to our father's needs in a servile way, we learned to cater to our brother. When I tease him that he did not have six sisters, he had six slaves, he denies the power and privilege that were his. The one space where we could exclude him was the world of the upstairs pink rooms. That space was off limits to him. Now and then he would, by invitation from his sisters and parental consent, be allowed to visit us there. Secluded in a private downstairs room, he felt cut off from the world of fun and good times that happened in the pink rooms. He resented us, our shared femaleness, that we never had to part with one another as he always had to leave his boy bonding behind when the nighttime came.

Living in a family with so many girls, we were always aware of difference. Sexist stereotypes were disrupted by the nature of our bodies and beings. Some of us were strong of body, athletic, and others were weak. Some of us were seen as sexy and cute, and others just plain. Some of us were brainy and others more interested in creative work. The strongest lesson that I learned coming to womanhood in a household with so many females was the recognition and appreciation of our differences. I feel tremendous gratitude for Rosa Bell, our mother's insistence on solidarity within difference. Despite our collective sexisms we were also bound by ties of learned sisterly bonding. We were taught by our mother to both share resources with one another and to settle our differences without trashing one another or holding on to sustained feelings of hostility. When we were together in our family house, we accepted our sisterly bonding as "natural." It was only later when we grew up and met many sisters who were not close to one another, who were bitter rivals, that we really learned to value our bonding—to appreciate its specialness.

Even though my sisters were participants in a dysfunctional family dynamic in which I was often scapegoated, persecuted, I did not blame them or feel tremendous anger toward them, since I felt that something was wrong with me. I wanted to be close. Sometimes I think it was this experience of bonding with a female group where we were so different from one another, we even looked different, that provided an important background for my early engagement with the feminist movement. As an undergraduate at Stanford involved in the women's movement, I encountered among peers and faculty that same suspicion about women gathering in groups that was so familiar in our childhood. I was impressed by the way in which the call for feminist sisterhood echoed the values Mama had taught us. While many of my peers talked about sisterhood, they were not as committed to the practice of sisterhood. Practicing sisterhood was work I had done for years in my family.

In the heat wave of contemporary feminism, I remember that our first concern as women gathering together to embrace liberation was not naming men as oppressors, or even calling out patriarchy. Our first focus was on ways women regard one another—the internalized sexism that shapes female-to-female behavior. Confronting that sexism was the prelude to becoming feminist—changing the ways we saw ourselves as women and the ways we looked at other women. Understanding that females could bond together in constructive ways even in the midst of sexism really strengthened my faith that feminist sisterhood could be realized.

When I began writing *Ain't I a Woman: Black Women and*

Feminism, I relied on the experiences of the black females in our family to guide and shape the direction of my speculative thought. As my commitment to feminist politics deepened, so did my relationships with the sisters I grew up with. When one of my sisters acknowledged her lesbianism, I was there to support and affirm her. When my sister G. married young without finishing her university studies, I was there to urge her on, to encourage her to return, finish her degree, and go on, to share feminist thinking. When A. was married to a violent man, I had Lenore Walker's *Battered Women* and my own experience to share. Although positively involved with all my sisters, it has been hardest for me to bridge the distance separating me and my older sister. As womanhood broke the hierarchial fascist power she had often used to dominate and control us in childhood, she more than any sibling became competitive for Mama's attention. Continuing her role of spy, she still works to bring home the information that will lead to parental disapproval. She is also the most conventional in her thinking about gender roles.

One of my youngest sisters was the first sibling to take the initiative to bring out in the open her participation in the collective persecution and scapegoating of me as a child. I vividly recall her coming to visit me at my small Cape Cod house in California and openly sharing, though it was painful, the feelings of envy and hatred that had made her a willing accomplice in the wounding that so hurt me as a child. The moment I left home for college I began the process of healing those wounds, of seeking the necessary mental health care that enabled me to process the past, to forgive and let go of the pain. When she came to see me, I was not the same troubled girl she had always known, the "crazy" one. We laughed together sitting in the sunshine as she exclaimed: "You're not crazy at all. You never were." She wanted forgiveness and I was glad that all was forgiven, that our sisterly bond could now be sweeter, stronger—deeper.

In her work as a therapist my sister V. has been most aware

of the need for women to recover who we were as girls together. Just recently we went down South together, sat on a porch swing in the sun, and remembered ourselves—girls together. Time brings us closer. We can talk about the rivalry that sisterly bonding did not enable us to name—the competition that was always lurking underneath the surface. I can share how much I envied her calmness, her athletic ability, her relationship to Dad. She envied me being the smart one. Luckily, we both know we are smart these days and affirm that understanding in our public interactions. My youngest sister, I often felt I never knew. She entered the family just as I was psychically leaving it and so I do not remember her girlhood. We came together first to relearn our childhood, to trace again the pattern of our bonding. When she travels with me to give a lecture for the first time, she is surprised at the woman I have become, that the world sees as a provocative strong voice. She remembers the sad suffering girl I was. She remembers my courage and my pain. I remember her as a smart little girl who dreamed of being a doctor, who always wanted to hang out with her older sisters, who always—always—left her behind.

These are the memories we laugh about sitting on the front porch. The day is hot and sticky. We have gathered as we often did in those pink rooms to tell our stories—to share our surprise at the women we have become—to talk about the way we were as girls and the way we are now. All of us know the joy of sustained sisterly bonding—that is the legacy Rosa Bell, our mother, gave us. This is the legacy we will pass on.

Maria Flook

The Boat Train

MY SISTER'S FACE floats in a dark square as I stand in the basement on a mound of soiled linen and look up the laundry chute. She leans deep into its sheet-metal frame; the plyboard lid blocks the bedroom daylight behind her until I can see only her face and her face repeated, mirrored on all four sides of the shiny burrow. Her blond hair falls in silky kinks on either side of her face, like curled ribbon.

I often went to the cellar to retrieve a doll I had punished and tossed into oblivion, but later wanted the doll forgiven. One of its eyes wasn't blinking and remained half-closed, half-open. There, I found my sister's face floating one floor above me. She scolded me for standing on my father's white Van Heusens. Her voice trailed off when she noticed our mother's seamless hose wound in a tight, erotic knob, like a nautilus perched on the pile of laundry. Finding our mother's female items in the subterranean washing room made us jittery; her lace undergarments were hints and markers suggesting that *sex was a highway,* and sooner or later my sister and I would get on it.

I reached for the silk mollusk.

"Don't touch that," Karen said. I looked up the silver chute and saw my sister's face. She smiled. Our childhood was safe in that tight mirrored flume, safer than it would ever be.

• • •

MY SISTER KAREN disappeared when she was fourteen years old. The *Wilmington Journal* ran a photograph of Karen with the word *Runaway?* beneath her face. The newspaper put a question mark after the word, asking readers to consider her case a local mystery. The next day they ran the same picture. The caption asked, *Dead or Alive?* It was 1964; I was twelve years old and the last person Karen had talked to. She told me, "I'm going to the corner, want anything? You want your Teaberry gum?"

I was at the kitchen table, writing five sheets of detention homework. I looked at my sister. I saw she was dressed up. She was wearing smoky nylons and low heels which shifted her posture forward. Her lipstick was frosted salmon-pink, and on her face she was wearing matte powder which erased her features.

"I don't have any money," I told her.

Karen said, "Well, I don't have enough for both of us."

"Forget it," I said.

"I'm going to the drugstore," Karen said once more, and she had her hand on the doorknob too long a time, I thought, before turning it.

The FBI visited our house. When Karen hadn't returned after forty-eight hours, the local Penny Hill Police assumed it was "bigger" than they were used to and the federal investigators were directed to our quiet neighborhood. My father laid out some of Karen's report cards with the teachers' comments and after these documents were reviewed, I was asked to leave the room. I wasn't reluctant to be dismissed because I knew I could hear everything the agent said by putting my head in the dining room chimney. Inside the mortared shaft, their conversation was amplified. I heard my mother sniffling. She ripped a tissue from its hollow box, and another. She was giving a performance. The agent was talking about whether or not my sister was a virgin and this upset my mother.

"It's these days," my father was saying to her, and the FBI agent agreed. He wanted a list of Karen's boyfriends. Karen didn't have any, my mother said flatly as if disproving his previous assumption.

"None? Are we sure?" my father said, since he had already taken sides with the FBI authority.

"If she had had any boyfriends, do you think she'd have been so gloomy all the time?"

"Love is strange," the FBI man said. I was asked to return to the room to relate the details of Karen's departure. I told the government official that Karen didn't take a suitcase.

"We have all the suitcases," my father told the man.

The agent said, "She could have hidden a grip in the bushes."

"She didn't take anything," I said.

"We have all the suitcases," my father said another time. It was getting ridiculous, as if they had lost sight of exactly what was missing. The man looked grim but he assured my father that some girls ran away with just the clothes on their backs.

Karen and I had shared a room. Once I had drawn an imaginary line down the middle of the bedroom and if Karen put anything of her own on my side, I claimed it. When Karen was missing, all of her possessions were arranged in their proper places; there was no chance of them moving over the boundary and becoming my rightful property. I collected china horses and arranged them in formal rows across my dresser according to each one's temperament and confirmation. These prancing mounts no longer allured me, and from my bed I studied the treasures on Karen's bureau glass. I saw her golden paperweight, a fossilized chunk of amber sap in which tiny bubbles of air are trapped.

The hours with my sister were too short. Our union was brief; our entire history together could be reflected in the tiny oval of her hand mirror. In the night-light's dull arc, I could see my sister's comb and brush; I could see my sister's hair.

MY SISTER KAREN disappeared when she was fourteen years old. On November 29, 1964, she walked out the kitchen door, out of our neighborhood. She sat down in some man's flashy car and drove out of our town. For two strange elastic years, she went missing. No word came.

I tried to picture my sister dead. I invented a scene, but it was an exercise of the imagination that few twelve-year-olds engage in. I saw a hovering angel, its heavy, ragged wings flapping, but to visualize my sister's motionless body in a grassy trench along the Delaware River was an act of sororicide. I couldn't achieve that vision. It disturbed me more to believe she still survived, survived without thinking of me.

If my sister drove off in a detailed Chrysler pimp ride, if she set up housekeeping with moody grifters and addicted vets, outlawing with some oddball foster family, was that worse than the fact that she never came back to collect me? How did she decide to forget me?

I searched for my sister. By the age of thirteen, I took off on weekend expeditions. I entered the same world my sister occupied and merged with lanes of traffic she might have traveled in. I made my own transitions, singular or imitative? My sister and I evolved synchronically. In our anonymity to each other we grew codependent, we grew closer. Now, in my early forties, my sister's disappearance remains in a dreamy stasis at the core of each decade. If I were to reactivate a search, where would I start? Which one of us will surface first, in what double mirror?

Three decades later, I have started to review what true knowledge I have of my sister's disappearance and what her disappearance created in us. When one child goes missing, the remaining child is left untethered in a peculiar way. I have seen a dog pull free from its collar and in its sudden freedom shudder, as if any connection it had to the world remained in the coil of leather.

The first minutes of freedom are unsettling.

When my sister disappeared, the physical world was immediately altered. The next morning after she was gone, the refineries at Marcus Hook spewed microscopic droplets of oil across the leeward neighborhoods. Our picture windows filmed; our hair sagged with petroleum mist as we stood at the bus stop. The sun itself was masked, as if behind a vinyl shower curtain. Natural laws seemed to reorganize and shift.

At night, Karen's closet door wouldn't latch and drifted loose. I saw her dresses hanging on the closet pole; their shoulders slumping off the hangers seemed animate and shrugging. I got out of bed to shut the door and again it fell open as if the room itself were turning and the wall was rotating to become the ceiling. I propped a pair of shoes against the door frame, Karen's Cordovan Weejuns with spidery tassels as if she had just stepped out of them.

That same week, a neighbor drove his car through a plate-glass slider. I went directly to the scene with my father, who penned measurements for a replacement door. The car was sitting on the plush carpet until insurance inspectors arrived. I felt the cold air rushing through the interior rooms of our neighbor's house.

My sister's disappearance had that same effect on ours. A window had broken open. Her disappearance was an assault on my security and yet, at the same instant, an alarming expanse was created, a chilly spectacle of freedom.

A missing child and a car in someone's living room have immediate shock value. When my sister disappeared, I was exposed to a new exterior world and the treacherous interior landscape of the wounded psyche. Delicate root systems had been disturbed, unearthed, left to the harsh elements. I was jostled and freed by a *charmed* destructive force, from every tether of childhood.

Absence is a fat seed.

When a loss occurs, it occurs in perpetuity; it keeps regenerating like a flowering vine. My sister's departure lengthened. Even after her eventual return, her exit tunneled farther than her reentry. What vanished once, keeps vanishing, in perennial mutations.

What happened to my sister, in fact, happened to me. My sister walks ahead of me through these pages. She's holding a shoe box of scraps, notes with her half of the story. I am writing this down as it happens. Sometimes I can't tell who is pulling whose puppet strings.

ONE SCHOOL NIGHT IN WILMINGTON. I hold a hand mirror extended as Karen brushes my hair. I watch my reflection as my sister pulls the bristles over the crest of my scalp, scouring my accentuated widow's peak. She angles the untame strands until my mane is plowed and parted. If I turn the mirror slightly I can see Karen's face, a pink barrette between her teeth. The lorgnette circle is a great abyss. Even a fleck of silver nitrate tells too much. She fastens the clasp around a clump of my hair and tugs the hunk tight until the roots at my temples are stinging. This hand mirror often comes back to haunt me. It is like a silver garden pond in memory, a bright oval of light splashed upon the ceiling of the psyche.

IN 1956, WHEN the S.S. *Andrea Doria* was rammed by the *Stockholm,* my sister and I were at home, in the suburbs of Wilmington, asleep in our horsehair beds. I was four years old, my sister was still six. Two weeks earlier, we had returned from Italy, where my father was employed by Fiat. My father had actually booked passage on the doomed ship, but he used his Fiat office to wedge us on an earlier crossing aboard the *Julius Caesar,* another ship from the same line. We kept our original ticket vouchers for the *Doria,* complete with the historic dates and cabin numbers. During our childhood, our mother often extended an end table drawer and fanned open the tickets. "You girls would have died," she told my sister and me. She didn't say "could have," she said "would have," as if a plan, greater than her own making, had been foiled. "*Your* cabin was on the side which was rammed. We couldn't have saved you. We would have been dancing upstairs in the ballroom. The dancing was terrific on those Atlantic crossings. Big-name bands. The floors were waxed to a turn. It was perfect. Little girls would have been in bed. The steward kept your names on a card."

The fact that my sister Karen and I should have been broadside of a Swedish liner has always alarmed me. I imagine the dense fog that squeezed the light from the liner's portholes. I can picture the taut little bunk I would have shared with my sister, and our one linking desire for shore and safety—for our parents to finish their indulgent night and to come check on us. The steamship incident was not merely a brush with misfortune; rather, it symbolized our dangerous journey through youth with parents who seemed under the spell of an intense erotic sorcery. This was the challenge of our household—how to maintain family life against a backdrop of carnal spectacles. Our mother's roiling jealousies and hungers swarmed the calendar. She was not Cinderella who had lost a slipper—she *was* the empty slipper. Her beauty created a lifelong fiasco for our father, and for us. We lived in our mother's element the way fish can live in a mesh bucket in the river, zigzagging with the current in the confines of a trap.

I have often thought our mother's unspeakable beauty was a curse to her. I have seen her avert her eyes from mirrors in public places, mirrors in lobbies or restaurants, as if she feared she might be devoured by her own famished expression. If any of our family instincts surged, our schemes toward nuclear unity were immediately quelled by our mother's rigid program of romance with our father. Children were intrusions and were quickly siphoned off to boarding schools or mental institutions, then into boot camp and marriages for better or for worse. Each one of us was ingeniously and prematurely dispersed. Unlike other species, we could make no migratory formations, no collective mass. We scattered.

There has always been a struggle in my household between our family allegiances and our erotic pursuits. Our mother spent a great deal of time sitting in our father's lap, or resting her hip against the arm of his chair, her arms around his neck. She usurped her children's rights to this ritual. If we sat at his feet she shooed us away. Karen and I were allotted only one good-night kiss, which our mother performed hurriedly, gracelessly, with her hands knotted behind her back. She was so erect and uncomfortable, she might have been administering inoculations. My sister Karen was two and a half years older than me. I was "littlest" but very canny, and I suffered these small rations better than she. We each took the icy clay mined from our mother and built our fortresses with it. My "tomboy" shell was thick. But in the absence of maternal nurturing my sister Karen grew more and more disconsolate. When our mother leaned, perfunctorily, over Karen's pillow to deliver her arid smooch, Karen turned away. She tugged the sheet over her head.

In junior high school, Karen hoarded money from our father's desk and gave it away to win momentary friendships, just as she would, in one year's time, square receipts with a pimp. I thought her looting of my father's money drawer was a sign of something very serious. She didn't show remorse for the pilfering she did. I watched her seek shelter in outsiders, having no vision of herself without a circle of cheap admirers. At night, in our shared room, Karen stared at herself in the closet mirror, as if she waited for her image to evaporate like steam. Once, she had read to me from a book in which the experts all agreed, in a unanimous statement: no one has ever successfully developed a snapshot of a ghost.

IN 1964, THE SUMMER before Karen disappeared, we were again booked for another transatlantic crossing. My father was working in industrial supply and he took us to Europe for an extended business trip. At the end of August, we were scheduled to take the boat train from Paris to Le Havre. We could have flown TWA, but my father had purchased a Citroën for our mother's fiftieth birthday and they had to bring it back on the liner S.S. *France.* An automobile could not be shipped to the states on the ocean liner unless accompanied by valid ticket holders.

During those weeks in Europe, I noticed a change occurring in my sister. A silence overtook her; she not so much suffered its condition but employed it. She no longer took the chocolate wafers from which I had licked off all the frosting, nor the pretzels, the denuded knots after I had licked off the salt. These snacking rituals between us had ended with her adolescence. Our childhood bond was waning but a new connection was emerging. She was on the brink of womanhood with all its trompe l'oeil, false doors and dangers; I was one step behind her and for the time being acted as her valet or assistant.

We were extra baggage to our mother. She didn't care to show us ruins or paintings. We were pulled along to get what we could from it while our father did business. My favorite pastime that summer was swiping my mother's unfiltered Gitanes and smoking them in the bathrooms of the small hotels we stayed in. Mornings, I went into my parents' bedroom to dunk my brioche in their pot of coffee. My father was in the salle de bains shaving. I saw another empty Maalox bottle in the trash basket when I looted the carton of cigarettes. My father's stomach condition wasn't getting any better, but our mother played it down; she said everyone has a "physical weakness." I wondered what my physical weakness might be. She said, "Girls have bladder complaints." This was news to me. I had never heard the term "complaints" for physical aches and pains, and I pictured an internal organ making acid remarks and grumpy asides, bitching and moaning. When she turned her back to sit on the edge of her bed and paint her toenails, I sunk the pack of cigarettes in the waistband of my underpants. I watched my mother's back, her small waist and the flare of her hips highlighted by her worn satin peignoir robe. Just as Karen had learned from her, my mother started her day with some sort of cosmetic ritual. Seeing my mother performing her morning toilette always unnerved me. Her sexuality was brimming, no dressing gown or bathrobe could disguise it. I always dressed hurriedly and went to play on the old-fashioned elevator—reaching through the accordian gate to finger the thick green lubrication on the cable. I smeared the grease from my fingers on the inside hem of my shorts.

The last week in Paris, waiting to take the boat train, Karen left the hotel every night. She climbed out the third-floor window and went backward down the fire escape, which dropped her in full view of the front office. The evening manager chose to ignore her. Karen had met an Iranian boy, Imran Manzoor, and they "dated" like this. She brought me along, perhaps fearing I might squawk if I stayed behind, but I think she wanted me there for company. She was embarking on the perilous activity of fighting off loneliness with lust. I was her tolerant kin; she wanted my intact purity nearby as she endeavored otherwise. Whether she cleaved to my tomboy image or flaunted herself before it, I couldn't tell. I waited on the sidewalk as she and the boy crumpled to their knees in an alley behind a pharmacy and he pumped her head above his crotch. Once, she moved her head away and I saw the glistening phallus, wet from Karen's saliva, but mostly I watched the traffic going by in the street and practiced my inhalation technique with the remaining cigarettes in the pack. After the boy had finished, he walked us around the block a few times which reminded me of a hot walker at a racetrack, a youth who leads horses in a circle to cool off the sweat. Then Imran stopped us in front of our hotel and my sister slipped back into her girlhood, as if the boy had snapped his fingers. She climbed the wrought-iron ladder into our hotel bedroom, pulling me up behind her. My sister brushed her teeth for longer than necessary. She told me she didn't want to use the bidet. It was a disgusting invention, why should she try it? After all, she was still a virgin.

I thought, how could she still be a virgin when she took his thing in her mouth? I didn't take her to task about it, although I was sure she was mistaken. We played cards for an hour, then turned out the light and discussed the girls we knew stateside, classmates at the junior high school, listing their weaknesses and then their endearing traits.

For the last several nights in Paris, I trailed behind the couple. I was impressed by my older sister—how had she attracted this stranger, handsome and lithe with deep saffron-toned skin? He handed me cigarettes and occasionally would light them for me. I started to inhale without the immediate cough. I was learning the style of it, then the nicotine assumed its importance.

One morning in our hotel room, Karen was taking a bath in the giant porcelain tub, deep as a sea. She washed her hair and reclined beneath the surface to rinse out the suds. She held her breath and went under. Her wavy hair floated like golden kelp. I walked into the other room and smoked a half pack of Gitanes, lighting a new one each time the cigarette was only halfway consumed. I threw the lighted butts out the balcony window. Later, I learned that the hotel's doorman, really not much older than a boy, was standing on the sidewalk beside an urn of flowers. My cigarettes fell onto his hair and shoulders, sometimes falling onto the pavement and rolling off the curb. He picked up the smoldering butts and looked up at our window. I was already inside lighting up another and had no idea I was showering sparks upon the epaulets of the uniformed victim. His supervisor saw him holding cigarettes in his hand and came outside to scold him. He was not permitted to smoke on the job. The boy explained what had happened, but his boss didn't believe him.

The young doorman and the concierge appeared at our room. Karen was wrapped in a bath sheet, tucking her hair around giant foam rollers. The concierge had come with the youth to inspect the situation. They looked at my sister, the moist sheet loosening around her curves as she lifted her arms to insert a bobby pin across the pink foam rubber. In pantomime, the boy explained to his employer how the cigarettes originated from our balcony, in an endless strafing, he was sure of it. He pretended to smoke an invisible cigarette, then he walked to the window and tossed it off. He struck an imaginary match and inhaled again. His performance was comical and since I had consumed the last real cigarette and had discarded the cellophane packet, it seemed ridiculous. There wasn't a dirtied ashtray to confirm the doorman's accusation.

The manager left us, called to the telephone, but the boy remained. He was looking at my sister. She was smiling at his foolishness.

She stood up and walked across the room, her hips pulled left and right just a little, enough to intimate she had the floor if she wanted it. She told him, "I don't smoke. It was her." She pointed to me and smiled the way a dog lover smiles at a puppy who has chewed a slipper. "It's on her breath. Go see. She shouldn't be smoking those things, should she?"

The doorman didn't bother to come over to me and investigate my smoky tonsils. He was already moving the palms of his hands over Karen's breasts, keeping his fingertips lifted off her flesh. Her breasts were released from their dewy sarong and the sheet fell to the carpet. He spoke in French, some words I thought I understood only from their heat. I went out to the balcony and looked at the foreign cars going by in the street. I searched for American models and saw a Ford Fairlane parked below the hotel, its tires rolled onto the sidewalk to afford room to the narrow street.

After a few moments, Karen pushed the doorman away and he went out of the room, his face still flushed with his greed. Karen said, "Mare, try not to get us in another jam like that." I promised to flush my butts. Once, when our mother came in unexpectedly, I crammed the lighted stub in the toe of my shoe and later suffered for it. The tips of my toes were burned, three pale blisters swelled until they burst, revealing the raw tips underneath.

ALL SUMMER, I was witness to my sister's carnal exchanges with members of the service industries in Italy and France. Busboys, cabdrivers, vending machine operators. She pulled me along on bizarre hikes into stockrooms and kitchens, or out to the streets and into the Métro. Once, a man drove us in his Renault to Bois de Vincennes where he made me wait on a bench stained with bird milk while he took Karen into the dark arbor for an hour.

"What happened?" I asked her.

"He couldn't."

"Couldn't what?"

She looked at me. She was gauging her responsibility. What should or shouldn't she explain to me? "What have you had to eat?" She always tried to consider whether my stomach was empty or not. Still other times, we walked or took the train and prowled after hours in the formal gardens of Tuileries and Champs-de-Mars. Karen scolded me for having such dirty hair. "I'm ashamed to be seen with you! How can you go around like that, you oil rag."

Despite her criticism, I continued to practice hygiene habits unacceptable to my sister. She tried to teach me the White Rain doctrine, "wash, rinse, repeat," but I wanted my hair dirty. I was twelve and experiencing rosy panty stains. I was concerned that menstruation would make me lose my hard, angular figure. I started hunching my shoulders a little to hide my own bustline, which manifested in two ridiculous conical lumps. Karen's breasts were full and heavy. I refused to plunge into the transformation and I rejected feminine ritual. My hair was greasy and hung in several limp hunks. I grew up on the TV shows *Have Gun Will Travel* and *Rawhide*, identifying with the cowhands and not the prairie maidens. I was "horse crazy." Fathers call it "horse crazy" when girls love horses but it's just out of jealousy; I still believe my relationships with horses were sane friendships. From western heroes, I graduated to secret agents, James Bond and Napoleon Solo. I was not "in love" with Bond, I wanted to be Bond. The summer of '64 was my last stand. And yet, I couldn't deny my fascination for what was happening to my sister. I listened to the cooing notes coming from the Iranian boy, his breathing brisk and humid, startled at his release. I was excited by the structure of his authority with Karen until that one wild, uncontrolled moment when it shifted to her, and she was superior to him.

Back in our hotel room, we traded French-edition Archies until we turned out the light. If I had trouble falling asleep, Karen told me, "Think of a field of daisies."

Think of a field of daisies. I wondered if that's what Karen saw when she shut her eyes. If it wasn't what Karen was seeing, wasn't it kind of her to think it up just for me?

Even if she had cured my insomnia at night, during the day Karen was moody and sad-eyed, and I couldn't cheer her. On a car trip to Lyon, she sat in the backseat and fingered the velveteen hand rest or plucked the lid of the ashtray open and shut. She was "depressed."

Our mother told her, "What have you got to be depressed about? What in the world ever happened to you?"

I was easily bribed by ice cream and laughed readily, enough to amuse my parents and make them think I was happy. I wasn't really certain I wasn't happy, although I was beginning to see the outlines of a personal despair I had yet to greet head-on. Our parents understood Karen's silence as a surly disregard for the privileges they showered upon her.

At dinner one night, my father became irritated at Karen's silent smirk and he hit her. I saw he was going to strike her when his face turned garnet and his fork quivered as if all his self-control were balanced on its tines. Yet, it was my mother who had orchestrated his display. She glared at him, shifting her posture, adjusting her weight almost imperceptibly upon her seat-bones. His anger wasn't even caused by Karen, it was a combination of Karen's remote unhappiness and my mother's impatience with him for not putting Karen in her place. He couldn't find middle ground between these polarities and finally he turned against Karen. He lost control abruptly, like when a teeter-totter loses its counterweight and crashes. He smacked her.

Earlier that summer, in Venice, my father had knocked Karen off a canvas director's chair in the Plaza San Marco. The fragile chair collapsed around Karen like wild, spindly stork legs. It happened after a grueling day. We had spent a long, blistering afternoon at Lido Beach during which Karen had run off with a man, riding on the back of his motorcycle while my mother and I sunbathed. Karen just disappeared off the crowded beach. Perhaps she had drowned. Our mother said, "I bet she's out there with all those cabin cruisers. She swam over there for a hand-out!" We scanned the anchored pleasure boats, the gaudy clusters of swimmers and tourists, but couldn't find Karen anywhere. At dusk, the beach was closed and I waited at the Lido police office with my mother as my father filled out the forms and gave my sister's description. "Missing Persons" was not the forte of this particular police barracks and the officers weren't reassuring.

I went outside and bounced pebbles on the slate sidewalk. I wondered if my sister had really drowned in the sea, but I was certain she had not.

After several hours, word came that an American girl had been stopped for riding a motorcycle wearing only a two-piece bathing outfit. Riding mopeds dressed in indecent attire wasn't permitted by law. Karen had a serious pipe burn on her inner ankle where she had touched the exhaust. The next day, we were both grounded in our hotel room four floors above the dirty canal. There was a nest of ants in the window box and I passed the time plucking them off the geranium leaves and throwing them into the water. Karen was in pain from the pipe burn and she whimpered now and then from the dark interior of our bedroom. She wasn't complaining. She seemed to expect these war wounds. I could tell that she expected to suffer more injuries until either she or her field of enemies surrendered.

TWO DAYS BEFORE we were scheduled to take the boat train, our father discovered our nightly sojourns with Imran. When we came back to the fire escape and looked up, our windows were blazing and molten voices showered down on us. I recognized my mother's livid accusations and my father's steady reprisals against himself. Karen decided to take the lift like a civilized person and face the music head-on.

My parents had made a preliminary conclusion: Karen was "uncontrollable" and needed a psychiatric evaluation. My father decided to take her home to Philadelphia, where a medical sleuth could figure out what was making her act this way.

Of course, there was the matter of the Citroën.

My mother and I would have to cross on the S.S. *France* in

order to ship the car home. My parents wouldn't have their romance on board the luxury liner, because of Karen.

I hated to see my sister leave with my father. His face was ashen from the ordeal of making several transatlantic telephone calls. He kept getting cut off. At last, he was connected to the Pennsylvania Institute, a swank psychiatric hospital, and after some explanation he made arrangements for my sister to be seen.

I watched the two of them get into a taxi, my father in his familiar striped suit, my sister in her rayon travel dress, a drip-dry shift that came in its own plastic envelope. When my father had kissed me, I could taste the chalky residue of his antacid on his lips; it left a telltale minty dust at the corners of his mouth. His stomach trouble had worsened all summer. He often pressed his fist against his diaphragm as if the inflamed ulcer was a trapped bird he could dislodge from his rib cage if he tapped his knuckles at the exact place where the pain emanated. Both Karen and my father looked relieved to be rid of us. Even at twelve, I understood that my father deserved a little respite from his wife's scrutiny. He might take a high road with Karen, if left to himself.

I already felt lost. Karen had been monosyllabic all summer, but I cherished her company. Each night, I fell asleep listening to the hollow rustle of her hairbrush as she pulled it through her tamed hair one hundred times. I was used to the smell of her acne lotion, a vinegar odor which remained all day on the rolled pillows. When she was gone, I was left alone at the hotel for a whole day while my mother visited cousins on the Right Bank. My mother left me to prowl the park by myself. I certainly wasn't going to solicit men's attentions like Karen. I went into the park, wandering in and out of the prams and bicycles. I tried to buy an ice cream cone, a "double," but I had the old currency. The country had just changed the franc, and the large piece I held in my palm was defunct. Karen knew the currency and would have avoided these embarrassments with vendors.

The morning before we were to take the boat train, my mother made a private appointment at Galleries de Lafayette to buy a few high-fashion cocktail dresses. We arrived at the store at nine o'clock. A manager told us where to report for the scheduled showing and fittings. The private salon was upstairs and we would have to take the escalator. My mother started up the escalator and suddenly turned round. She bumped me and we both jumped off. Her face was white as a sheet and her eyes looked swimmy.

She couldn't bring herself to ride the flowing stairway.

"What's the matter?" I said, but I knew she was frightened. This had happened before at other department stores in the States. It had happened at Lord & Taylor, where the mechanical stairs had a white tread that looked remarkably like giant teeth in an opened jaw. My mother could ride the "Down" escalator, but she refused to ascend on the motorized runway. She seemed frightened of riding higher and higher to an unfamiliar level, never sighting her destination until the last moment when the stairway crested and the silver risers disappeared. She disliked the way an escalator delivered her at the threshold of the unknown, even if a sign announced LINENS AND LINGERIE.

Someone showed us to a stairwell and we hiked up the marble landings until we reached the third floor where we were greeted by two gorgeous saleswomen, like Chanel models. My mother was perspiring, and she dabbed at her face with one of my father's handkerchiefs. She passed the crumpled linen beneath her nose once and again, as if she wanted the smell of him; his smell would snap her out of it.

In the fancy salon, I sat on a plush chair and watched the two women dress my mother in a fiery lamé jersey gown, then in a gauzy dress of metallic net. She was looking only at "gold" dresses. Seeing my mother revolving before the mirrors in the provocative gowns led me to a new recognition. I watched the saleswomen dressing and undressing my mother in these golden frocks, tucking waistbands, fastening the tiny hook-and-eye closures, peeling necklines away from shoulders. I realized that *the highway* was long; it was its own destination. My mother was still traveling on it; as if on a conveyor belt, she could ride it without thinking. She could pull out her compact and fix her lips and still keep traveling. God forbid there should ever be an "Up" escalator along the way.

My mother had been an only child. Her father died before I was born, and my French grandmother rarely visited. I knew my grandmother only from the boxes of Domino sugar cubes she sent in the mail, whole cartons of sugar dots which I fed to the horses at Highland Stables. Why my grandmother sent pounds and pounds of cubed sugar to our household was a mysterious delight. I filled the sugar bowls on the silver tea service and hoarded the remaining boxes.

When her mother was dying, my mother took Karen and me to Chicago to wait at her deathbed. She pushed me into my grandmother's sickroom and left me standing at her footboard; she and Karen waited in the doorway. My grandmother asked me to sing the whimsical French love song "Dites-moi Pourquoi." *Tell Me Why*. I sang it without a glitch. My singing French was perfect. The old woman, skinny and weak from diabetes, peered at me, her quilt up to her chin. She seemed buried already. I sang the French lyrics, my heart spilling out. The old woman appeared so sweet and contrite, how could my mother hate her?

Hate her own mother?

If my mother hated her own mother, might I, too, fall to that fate? I looked at my grandmother who looked at my mother who looked at my sister, Karen. I did not yet recognize my station on that shriveling vine. The fruit of that vine was indeed as fragile and easily blemished as squash blossoms, which emerge and wither in a period of hours.

After her mother's death, my mother told me that her parents had routinely locked her in their Chicago apartment with a padlock each night and left her alone when they went to run their restaurant. Her parents had been industrious French immigrants and had worked long hours serving Continental cuisine to business clients who tired of the bland Irish and Polish entrées on local Chicago menus. Afternoons, she did her homework at the restaurant, her books spread across one of the empty tables. She was given her dinner at the restaurant and at seven she was sent home.

There, her father locked her in the apartment. She looked out the front window and watched her parents walk down the sidewalk, arm in arm, until they crossed the street and turned the corner. Then she banged the wall to rouse the neighbor who tried to soothe her through the door although he didn't have a key to free her. My mother told me that being locked inside those small, familiar rooms in a monotony of domestic landmarks was more tortuous than being left abandoned on an open plain. She enjoyed telling me these stories and seeing my alarmed reaction. More than once she told me about her father's fit of violent anger when he heaved her bicycle down the basement stairwell. The bicycle was destroyed; its frame was hideously bent, its wheels skewed.

Then he forced her to ride it.

If she ever complained or caused trouble, he took out the misshapen bicycle and insisted that she try to balance it.

My mother purchased three dresses and a French bathing suit she later discovered was "Made in Israel," and not in Paris as she had thought. I pictured Karen at home with my father. How was she surviving her interrogation? I heard mention of an "ink-blot test" my sister might be asked to take during one of her examinations. I didn't know exactly what kind of procedure it was and confused it with "Chinese water torture," which was described in an Ian Fleming paperback. I pictured my sister strapped to a bed and balls of indelible ink dripping onto her forehead until her golden hair was saturated, her oat straw eyebrows permanently stained.

The train trip to Le Havre was crowded but somber. The wheels rolled over the track in a remote, clattering dirge. I didn't want to spend five days at sea with my mother. The sea was so vast and empty; certainly our unhappy souls would be mirrored in it. My mother tried to stop my whining about Karen and told me there were two swimming pools on board, one freshwater, one seawater. But what fun would I have without Karen, who always spread her legs apart so I could swim through the underwater bridge?

On board the ocean liner, I suffered a momentary queasiness when I could no longer sight land, its thin green line evaporating. I watched the horizon from huge porthole windows in our luxury suite, which was a mistake. We were placed in a stateroom after a glitch in booking. Our modest cabin was already occupied by newlyweds. The young wife opened the door in her slip; she was already unpacked.

"This will do fine," my mother said, when the steward showed us the opulent accommodations. "Look at these windows," she said. But I didn't like seeing the breadth of the ocean without Karen. If I should fret about sinking, Karen would have said, "Think of a field of daisies."

Later that evening, my mother and I were seated at dining hour beside another single mother and her son. The boy was twelve years old like me; his hair was the color of glossy fishing line, almost like a Barbie doll. His name was Sandy Crow and he was related to the famous Texas tycoon Trammel Crow. Our two separate tables were arranged so that we ate our meals elbow-to-elbow. After our first discomfort at meeting, lifting our silverware in clumsy tandem, the boy and I ran around all decks together. We swam in the saltwater pool, although I secretly promised Karen I wouldn't enjoy it. Of course, I didn't dare swim between the millionaire's legs. During one of our water games, I lost a signet ring Karen had given to me from her own jewelry box. I mourned the loss of it, especially since I didn't know if Karen had wanted it back. At dinner, I was shocked to find the ring centered on the stiff white lily petals of my dinner napkin. Sandy had snorkeled for the ring and found it.

My mother was impressed by his attention to me. She warned me to get his address and make a pen pal of him, his family were millionaires. I wanted to tell Karen about the boy and the minor stirrings I was feeling. Most of all, his name upset me. How could such a blond and airy nickname like "Sandy" be followed by the common coal-black scavenger "Crow"? Was this a typical trap the masculine world concocted? This dichotomous lesson seemed to have some broader meaning, perhaps Karen and I could later discuss it.

On the second day in open water, my mother suffered from a severe attack of "gout." The ship's physician came to our cabin at midnight. My mother asked the doctor to palpate and knead her thigh, which she claimed was knotted in spasms, but it looked smooth as silk. She suffered from night sweats and palpitations. Her pulse was racing. The doctor listened to her heart with a stethoscope and gave her three little pills of nitroglycerin. If she had further discomfort she should dissolve one of these pills under her tongue. Two other nights, she called the ship's doctor to her bedside, and the last night I slept through. My mother never again suffered from "gout." It was a transient, deep-Atlantic condition. Home in Wilmington, the Chemical Capital of the World, gout was a minor complaint compared to the brain tumors emerging in the neighborhoods bordering the pigment plants and the Du Pont Experimental Station. The first inklings of my mother's heart disease had been couched in dreamy fantasy—the cabin shifted slightly in the rocky seas, the doctor whispered in a slow, exact French. He told my mother that she exhibited a dangerous predisposition to a massive coronary. She made light of it and asked him to massage the spasm in her leg.

IN PHILADELPHIA a psychiatrist named Dr. Benvenuto interviewed Karen and decided that she would be better off in boarding school. He told her, one-to-one, that he just might be delivering her from the evil environment which nurtured her symptoms of promiscuity.

I didn't believe the plan was for my sister's sake alone. My mother tried hard to pretend she had mixed feelings about Karen's imminent departure, but she was actually quite chipper. She seemed renewed by a peculiar domestic energy—the same "nesting reflex" some women feel prior to the *birth,* not the departure of, a child. She helped Karen collect her possessions and put what she didn't want into boxes for Goodwill. Nothing was left in Karen's bureau drawers, as if Karen was leaving home forever and not just for the fall semester. They stripped her bed and folded the blankets. The blankets were stored on the top shelf in the closet, too close to the lightbulb. The wool was scorched and emitted an acrid odor. My mother discarded the charred covers so that even Karen's bedding was removed from the room where she had once slept.

"Boarding school is a privilege," my mother told Karen. "It's a springboard."

I tried to imagine this "springboard," and could not see anything but an empty swimming pool. My mother took Karen to Wanamaker's and Strawbridge's to buy her the appropriate girl's prep school attire to match the required uniform. Karen received a mimeographed list from Greer School explaining what was expected. "Six pairs kneesocks, forest green. Dickies acceptable. Forest green or nut brown."

"Nut brown?" I asked Karen. "What's that?"

"Squirrel shit color, I guess," Karen told me. Karen was

irritable those days before she went to Greer School. She didn't necessarily want to stay at home any longer, but she didn't much like the idea of the school our parents had found for her, which emphasized "Equestrian Arts." Together, Karen and I had attended Boots and Saddles day camp, but Karen wasn't a good rider. She was a little hippy and didn't have the sexless flexibility of an athlete. I continued to take lessons at the rat-infested riding academy and spent much of my time mucking out stalls. When the exterminators came every month, they let me look through their ultraviolet lenses which illuminated rats' urine trails. I held the contraption in front of my eyes. The barn was crisscrossed with a thousand electric paths from the hayloft to every feed bin, every rail and gate; even the benches where we sat and the telephone receiver were scrawled with dried urine. I was curious about these invisible rat trails—I imagined our human thoughts, our deepest spiritual desires and worse, our unhappy prayers for the deaths of our enemies. Perhaps our secrets excreted unreadable stains, a magic waste on everything we touched.

I told Karen, "Greer School must have at least one gentle nag that's easy to trot."

"I don't want to sit on a horse at all."

MY FATHER DROVE the new Citroën. Its trunk was packed with my sister's possessions: six pairs of forest-green socks. New pajamas with a matching robe. Karen swore she would never wear these matching items at the same time. The school was located in a remote section of mountainous terrain in western Pennsylvania. The campus buildings looked Gothic and cold. Although I teased my sister about her new surroundings, my heart was in my throat. How could we drive off and leave her there like that? Our parents went inside an office to sign forms and write further deposit checks for school books and gym clothes. Karen and I walked through the stables. A horse stood at a stall gate;

he shoved his head over the rail and we stroked its velvet muzzle.

"Well, this is it," Karen said.

She might have meant "This is good-bye for now" or "good-bye forever." She hinted at an immediate finality that I was unwilling to accept.

I told her, "You'll be back in a couple months. You could get yourself expelled."

Karen shrugged. "I don't really want to go home."

I tried not to feel stung.

Karen didn't see herself merging with the college preparatory crowd, nor did she imagine returning to the world she had left that morning. She smiled at me. It was a strange, enlightened expression. She looked as if she had a baby aspirin dissolving on her tongue, its sweetness overpowered by the bitter ingredient. All of her childhood seemed condensed in this little pill. Soon it would be only a pink stain on the roof of her mouth.

KAREN'S MONTHS at Greer School were not successful. She couldn't manage her classroom duties or get along well in the dormitory. She often had headaches and was sent to the infirmary, where she had to lie on a green leather couch with a cold pack on her forehead. If she lifted the ice off her brow to regulate its cold, the nurse scolded her and she had to replace the rubber bag although it made her headache worse.

In late November, Karen walked away from the Greer campus. She followed the gravel shoulder on the county road. She told me it was painful but she had managed to walk three miles in her Cordovan loafers, which chafed until her heels had swollen red knots and pink stripes crept up her Achilles tendons. She got as far as a VFW, where she entered the kitchen door and told the woman who cooked that she'd like to find work. The cook took one look at her and knew Karen had come from the girls' school.

But Karen looked serious about working; Karen's desperation gave her an older appearance, an earned maturity. The cook gave Karen a colander of potatoes to peel for the "Hunters' Banquet" scheduled for later that evening. The potatoes were to be added to the venison stew. The cook showed Karen the big table of deer meat already coarsely chopped. The meat looked strange, a deep purple heap of cubes with whorls of gristle. Karen knew she was going to be sick, and she stepped outside the kitchen door before she retched. Nothing came up. She went back into the VFW kitchen and started to scrape the potatoes.

By dusk, Karen had performed many tasks for the cook and started to understand she had been manipulated by the older woman. She left the building, heading out the front door where men had already assembled for their party. She caused quite a ripple, and a man followed Karen outside. He put her in his car. It was one of those El Camino sedans with an altered cab, half car, half pickup. "Where to?" he said.

"You tell me," she told him.

MY PARENTS RECEIVED a telephone call from the headmistress at Greer School. She told my parents that Karen was in the hospital with "bladder troubles." Somehow, Karen's urinary tract had been traumatized and she needed a catheter. In two days, Karen was discharged from the hospital and she returned to Wilmington. The following business day she was reenrolled in the high school.

"You had your opportunity," our mother said, "now you have to go back to the high school and face the teachers." She looked truly alarmed by the idea as if she herself would be forced to stand at the front of the classroom and explain why Karen had returned.

In bed that night, Karen said, "I can't stand another day."

"Can't you just ignore her?" I said.

"How?"

"Tell her this: 'I'm rubber, you're glue. Whatever you say bounces off me and sticks to you.' "

Karen looked at me again, as if I was a kitten fighting in a paper bag. "Do those rhymes work for you?"

I had never stopped to ask myself how I survived our mother's belittling remarks. I suppose I avoided her company and stayed late hours at the riding stables, shoveling manure in exchange for time in the saddle.

KAREN GAVE ME three pairs of her forest-green kneesocks but the elastic was stretched and they didn't stay up. Karen was a little heavier than me, and our figures were in sharp contrast. Our mother decided to get Karen some diet pills. The next Thursday, I went with Karen to the family doctor. I waited in the room outside where they had the Norman Rockwell. When my sister came out I could smell the syrups and alcohol from the open bottles the doctor kept on his desk. Karen was holding a prescription which had the words *Marbles, three times a day* scrolled across it. The doctor didn't prescribe diet pills after all. Karen didn't say anything as our mother paid the doctor and he put the cash right in his pocket. Karen had been crying. I could see it right off because Karen had the kind of eyelashes that kept the tears in place long after there was any cause.

Driving home, we stopped at the five-and-ten, but Karen wouldn't get out of the car. I went in with my mother because I liked the aisle with the white mice; the hairless baby rodents suckling their mother looked like a row of worn-down pink erasers. My mother wasn't in a mood to poke around. We came outside with a fifty-cent bag of marbles. In the car, I said, "Three times a day isn't too bad." I was just prying.

"If you have to know, your sister has flat feet. She has to pick up the marbles with her toes."

"Shit," Karen said.

I said, "I think it's good we bring it all out in the open."

"It's none of your business," Karen said.

"You're my sister."

"It's my flat feet."

"It's nothing to cry about," our mother said.

"It's not polio or anything," I told her.

We bickered until our mother said, "Your father." She often said these words, *Your father,* when Karen and I argued. It meant that we should stop what we were doing and think of him, but he was difficult to picture in my mind. Instead, I pictured his big chair in the corner of the living room. It was a new recliner. With his legs extended I could never approach my father or sit in his lap. This had me feeling sorry for myself and I forgot about Karen's condition.

Karen practiced with the marbles in the privacy of our bedroom. She had a tin wastebasket and she picked up the marbles with her toes and dropped them in the can. We could hear it throughout the house. We could hear it out on the sidewalk, a sad *plink, plink, plink.*

One day Karen took an ink pad and she made some footprints on a paper bag. They were flat as ever. I couldn't keep out of it and my own high arch left only a thin crescent on the paper. It made me feel guilty and I tried to remind Karen of my own frailties. I reminded her that I had been a preemie and had spent weeks in an incubator. I believed this first encounter had a lasting effect on me. In my first month of life, the only contact I had was with awkward rubber hands. Nurses inserted their arms in huge sleeves, like Playtex Living Gloves, attached to the heated cubicle. No one held me. At twelve, I was still too skinny and had to take an elixir to increase my appetite, but this was the wrong example to make because Karen, along with her flat feet, had a low center of gravity and it made her feel clumsy. "Oh, never mind," she told me, and she crumpled our footprints and threw them in the waste can.

Karen returned to the high school. It wasn't easy for her, and she looked haunted by her experiences there when she came home in the late afternoon. At the end of one week in the high school, she sat across from me at the kitchen table, swirling a glass of Tab, but she didn't lift the cola and drink it.

She went away to change her clothes. She returned in ten minutes and told me, "I'm going to the corner, want anything?"

I said, "With what money?" Karen could have loaned me a dollar. She had started working an after-school job behind the soda counter at Holiday Lanes, but I didn't ask for charity. I might have pulled my jacket from its hook and trailed her, the same way I followed Karen and Imran those nights in Paris. But I didn't go with her. She didn't ask me. I watched her hand on the kitchen door, the way she pinched the knob and released it. Karen walked down the sidewalk. It was only three blocks to the Philadelphia Pike, where she waited on the corner of Silverside Road, in front of Harry's Liquor Mart. Then she sat down in someone's Glo-Waxed Chrysler.

JUST AS WE RODE the boat train to Le Havre, again my mother and I were thrown together. We sat facing front without talking. We watched television. The screen showed the chalk outline of a body. It was a detective series and it usually started out this way. Two months had passed with no word about my sister. I was still waiting for Karen to call me. I saw the chalk outline and told my mother, "Look, it's Karen." It was just another way I learned to hurt myself by trying to harm others. I was becoming mean-spirited in my new adolescence, weary of it already. I didn't flinch when my mother stood up in a tide of anger, flicked the television off, and turned to face me.

• • •

SHE COUNTS NINE lighted windows outside in Bailey's Trailer Village. Each smeary humid square, yellow as taffy. People stay up pretty late. Each of these units seems to have its own clock. People work all hours but you wouldn't know it from what they have to show for it. Every trailer looks junked. Some are skirted with cheap plywood to hide the hitch and undercarriage, but the skirts warp from the humidity or heave with the frost. The neighbors don't have much in the way of landscaping, just a pine sign that says "Never let your hitch get rusty."

The box heater is useless, the heat can't work its way from end to end. It's a 1953 Troutwood. The walls are thin and bellow in the wind. The air slips in and out through rusty rivet circles, like a colander. Each room opens up into the next and she can look down a narrow corridor, through all three archways, room to room in one clear sweep. The ceiling is smooth, lacquered birch veneer. It's like being inside a seashell.

The floor is crowded with new cartons of S&H green stamps, stolen from a box trailer lock-up. Glued into books, they get him silverplate items and small appliances. He puts her to work and teases her; he calls her a Minor in Need of Supervision.

He makes a production about getting rid of her old clothes. She has goose pimples while he tears her skirt into little strips; its acetate lining is shredding unpredictably. He's pulling the seams apart the way her father used to tear rags for the car wash. He tells her he is forty-six years old but he's gray already. His side-burns are curly like little silver pasta twists. He tugs the left side and the whiskers uncoil like a spring until he lets go and it snaps tight again. His lips are hot and his breath is tarry from Pall Malls, that much she learned in the first five minutes.

She just can't stop laughing.

He's snipping her blouse with a meat scissors and feeding the scraps to the blazing ring on the compact gas range.

"You're crazy," she tells him.

He burns ribbons of her clothes and wipes the ash from the enamel stovetop with a wet rag. The greasy NuTone sucks away the smoke. There is nothing left of her belongings.

"It's a good feeling, isn't it?" he tells her.

"I guess. But shoot, I'm freezing."

He hands her a large bag from Sears. She has been waiting all afternoon to take a peek but he wouldn't let her open it. She pulls the sweaters and slacks from the tissue paper. Silky triangles fall to the floor, new panties with tiny hearts and polka dots. A pink jersey nightgown with eyelet lace at the collar. Meanwhile, she is shivering, naked as a cashew. She starts to put on her new clothes but he won't let her. He wraps her up in an electric blanket. He puts the big dial into her hands. She rolls her eyes, but she stops them halfway. She's breaking that childish habit. He walks her to the other end of the trailer. He plugs the blanket cord into a socket. She stands before him, the wire mesh in the automatic blanket starts to heat up.

"You'll need more things," he tells her "We'll get it."

She nods.

"You're here now, we're clear on that?"

"Sure," she tells him. "Where am I going to go?"

"Shit, honey, if you left your own home, you can break away anytime."

"I'm here now."

"That's what we're saying."

Joy Williams

Traveling to Pridesup

OTILLA COOKED UP the water for her morning tea and opened a carton of ricotta cheese. She ate standing up, dipping cookies in and out of the cheese, walking around the enormous kitchen in tight figure eights as though she were in a gymkhana. She was eighty-one years old and childishly ravenous and hopeful with a long pigtail and a friendly unreasonable nature.

She lived with her sisters in a big house in the middle of the state of Florida. There were three of them, all older and wiser. They were educated in northern schools and came back with queer ideas. Lavinia, the eldest, returned after four years, with a rock, off of a mountain, out of some forest. It was covered with lichen and green like a plum. Lavinia put it to the north of the seedlings on the shadowy side of the house. She tore up the grass and burnt out the salamanders and the ants and raked the sand out all around the rock in a pattern like a machine would make. The sisters watched the rock on and off for forty years until one morning when they were all out in their Mercedes automobile, taking the air, a sinkhole opened up and took the rock and half the garage down thirty-seven feet. It didn't seem to matter to Lavinia, who had cared for the thing. Growing rocks, she said, was supposed to bring one serenity and put one on terms with oneself and she had become serene so she didn't care. Otilla believed that such an idea could only come from a foreign religion, but she could only guess at this as no one ever told her anything except her father, and he had died long ago from drink. He was handsome and rich, having made his money in railways and grapefruit. Otilla was his darling. She still had the tumbler he was drinking rum from when he died. None of Father's girls had ever married, and Otilla, who was thought to be a little slow, had not even gone off to school.

Otilla ate a deviled egg and some ice cream and drank another cup of tea. She wore sneakers and a brand-new dress that still had the cardboard pinned beneath the collar. The dress had come in the mail the day before along with a plastic soap dish and three rubber pedal pads for the Mercedes. The sisters ordered everything through catalogs and seldom went to town. Upstairs, Otilla could hear them moving about.

"Louisa," Marjorie said, "this soap dish works beautifully."

Otilla moved to a wicker chair by the window and sat on her long pigtail. She turned off the light and turned on the fan. It was just after sunrise, the lakes all along the Ridge were smoking with heat. She could see bass shaking the surface of the water and she felt a brief and eager joy at the sight—at the morning and the mist running off the lakes and the birds rising up from the shaggy orange trees. The joy didn't come often anymore and it didn't last long and when it passed it seemed more a part of dying than delight. She didn't dwell on this however. For the most part, she found that as long as one commenced to get up in the morning and move one's bowels, everything else moved along without confusing variation.

From the window, she could also see the mailbox. The flag was up and there was a package swinging from it. She couldn't understand why the mailman hadn't put the package inside. It was a large sturdy mailbox and would hold anything.

She got up and walked quickly outside, hoping that Lavinia wouldn't see her, as Lavinia preferred picking up the mail herself. She passed the black Mercedes. The garage had never been rebuilt and the car had been parked for years between two oak trees. There was a quilt over the hood. Every night, Lavinia would pull a wire out of the distributor and bring it into the house. The next morning she would put the wire back in again, warm up the Mercedes, and drive it twice around the circular driveway and then down a slope one hundred yards to the mailbox. They only received things that they ordered. The Mercedes was fifteen years old and had eleven thousand miles on it. Lavinia kept the car up. She was clever at it.

"This vehicle will run forever because I've taken good care of it," she'd say.

Otilla stood beside the mailbox looking north up the road and then south. She had good eyesight but there wasn't a thing to be seen. Hanging in a feed bag off the mailbox was a sleeping baby. It wore a little yellow T-shirt with a rabbit on it. The rabbit appeared to be playing a fiddle. The baby had black hair and big ears and was making small grunts and whistles in its sleep. Otilla wiped her hands on the bodice of her dress and picked the baby out of the sack. It smelled faintly of ashes and fruit.

Inside the house, the three sisters, Lavinia, Louisa, and Marjorie, were setting out the breakfast things. They were ninety-two, ninety, and eighty-seven respectively. They were in excellent color and health and didn't look much over seventy. Each morning they'd set up the table as though they were expecting the governor himself—good silver, best china, egg cups, and bun cozy.

They settled themselves. The fan was painted with blue rustproof paint and turned right on around itself like an owl. The soft-boiled eggs wobbled when the breeze ran by them.

"Going to be a hot one," Lavinia said.

The younger sisters nodded yes, chewing on their toast.

"The summer's just begun and it appears it's never going to end," Lavinia said.

The sisters shook their heads yes. The sky was getting

brighter and brighter. The three of them, along with Otilla, had lived together forever. They weren't looking at the sky or the empty groves which they had seen before. The light was changing very fast, progressing visibly over the tabletop. It fell on the butter.

"They've been tampering with the atmosphere," Lavinia said. "They don't have the sense to leave things alone." Lavinia was a strong-willed, impatient woman. She thought about what she had just said and threw her spoon down irritably at the truth of it. Lavinia was no longer serene about anything. That presumption had been for her youth, when she had time. Now everything was pesky to her and a hindrance.

"Good morning," Otilla said. She walked to the wicker chair and sat down. The baby lay in her arms, short and squat like a loaf of bread.

Lavinia's eyes didn't change, nor her mouth nor the set of her jaw. Outside some mockingbirds were ranting. The day had gotten so bright it was as if someone had just shot it off in her face.

"Put it back where you got it," she said slowly.

"I can't imagine where this baby's from," Otilla said.

The baby's eyes were open now and were locked on the old woman's face. Lavinia spoke in a low furious voice. "Go on out with it, Otilla." She raised her fingers distractedly, waving at the baby as though greeting an old friend.

Otilla picked the baby up and held it out away from her and looked cheerfully at it. "You're wetting."

"My God," Marjorie said, noticing the affair for the first time.

Otilla shook the baby up and down. Her arms were skinny and pale and they trembled a bit with the weight. The baby opened its mouth and smiled noiselessly. "You're hollow inside," Otilla said. "Hollow as a bamboo. Bam Boo To You Kangaroo."

She joggled the baby whose face was static and distant with delight. "Bamboo shampoo. Bamboo cockatoo stew."

"My God," Marjorie said. She and Louisa got up and scraped off their plates and rinsed them in the sink. They went into the front room and sat on the sofa.

Otilla held the baby a little awkwardly. Its head flopped back like a flower in the wind when she got up. She had never touched a baby before and she had never thought about them either. She went to the drainboard and laid the baby down and unpinned its diaper. "Isn't that cute, Lavinia, it's a little boy."

"You are becoming senile," Lavinia said. Her fingers were still twitching in the air. She wrapped them in her napkin.

"I didn't make him up. Someone left him here, hanging off the postbox."

"Senile," Lavinia repeated. "Who knows where this baby has been? You shouldn't even be touching him. Perhaps you are just being 'set up' and we will all be arrested by the sheriff."

Otilla folded a clean dish towel beneath the baby and pinned it together. She took the dirty diaper and scrubbed it out in the sink with a bar of almond soap and then took it outside and hung it on the clothesline. When she came back into the kitchen, she picked the baby off the drainboard and went back to her chair by the window. "Now isn't that nice, Lavinia?" She didn't want to talk but she was so nervous that she couldn't help herself. "I think they should make diapers in bright colors. Orange and blue and green . . . Deep bright colors for a little boy. Wouldn't that be nice, Lavinia?"

"The dye would seep into their skin and kill them," Lavinia said brusquely. "They'd suffocate like a painted Easter chick."

Otilla was shocked.

"You accept things too easily, Otilla. You have always been a dope. Even as a child, you took anything anyone chose to give you." She got up and took the distributor wire of the Mercedes out of the silverware tray. She clumped down the steps to the automobile, banging the screen door behind her. A spider dropped from the ceiling and fell with a snap on the stove. Otilla heard the engine turn over and drop into idle. The screen door banged again and Lavinia was shouting into the darkened living room.

"We are going in town to the authorities and will be back directly."

There was a pause in which Otilla couldn't hear a thing. Her arm was going to sleep. She shifted the baby about on her lap, banging his head against her knee bone. The baby opened his mouth but not his eyes and gummed on the sleeve of his shirt. "Excuse me," she whispered.

"No, no," Lavinia shouted at the living room. "I can't imagine how it happened either. Someone on their way somewhere. Long gone now. Pickers, migrants."

She came back into the kitchen, pulling on a pair of black ventilated driving gloves. Lavinia was very serious about the Mercedes. She drove slowly and steadily and not particularly well, looking at the dials and needles for signs of malfunction. The reason for riding was in the traveling, she always said, for the sisters never had the need to be anyplace. Getting there was not the object. Arrival was not the point. The car was elegant and disheartening and suited to this use.

"Where are we going?" Otilla asked meekly.

"Where are we going," Lavinia mimicked in a breathless drawl that was not at all like Otilla's voice. Then she said normally, "We are going to drop this infant off in Pridesup. I am attempting not to become annoyed but you are very annoying and this is a very annoying situation."

"I think I would like to keep this baby," Otilla said. "I figure we might as well." The baby was warm and its heart was beating twice as fast as any heart she had ever heard as though it couldn't wait to get on with its living.

Lavinia walked over to her sister and gave her a yank.

"I could teach him to drink from a cup," Otilla said, close to tears. "They learn how to do that. When he got older he could mow the lawn and spray the midge and club-gall." She was on her feet now and was being pushed outside. She put out her free hand and jammed it against the door frame. "I have to get some things together, then, please Lavinia. It's twenty miles to Pridesup. Just let me get a few little things together so that he won't go off with nothing." Her chin was shaking. She was hanging fiercely onto the door and squinting out into the sunlight, down past the rumbling Mercedes into the pit where the rock had fallen and where the seedlings, still rooted, bloomed in the spring. She felt a little fuddled. It seemed that her head was down in the cool sinkhole while the rest of her wobbled in the heat. She jammed the baby so close to her that he squealed.

"I can't imagine what you're going to equip him with," Lavinia was saying. "He can't be more than a few months old. We don't have anything for that." She had stopped pushing her sister and was looking at the car, trying to remember the route to Pridesup, the county seat. It had been five years since she had driven there. Somewhere, on the left, she recollected a concentrate canning factory. Somewhere, also, there was a gas station in the stomach of a concrete dinosaur. She remembered stopping. Otilla had used the rest room and they had all bought cold barbecue. No one ever bought his gasoline, the owner said. They bought his snacks and bait and bedspreads. Lavinia had not bought his gasoline either. She doubted if the place was there now. It didn't look as though it had five years left in it.

"Oh just a little apple juice and a toy or something."

"Well, get it then," Lavinia snapped. She couldn't remember if she took a right or a left upon leaving the driveway; if she kept Cowpen Slough on her west side or her east side. The countryside looked oddly without depth and she had difficulty imagining herself driving off into it. She went into a small bathroom off the kitchen and took off her gloves and rinsed her face, then she went out to the Mercedes. She sat behind the wheel and removed some old state maps from the car's side pocket. They were confusing, full of blank spaces. Printed on the bottom of the first one were the words *Red And Blue Roads Are Equally Good.* She refolded them, fanned herself with them, and put them on the seat.

Otilla got into the car with the baby and a paper bag. The baby's head was very large compared to the rest of him. It looked disabling and vulnerable. Lavinia couldn't understand how anything could start out being that ugly and said so. His ears looked like two Parker rolls. She moved the car down the drive and unhesitatingly off onto the blacktop. They drove in silence for a few minutes. It was hot and green out with a smell of sugar on the air.

"Well," Otilla said, "it doesn't seem as though he wants anything yet."

Lavinia wore a pair of enormous black sunglasses. She drove and didn't say anything.

"Look out the window here at that gray and black horse," Otilla said. She lifted the baby up. He clawed at her chin with his hand. "Look out thataway at those sandhill cranes. They're just like storks. Maybe they're the ones that dropped you off at our house."

"Oh shut up. You'll addle the little bit of brain he has," Lavinia yelled.

"It's just a manner of speaking, Lavinia. We both know it isn't so." She opened the bag and took out a piece of bread and began to eat it. The baby pushed his hand into the bread and Otilla broke off a piece of crust and gave it to him. He gnawed on it intently without diminishing it. In the bag, Otilla had a loaf of bread, a can of Coca-Cola, and a jar of milk. "I couldn't find a single toy for him," she said.

"He'll have to do with the scenery," Lavinia said. She herself had never cared for it. It had been there too long and she had been too long in it and now it seemed like an external cataract obstructing her real vision.

"Lookit those water hyacinths," Otilla went on. "Lookit that piece of moon still up there in the sky."

Lavinia gritted her teeth. There had not been a single trip they had taken that Otilla had not spoiled. She talked too much and squirmed too much and always brought along food that she spilled. The last time they had driven down this road, she had had a dish of ice cream that had been squashed against the dashboard when the car had gone over a bump. Lavinia braked suddenly and turned the Mercedes into a dirt side road that dropped like a tunnel through an orange grove. She backed up and reversed her direction.

"Where are we going now, Lavinia?"

"We're going to the same place," she said angrily. "This is simply a more direct route." The baby burped softly. They passed the house again, planted white and well-to-do in the sunlight. Embarrassed, neither of them looked at it or remarked upon it.

"I think," Otilla said formally, "that we are both accepting this very well and that you are handling it okay except that I think we could have kept this baby for at least a little while until we read in the paper perhaps that someone is missing him."

"No one is going to be missing him."

"You're a little darlin'," Otilla said to the baby, who was hunched over his bread crust.

"Please stop handling him. He might very well have worms or meningitis or worse." The Mercedes was rocketing down the middle of the road through hordes of colorful bugs. Lavinia had never driven this fast. She took her foot off the accelerator and the car mannerly slowed. Lavinia was hot all over. Every decision she had made so far today seemed proper but oddly irrelevant. If she had gone down to the mailbox first as she had always done, there would have been no baby to find. She was sure of that. The problem was that the day had started out being Otilla's and not hers at all. She gave a short nervous bark and looked at the baby who was swaying on her sister's lap. "I imagine he hasn't had a single shot."

"He looks fine to me, Lavinia. He has bright eyes and he seems clean and cool enough."

Lavinia tugged at the wheel as though correcting a personal injustice rather than the car's direction. "It's no concern to us what he's got anyway. It's the law's problem. It's for the orphanage to attend to."

"Orphanage? You shouldn't take him there. He's not an orphan, he has us." She looked at the pale brown veins running off the baby's head and faintly down his cheeks.

"He doesn't have us at all," Lavinia shouted. She started to gag and gripped her throat with her left hand, giving it little pinches and tugs to keep the sickness down. There had never been a thing she'd done that hadn't agreed with her and traveling had always been a pleasure, but the baby beside her had a strong pervasive smell that seemed to be the smell of the land as well, and it made her sick. She felt as though she were falling into a pan of bright and bubbling food. She took several breaths and said more calmly, "There is no way we could keep him. You must use your head. We have not had the training and we are all getting on and what would happen is that we would die and he'd be left." She was being generous and conversational and instructive and she hoped that Otilla would appreciate this and benefit from it even though she knew her sister was weak-headed and never benefited from things in the proper way.

"But that's the way it's going to be anyway, Lavinia."

The air paddled in Lavinia's ears. The Mercedes wandered on and off the dusty shoulder. The land was empty and there wasn't anything coming toward them or going away except a bright tin can, which they straddled. "Of course it is," she said. "You've missed the point."

Lavinia had never cared for Otilla. She realized that this was due mostly to preconception, as it were, for she had been present at the awful moment of birth and she knew before her sister had taken her first breath that she'd be useless. And she had been. The only thing Otilla ever had was prettiness and she had that still, lacking the sense to let it go, her girlish features still moving around indecently in her old woman's face. Sitting there now in a messy nest of bread crusts and obscure stains with the baby playing with her dress buttons, Otilla looked queerly confident and enthusiastic as though at last she were going off on her wedding day. It disgusted Lavinia. There was something unseasonal about Otilla. If she had been a man, Lavinia thought, they might very well have had a problem on their hands.

Otilla noisily shook out one of the road maps. Down one side of it was a colorful insert with tiny pictures of attractions—fish denoting streams, and women in bathing suits, and llamas representing zoos and clocks marking historical societies. All no bigger than a thumbnail. "Why this is just charming," Otilla said. "Here we have a pictorial guide." The baby looked at it grimly and something fell runny from his mouth onto a minute pink blimp. "This is the first time we have had a real destination, Lavinia. Perhaps we can see these things as well." She rested her chin on the baby's head and read aloud, " 'Route S40 through the Pine Barrens. Be sure to see the *Produce Auction, Elephant House, State Yacht Basin Marine View Old Dutch Parsonage Pacing Racing Oxford Furnace Ruins.*' Why just look at all these things," she said into the infant's hair. "This is *very* helpful."

The two regarded the map carefully. "See this," Otilla said excitedly, pointing to a tiny ancient-looking baby with a gold crown on his head. "*Baby Parade. August.* That's for us!" Then she fell silent and after a few miles she turned to Lavinia and said, "This is not for our region at all. This is for the state of New Jersey."

Lavinia was concentrating on a row of garish signs advertising a pecan shop. She'd been seeing them for the last half hour. *Free Ice Water* one said *Lettus Fill Your Jug. Neat Nuts* one said. *Ham Sandwiches Frozen Custard Live Turtles.* She thought she'd stop and discreetly ask the way to Pridesup. *Pecan Clusters Pecan Logs Pecan Pie Don't Miss Us!*

Otilla was picking through the remaining maps when the baby tipped off her lap and into Lavinia's side. Lavinia stomped on the brakes and beat at him with her hand. "Get away," she shrieked, "you'll break my hip!" She tried to pull her waist in from the weight of his head. His smell was sweet, fertile, like an anesthetic and she felt frightened as though someone had just removed something from her in a swift neat operation. She saw the dust motes settling like balloons upon the leather dashboard and white thread tangled in the baby's fingers. *Slow Down. You're Almost There Only 2000 Yds.* The baby's face was wrinkling her linen and his hand was fastened around the bottom of the steering wheel.

"Lavinia, you'll frighten him," Otilla said, pulling the baby back across the seat. She arranged him in her lap again and he instantly fell asleep. The Mercedes was almost at a standstill. Lavinia pressed on the gas and the car labored forward, out of gear, past an empty burnt-out shack. *Six Lbs For $1 Free Slushies For the Kiddies.* The door to the place was lying in the weeds.

"That's all right, that's all right," Lavinia said. She took off her sunglasses and rubbed the bridge of her nose. The fingers of her gloves were wet. The engine was skipping, the tachometer needle fluttered on 0. She stopped the car completely, shifted into first, and resumed. *You've Gone Too Far!* a sign said. She felt like spitting at it. Otilla had fallen asleep now too, her head slightly out the window, her small mouth shining in the side-view mirror. Lavinia picked up a piece of bread, folded it into an empty sandwich, and ate it.

When Otilla woke, it was almost dark. The baby had his fingers jammed into his mouth and sucked on them loudly. Otilla unscrewed the top of the mason jar and pushed the lip toward him. He took it eagerly, sucking. Then he chewed, then he lapped. Enough drops went down his throat for him to think it was worthwhile to continue. He settled down to eating the milk that was slapping his cheeks and sliding down his chin back into the jar.

They were on a narrow soft road just wide enough for the car. Close on either side were rows and rows of orange trees, all different shades of darkness in the twilight.

"It's like riding through the parted waters, Lavinia."

Her sister's voice startled her and Lavinia gave a little jump. Her stylish dress was askew and her large faded eyes were watering.

"You woke up to say an asinine thing like that!" she exclaimed. All the while Otilla and the infant had been sleeping, she had driven with an empty mind and eye. She had truly not been thinking of a thing, and though she was lost and indignant and frustrated she did not feel this. She had driven, and the instructions she had received cautiously from the few people she had seen she wrote down on the back of a pocket calendar. When she left the people, they became bystanders, not to be trusted, and she drove on without reference. And the only sounds she heard were the gentle snappings somewhere in her head of small important truths that she had got along with for years—breaking.

She had not looked at the car's equipment, at its dials and numbers, for a long time because when she had last done so, the odometer showed her that they had driven 157 miles.

"How long have we been traveling, Lavinia?"

"I don't know." She remembered that when she had bought the Mercedes, the engine had shone like her silver service. She remembered that there had been one mile on the odometer then. Sitting in the showroom on a green carpet, her automobile had one mile on it and she had been furious. No one could tell her why this was. No one could explain it to her satisfaction.

"Well," Otilla said, "I suppose Louisa and Marjorie have eaten by now." She looked out the window. A white bird was hurrying off through the groves. "This is an awfully good baby," she said, "waiting so long and being so patient for his meal. And this being not the way he's accustomed to getting it besides." She looked behind her. "My, they certainly make these roads straight. It seems like if we had intended to, we could be halfway to New Jersey by now, on our way to seeing all those interesting things. We could stay in a New Jersey motel, Lavinia, and give the baby a nice bath and send out for supper and I've even heard that some of those motels are connected with drive-in theaters and we could see a film directly from our room."

The soft sand tugged at the car's wheels. The stars came out and Lavinia pulled on the headlights.

"Lavinia," Otilla said softly. "I have twelve hundred dollars sitting in the teeth of my mouth alone. I am a wealthy woman though not as wealthy as you and if you want to get there, I don't understand why we just don't stop as soon as we see someone and hire us a car to Pridesup."

"I have no respect for you at all," Lavinia said.

Otilla paused. She ran her fingers over the baby's head, feeling the slight springy depression in his skull where he was still growing together. She could hear him swallowing. A big moth blundered against her face and then fell back into the night. "If you would just stop for a moment," she said brightly, "I could change the baby and freshen up the air in here a bit."

"You don't seem to realize that I know all about you, Otilla. There is nothing you could ever say to me about anything. I happen to know that you were born too early and mother had you in a chamber pot. So just shut up, Otilla." She turned to her sister and smiled. Otilla's head was bowed and Lavinia poked her to make sure that she was paying attention. "I have wanted to let you know about that for a long long time so just don't say another word to me, Otilla."

The Mercedes bottomed out on the sand, swerved and dropped into the ditch, the grille half-submerged in muddy water and the left rear wheel spinning in the air. Lavinia still was steering and smiling and looking at her sister. The engine died and the lights went out and for an instant they all sat speechless and motionless as though they were parts of a profound photograph that was still in the process of being taken. Then the baby gagged and Otilla began thumping him on the back.

Lavinia had loved her car. The engine crackled and hissed as it cooled. The windshield had a long crack in it and there was a smell of gasoline. She turned off the ignition.

Lavinia had loved her car and now it was broken to bits. She didn't know what to think. She opened the door and climbed out onto the road, where she lay down in the dust. In the middle of the night, she got back into the car because the mosquitoes were so bad. Otilla and the baby were stretched out in the back so Lavinia sat in the driver's seat once more, where she slept.

IN THE MORNING, they ate the rest of the bread and Otilla gave the baby the last of the milk. The milk had gone sour and he spit most of it up. Otilla waded through the ditch and set the baby in a field box beneath an orange tree. The fruit had all been picked a month ago and the groves were thick and overgrown. It was hard for Otilla to clear out a place for them to rest. She tried to fan the mosquitoes away from the baby's face but by noon the swarms had gotten so large and the bugs so fat and lazy that she had to pick them off individually with her fingers. Lavinia stayed in the Mercedes until she felt fried, then she limped across the road. The sun seemed waxed in the same position but she knew the day was going by. The baby had cried hard for an hour or so and then began a fitful wail that went on into the afternoon.

Every once in a while, Lavinia saw Otilla rise and move feverishly through the trees. The baby's weeping mingled with the rattle of insects and with Otilla's singsong so that it seemed to Lavinia, when she closed her eyes, that there was a healthy community working out around her and including her in its life. But when she looked there was only green bareness and an armadillo plodding through the dust, swinging its outrageous head.

Lavinia went to the Mercedes and picked up the can of Coca-Cola, but she couldn't find an opener. The can burnt in her hand and she dropped it. As she was getting out of the car, she saw Otilla walk out of the grove. She stopped and watched her shuffle up the road. She was unfamiliar, a mystery, an event. There was a small soiled bundle on her shoulder. Lavinia couldn't place the circumstances. She watched and wrung her hands. Otilla swerved off into the grove again and disappeared.

Lavinia followed her giddily. She walked hunched, on tiptoe. When she came upon Otilla, she remained stealthily bent, her skirt still wadded in her hand for silence. Otilla lay on her back in the sand with the baby beside her, his bug-bitten eyelids squeezed against a patch of sky that was shining on them both. The baby's mouth was moving and his arms and legs were waving in the air to some mysterious beat but Otilla lay motionless as a stick. Lavinia was disgusted to see that the top of Otilla's dress was unbuttoned, exposing her gray stringy breasts. She picked up a handful of sand and tried to cover up her chest.

The baby's diaper was heavy with filth. She took it off and wiped it as best she could on the weeds and then pinned it around him again. She picked him up, holding him carefully away from her, and walked to the road. He was ticking from someplace deep inside himself. The noise was deafening. The noises that had seemed to be going on in her own head earlier had stopped. When she got to the car, she laid him under it, where it was cool. She herself stood up straight to get a breath, and down the road saw a yellow ball of dust rolling toward her at great speed. The ball of dust stopped alongside and a young man in faded jeans and shirt, holding a bottle of beer, got out and stared at her. Around his waist he wore a wide belt hanging with pliers and hammers and cords.

"Jeez," he said. He was a telephone lineman going home for dinner, taking a shortcut through the groves. The old lady he saw looked as though she had come out of some Arabian desert. She had cracked lips and puffy eyes and burnt skin. He walked toward her with his hand stretched out, but she turned away and to his astonishment, bent down and scrabbled a baby up from beneath the wrecked car. Then she walked past him and clambered into the cab of his truck by herself and slammed the door.

The young man jumped into the truck and smiled nervously at Lavinia. "I don't have nothing," he said excitedly, "but a chocolate bar, but there's a clinic no more'n ten miles away, if you could just hold on until then. Please," he said desperately. "Do you suppose you want this?" he asked, holding out the bottle of beer.

Lavinia nodded. She took the chocolate and put it in the baby's fist. He cried and pushed it toward his mouth and moved his mouth around it and cried. Lavinia pressed the cool bottle of beer against her face, then rolled it back and forth across her forehead.

The truck roared through the groves and in an instant, it seemed, they were out on the highway, passing a sign that said WORSHIP IN PRIDESUP, 11 MILES. Beyond the sign was a field with a carnival in it. Lavinia could hear the sweet cheap music of the midway and the shrieks of people on the Ferris wheel. Then the carnival fell behind them and there was just field, empty except for a single, immense oak, a sight that so irritated Lavinia that she shut her eyes. The oak somehow seemed to give meaning to the field, a notion she found abhorrent.

She felt a worried tapping at her shoulder. When she looked at the young man, he just nodded at her, then he said, an afterthought, "What's that baby's name? My wife just had one and his name is Larry T."

Lavinia looked down at the baby, who glared blackly back at her, and the recognition that her life and her long, angry journey through it had been wasteful and deceptive and unnecessary hit her like a board being smacked against her heart. She had a hurried sensation of being rushed forward but it didn't give her any satisfaction, because at the same time she felt her own dying slowing down some, giving her an instant to think about it.

"It's nameless," she whispered.

Joy Harjo

The Gift of Margaret

1.

MY SISTER, MARGARET, was born during the early weeks of 1955. I was three and a half years old. My brother Allen was eighteen months younger than me. We'd prepared for the baby by helping our mother sterilize baby bottles and nipples; we were impressed by the tiny clothes. The bassinet took up the corner in my parents' room. My brother was moved to my room. I sneaked smells of baby powder and baby oil and imagined being sister to a girl, just as the doll in my cradleboard. My mother said we were ecstatic when she brought the baby home, for she'd told us Margaret was a gift for my brother and me. Margaret was the name bestowed on this gift of birth. She was named for my mother's best friend, though my father's high school sweetheart was also named Margaret.

Margaret's birth marked the beginning of another era in our home. The pre-Margaret era was characterized by relative calm, perhaps a fiction, for my father drank heavily. He had a vicious temper and was cruel; I was afraid of his temper and ran to hide every afternoon when he came home from work. In this period, though, he kept his other romances from the house and there were large periods of normality, highlighted with trips to the lake with my mother's perfect fried chicken and potato salad.

During this period our mother stayed at home, cleaned, and sewed many of our clothes. She was submissive to my father's anger, couldn't face the reality that her dream of the perfect love, the kind of love she sang about as she washed and ironed, the love she imagined around my father, a tall good-looking Creek man, did not exist. Though she loved to dance and party as much as my father, my mother was monogamous, and preferred home to the raucous bars my father frequented in what had been Indian Territory. But the struggle was wearing thin when Margaret was born; routine masked a rupture.

My first memory of Margaret is this: a kind elderly woman has been hired to baby-sit my brother, new sister, and me because my mother is working. This arrangement feels very strange, as if the house is lopsided, headed in an unknown direction. I'm helping her bathe Margaret and watch to make sure Margaret doesn't roll from the padded bench, as the woman fills a pan with water, tests it with her hand for heat. The tiny bathroom is hot with gas heat, and humid. I'm proud to be helping her with this new creature who is my sister. I feel alone with my sister and wonder what will become of us in this house.

Sister is a new name, which I am fitting myself to. It means protector of this infant who still wears the stub of her birth cord, something I'm quite intrigued with—its appearance and smell remind me of the newborn puppies who abruptly disappeared shortly after our dog had given birth. Margaret's tiny hands are not much larger than the dolls my brother and I doctor and feed dirt, when we're not running or building worlds of sand and earth. I feel intimate and exposed by this little sister. Though I had been prepared in the weeks before her birth no one could precisely touch this feeling. I wonder now, how did I understand the role? I had never been a sister. My mother had no sisters, only brothers. My father didn't talk to his sister because she hated being Indian, tried to pretend she was white though she was much darker than he.

When my brother was brought home from the hospital I bit him in a jealous fit, says my mother. That encounter is family legend. It characterizes my relationship with my brother. We love each other fiercely, yet stand back, on guard. I still imagine that the jagged birthmark he carries as a shield on his thigh was my doing, even after all this time. The birth of this sister had a different tone. Here was someone who would share, an equal. She would be treated the same as me. We were joined together by the nature of our sex, and this was no small thing in the Bible Belt. As well, my brother was a buffer between us.

I asked my mother recently about this memory I have of bathing my sister, while my mother was away at work. Her memory differs. She was working part-time for the Swift Packing Plant before Margaret's birth, then quit to look after the new baby. The elderly woman was someone my father hired to help my mother, but she stayed no longer than a few days because she felt my mother didn't need her, as she did everything herself. I wonder why this discrepancy in memory?

My version appears solid and real to me. When I return to that bathroom as the adult looking over the shoulder of the three-and-a-half-year-old, I still feel the biting absence of my mother, I feel adrift with my baby sister in a house that is being torn apart by my father's anger, by my mother's refusal to acknowledge the truth of the matter. The roof is beginning to break over us. Any one of us could disappear, just as the puppies disappeared. I didn't realize how much I knew of this until I spoke it, how difficult the disappearance of the fragile, soft puppies to my father's callous disposal of them—before their eyes were open—by the side of the road, how terrifying it was to love my sister when I thought I could lose her to the force that destroyed the puppies, to disturbance in the house.

By the time my second brother was born a few years later no one was there except for paid strangers who lived in with us while our mother worked as a cook and waitress in truck stops and restaurants, as our father gradually disappeared between rages with other women, often in our own house. These hired caretakers included people who could get jobs nowhere else: military retirees, unwed mothers, and women with addiction problems. Our little brother didn't learn to walk until he was two years old, and that was only because my aunt and uncle took him to live with them for a few months. The pressure of the lie engulfed us.

There were years that I can't remember much between Margaret's birth and the disintegration of this unwieldy form of nuclear family. My father left when we were eight, six, four, and two years old. Then my mother married a man who was manipulative and evil. I remember mowing the lawn of this strange man's house with my mother. Snakes literally covered the yard in hundreds. My mother told me in this instance they meant the presence of evil (snakes have two sides, as does everything in this world). Yet she went through with the marriage, and he married my mother, a mixed-blood Cherokee woman who had Indian children. He hated Indians and anything Indian and felt superior as a white man and made sure I knew this. When we begged her to leave him shortly after their marriage, he told her he would kill all of us before he'd let her go. We believed him. He forced my mother to play Russian roulette with a loaded gun in front of the children. We often hid together in the aftermath. Our lives felt tenuous, even worthless. I thought it would be better to be dead than to live the way that we were living. I began to hide knives, make plans, but my sister, Margaret, lived with grace through the dangerous years.

2.

IT IS AMAZING how two sisters can be brought up in the same family, but live very different lives. Each life has consequence and will leave its path through the human book of tales. Margaret's path is smooth, no tangles of character, the perfect daughter, as my mother reminded my brother Allen and me more than once. She was the opposite of me. I was "dark," tempestuous, or "high-strung" as my mother called it. My sister was so light I could see her blue veins through her milky skin. She was "dainty," my mother said. I knew that dainty was appreciated over high-strung. Margaret was the child who behaved, kept quiet during the hellish descent.

I questioned everything, including the style and manner of dress my mother preferred for me. I did not like lace and ruffles or other exaggerations of femininity and by the time I could complete sentences I refused to wear such concoctions. I felt my mother's strong disappointment. Margaret fulfilled this dream for her of female beauty. I remember a lavender organdy dress that had been at the back of my closet for years, one of my mother's last efforts to dress me prettily, waiting for Margaret to fit into it because I wouldn't wear it. My mother took it carefully down for a special occasion. As I pulled on my more tailored outfit, I asked Margaret as we dressed in our room, "How can you wear such a thing?" Margaret told me she didn't particularly like it. I encouraged her to wear something else, or say something. Within minutes of Margaret's first rebellion my mother came into my room, told me to leave Margaret alone. I had encouraged her bad behavior. Margaret wore the dress. Perhaps Margaret preferred those styles and wasn't honest with me, for she and my mother still have similar taste in clothes and environment.

My mother did not help Margaret's position with the rest of the children. She elevated her behavior as a model for the rest of us. Yet I can understand how Margaret's acquiescence made life easier for my mother, who struggled daily to get by. I wonder if the same Margaret would have emerged from a calmer sea? Yet I believe Margaret was praised for what was natural to her, and she did not take advantage of her position as the standard-bearer. She was steady, as if she already had her eyes on the way out, while my brother and I engaged with the fight.

When I look back through those hazy years I see my sister, the dutiful daughter gliding with grace through the mess. She sometimes disappears and no one can see her, for she's shaped herself carefully so she can sidestep the emotional mine traps that often snapped unexpectedly in our home. I wonder what I don't know about Margaret, for I often don't remember her when I travel back through patches of memory that cling together marking that particular era. I am engulfed by my own efforts to survive. A recurring dream I have is of sudden and disturbing memory. I suddenly remember I have a home with animals who depend on me for care. I have been away for a long time, weeks or months. They are starving, some have died. I hurry to this suddenly remembered place to feed them. Many have survived despite the terrible odds. I weep from shame of forgetfulness as I feed the poor things.

Margaret was the one of us four children who always appeared to have a "normal" life. I was kicked out of the house at sixteen, my brothers at fourteen and thirteen. Margaret was allowed to stay through high school. She even began calling our stepfather Father. My older brother and I didn't approve, we felt it was betrayal. Doesn't she remember how he treated us, his dislike of us? The violence, the threats? I don't remember her answer. I told myself she really didn't know our father, for he was virtually gone by the time of her conscious memory, yet I do remember him punishing her. And I cannot recall our father ever holding her. Nor do I remember any kindness from the man she was naming father.

Margaret joined school clubs, drank Cokes with friends, appeared to live casually, and succeeded in that world my brothers and I did not. We often envied her place. Now I understand it was not an easy position, not as easy as she made it appear to be.

That kind of technique is studied, hard work, of a relentless craft, a craft she must have studied while everyone was asleep.

3.

YEARS LATER MARGARET is a student at Northeastern State College in Tahlequah, Oklahoma, majoring in education. She has worked hard during summers, saved money for school, and has some support from the tribe. School wouldn't be possible without that, for our mother and stepfather did not offer her any kind of support whatsoever. (Neither did they attend any of our college graduations. Nor was there any acknowledgment of such achievements.) She is a member of the Christian student organization. Her friends are Christians whose lives are based on rules of the church which they do not question. Recreation is squirting each other's cars with shaving cream at red lights, eating hamburgers and singing hymns together. I understand the need for this apparent safety while the rest of the world is at an edge in the middle seventies. Rules are a harbor in a world of paradox, and are all that many of Margaret's friends know as children of the Bible Belt. They were raised that way. Margaret, however, has created this refuge for herself out of the wreckage.

I am living in New Mexico, attending the University of New Mexico as an art student, and am heavily involved with the national movement for Indian rights, as a member of the Kiva Club, an Indian student organization at the university, as well as the fringes of the American Indian Movement. Our work to bring consciousness to our peoples as well as to the larger system is grueling, inspiring, and we are making change. We revise history textbooks in schools, we march against injustices. We have seen people killed in the struggle.

I am working on large canvases of tribal leaders throughout history. I am raising two children: my son, who was born when I was seventeen, whose spirit I have always felt came directly from the killing fields of Vietnam, and a daughter who was born during the period of the Wounded Knee uprising. I am deeply struck by the difference in my life, when compared to my sister's life, yet it doesn't occur to me to question my sister with my outrage, to feel her out regarding this major shift of consciousness I am taking part in. I expect silence from her. And though I can question the larger travesties of genocide I cannot dig through the debris of the aftermath of my childhood with such an intimate participant. Not yet.

When I visit my sister during this time I bring my daughter, Rainy, who is still a baby in diapers and who delights in the company of her auntie, who has volunteered to watch her while I take part in a national Indian conference in the same town. Though I am within a few miles of my mother's house I am not allowed on the premises, nor is my name allowed to be spoken, since my outrage was written in a letter I wrote to my mother after my stepfather accused my thirteen-year-old brother of craziness and kicked him out of their home. My stepfather intercepted it, as he did all mail, no matter to whom it was addressed. In the letter I noted my stepfather was the crazy, not my brother. I was therefore exiled. My brother was sent to me in New Mexico.

My sister is still a member of that household. She goes home on weekends, keeps up the appearance of normality. Her participation doesn't appear to come between us. I know she is making family in the only way she knows how. She has always been on the inside of prevailing culture. She sacrifices to keep up appearances, walks boldly into the living room of a man who wished to destroy everyone, even Margaret, though he appears to love her most. Or does he just suffer her more easily because she is quiet, pleasing? I don't know if Margaret is capable of asking these questions at this time. She is vulnerable, concentrating on making her life out of pieces of the wreck.

At the gray of dawn I am throwing rocks at Margaret's window in the dorm to be let in. I smell of sweat, beer, rich earth, and river. I have taken part in long meetings for strategy, then I danced and sang through the night with fervent hope and desire for the new world, celebrated with others who are part of the awakening. I love the smell of the earth here, so rich, you can hear oil being made from the disintegrating bodies of creatures who lived before us. We did not die.

My sister unlocks the dorm and I crash until late morning. She accommodates me, never reproaches me with her doctrine, never tries to change me. She accepts and loves me. It is within this mutual love we are able to meet in the dissonance of our differences.

4.

MARGARET AND MELISSA, her daughter born on my birthday, have come to meet me while I'm in Oklahoma for a short trip to perform poetry at a college, high school, or conference. They always support me and have often been the only family members present at major life events. We drive to a lake my father used to take us to as children near Oklahoma City. It was only near large bodies of water that my father unwound. It is here I can hear him laughing without the cut of derision. It's a windy spring day and waves kick up tight curls of white foam on the lake. I remember the sandy bottom, see Margaret bobbing in a small orange life jacket between my brother and me. Melissa is barely a teenager, and hangs close to me. We always soak up our time together because it's rare and delicious. She listens with her whole body as we begin talking about growing up, our lives so different than her protected growing up as an only child in a sane family in the same community our great-grandfather Henry Marsey Harjo's allotted land was located. She has everything Margaret wanted.

I've been awakening to the intense roil of pain and history that informed me from childhood and beyond in an effort to understand it, so I can remake the raw stuff into something useful, for my son and daughter, my family and myself. The sustained atmosphere of terror originated with our father's physical and emotional abuse, which stemmed from self-hatred which has everything to do with the history and the manner in which the land was stolen, though history is no excuse for character, ever. One of my earliest memories is my father hitting my mother, throwing her against the tiled walls of the bathroom. He's hitting, then choking her. I am pounding at the back of his jeans. I can only reach as far as the pockets. I'm crying for him to stop.

It has to do with my mother's severe test of will and commitment, a test she took twice and involved us in her struggle. She sacrificed our safety for what she understood to be love and commitment for these men.

I want to know, what does Margaret do with the pain when it begins to overwhelm? What does she remember?

She answers with a laugh. (And Margaret has a distinctive laugh my daughter has inherited; it links them. Laughter makes the perfect link.) "I don't remember much at all. That's how I survived. The problem is I sometimes forget what I need to remember."

I think about all those unanswered events crowding around Margaret and their wish to be recognized. They make rumbles and other noises, though Margaret is cool and calm, perfectly coifed and dressed as we watch the lake. I think about the belt buckle mark and bruise on her thigh, about her being held aloft by one leg while being hit for some small forgettable thing. I still burn with the injustice of it. I've begun telling her these things she couldn't remember, checking her memory against mine, as I am this moment. I'm the catalyst in my family for memory and am fiercely trying to remember everything and question what the memories have given me.

I remember a terrible Saturday, and every weekend was terrible because then our stepfather was not at work. He parked in his chair, barked out orders, and berated everyone as we cleaned and picked up around him while he watched sports on television. My mother served him anything he wanted to eat and drink while we worked together on the house and yard. This particular Saturday I finally snapped after months of his disrespect of her, when he told her roughly that she wasn't attending to his needs fast enough. She had worked two full shifts cooking and waitressing the day before, had come home and cooked, while he watched television and read the paper, and was doing nothing now. I knew I would pay for my remarks but I still contend to this day it was worth it. With cleaning rag in hand I told him, "Why don't you buy her a pair of roller skates so she can get around faster?" The whole house went silent. I can still see Margaret flinching for me. I went to my punishment with satisfaction that the silence had been broken.

Margaret appears untouched in the warm afternoon as we trade memories, but for the tension I trace with my eyes around her jaw. Yet, some have a gift for walking through great disturbance, the density of evil, without it touching them, similar to the gift my mother has for growing plants. I also know that electricity is made from the force of stress, of these tests of fire. And electricity can be used for keeping us warm, lighting the night, as well as for burning down a house. Margaret has made her house of this electricity. I am writing and singing history with it. It is only later in life that I am able to construct a home of substance and beauty, after recalling the stories and walking through the terror with myself whole. I wonder what Margaret would write out of the silence. I wonder what silenced her so fully from the beginning.

5.

THREE YEARS AGO my sister and I stood at the Great Serpent Mound in Ohio, a distinctive effigy mound that was not plowed under by farmers who took the rest of the land surrounding this place of ceremonial significance by a people who were related to our ancestors. Margaret had joined me at a National Teachers of English Conference in Cincinnati and we'd found other willing participants to make the trek to this significant symbol. As we stood there in that sacred place I was aware that there was a larger meaning in this trek. I knew there was another turn in the road together. I could smell it but not see it as I knew that link binding us together as sisters was a potent and powerful thing, had unfolded into dimensions of grace from suffering. I was proud of both of us as we stood here so many years after the war: Margaret as an award-winning teacher, on many state boards and commissions, who teaches in a rural school in Liberty Mounds, Oklahoma, and me as a professor at the University of New Mexico, a published poet, speaker, and musician, working for Indian rights. We survived, even flourished, on different tracks, yet together.

We flew to Chicago together that afternoon, then parted ways. The next morning Margaret called before dawn with the news our stepfather had died quite unexpectedly. He was a hypochondriac and always had some ailment but we expected him to live forever because he was so relentless in his need to disturb the world around him. We were all so relieved. The release of years of tension was palpable over the wires. Another era had ended, marked by the justice of time, the image of the snake over the green Ohio valley Margaret and I had witnessed.

• • •

6.

ALL LIVING THINGS evolve and are involved in a pattern of struggle and release. This includes sisterhood. My sister and I came through the same door of our mother, we ate from the same earth. We began our lives together in the hills of northeastern Oklahoma. We lived through two violent eras, gave birth to our own children, to knowledge born from drastically different roads. I did not test myself against her, nor has she against me, though she told me once she felt I had been gifted with all the talents and looks, that she received what was left after the birth of my brother and me. I cannot remember major disagreement or dissension from her, though I can recall every unkindness I have uttered or exacted against Margaret. Once, before any of us were of school age, I chased her with poison ivy when I knew she would react to it. My brother and I had been accused of something we did not do and took unjust punishment for it, some rather small thing young Margaret had done, not worthy of severe punishment. I will never forget the effect of the poison, how she swelled up with its terrible juice. I've since not consciously added to the list of unkindness.

Our pattern of sisterhood makes an ongoing spiral, and within that spiral are our families, our communities, the earth, stars, all time. The spiral resembles two women carrying water through a battlefield in a rain of arrows. It resembles a long snake of relatives who walk through history, from the eastern hills of time immemorial. The light balances the dark. Wildness walks next to her steady sister. They make it to the other side together.

May 1994
for my sister

Letty Cottin Pogrebin

Sisters and Secrets

"HAVE YOU ANY BROTHERS OR SISTERS?"

It's a question I dread, yet people ask it all the time. At best, it's a caring question on the road to intimacy. We want to know more about one another's origins, to understand who we are and where we come from. At worst, it's fueled by conversational drought: "Where'd you grow up?" we ask when we run out of things to say. "Got any sisters or brothers?"

To most people, the answer is simple. "I'm one of four girls," they reply. "I have two brothers." "I'm an only child."

But when I get the question, I have to make a split-second decision. Do I finesse it and just say "I have two sisters," or do I take several minutes of my listeners' time, test their powers of concentration, and tell them the whole story? Sisterhood is such a complicated subject for me: it's about biology and family history, lies and love, identity, secrecy, and the gut-level truth that one distills not from facts but from feelings. Most of all, for me, sisterhood is about equality and acceptance. No other definition can contain my convoluted story.

I have two sisters but only one of them feels like a sister—Betty, who is fourteen years older than I. She's the sister who lived at home until the morning of her wedding; she left when she was twenty-one and I was seven. She's the sister who taught me how to tell time, the sister who set her hair in bobby pins and combed it in a pageboy, the sister who dated handsome boys in uniform and wore leg makeup during World War II when stockings were rationed, the person I've always called my sister, and thought of as my sister, my real sister, my only sister, even though I discovered when I was twelve that she was born of a different father and was in fact my half sister, whom my father adopted after he abandoned his own daughter, who was also my half sister but whom I never met until I was almost fifteen years old and she twenty-seven.

Are you with me? Let's try again.

By blood, I'm related equally to both of my sisters: Betty, born in 1925, is my mother's daughter by her first marriage. Rena, born in 1927, is my father's daughter by *his* first marriage. For years, my parents concealed their previous unions from me and most of their friends. The relatives cooperated in the ruse. Much later, when a cousin spilled the beans and my parents had to answer for their lies, they explained that when they were young, divorce was considered a scandal, a personal, if not moral, failure, especially for a woman. So, like thousands of others trapped in the mores of the time, they created a cover-up. After they married each other in 1937 and I was born in 1939, they moved to a new place and seized the opportunity to erase their prior lives and invent a more respectable family history. Their divorces vanished into thin air. The rough edges of their biographies were filed as smooth as a well-honed myth. They backdated their wedding to 1923 to accommodate Betty's birthdate. My father legally adopted Betty and at the same time became estranged from his own daughter, Rena. With a fresh slate, my parents could present themselves to their new community as a long-married couple with two daughters, Betty and me, her baby sister—a love child born to this long-married pair "after fourteen years of trying." In short, a normal, all-American family.

From the perspective of my early childhood, our family

seemed not just normal but enviable. I had this wonderful big sister who treated me like a living doll, adored me, indulged me, and then, when taking leave of her parents' home, made me the flower girl at her wedding. What more could a seven-year-old want? A kid doesn't question her family mythology. I never noticed that our family albums contained no pictures of my parents' wedding or that none of the photos showed Daddy and Betty in the same shot until she was fourteen. I was too busy lingering over the images I loved, like the one of Betty and me on the back porch in our summer outfits, she a fully developed young woman, and me a pudgy toddler imitating her grown-up pose; or dressed for a costume party—she looking sexy in an army cap and boots, and me in a grass skirt.

My memories of our time together are sparse but precious. I remember being the much-fussed-over mascot at her slumber parties in our finished basement, with her friends in their satin pajamas lounging on mounds of pillows, trying on lipstick, playing 78 rpm records, and talking about boys. It was Betty who taught me to eat spaghetti with butter and ketchup; hold the sauce. It was she who started me listening to "our" favorite radio shows—*Burns and Allen, The Easy Aces, Mr. Kean: Tracer of Lost Persons*—and keeping track of the top tunes on Martin Bloch's Make-Believe Ballroom. And thanks to her, I learned all the words to "Mares Eat Oats" and "Comin' in on a Wing and a Prayer" and "White Cliffs of Dover"—wartime melodies that somehow belong to my childhood as much as to her dating years.

Best of all, I remember our trip to a fabric store when she was engaged and shopping for her new life. The salesman mistook me for her daughter. "No, we're *sisters!*" Betty laughed, reaching down to hug my little-girl shoulders. "We're *sisters!*" I beamed, the fourteen years between us melting away as I basked in the status of an equal.

The day after Betty's wedding, my parents moved me into her room with its tiny rosebud wallpaper and mirrored dressing table swathed in an organdy skirt. I was thrilled, but I missed her terribly. Looking back, I suppose I might have preferred to have had a sister who was a contemporary, someone with whom I could play paper dolls and ring-a-levio, rather than a glamorous college girl living in a different world under the same roof. And with each passing year, as my parents' marriage became a battleground, I might have wished for a sister to huddle with at the top of the stairs when their arguments shook the house and I alone absorbed the bickering, the shouting and sobbing, the weeks of turgid silence.

The truth is, I don't remember ever wanting any other sister. Though Betty was years older and miles away, I cherished her for everything she was and everything she brought into my life, especially for giving me a brother-in-law—no other kid my age had one—for making me an aunt when I was nine, and for having four terrific babies before she turned thirty, thus fulfilling every female fantasy of the 1950s to the letter. I loved her husband, Bernie, who was the spitting image of the actor Glenn Ford and the most dashing of all her uniformed suitors, a man of gentle wisdom who always made me feel as if I'd invented sunshine. I loved their kids—to me, the cutest, smartest, most lovable children on earth. I visited often, dropping into their *Good Housekeeping* life as if into a dream, all the while studying my sister's world like a painting—foreground, background, light and shadow.

I watched her hang curtains, file recipes, tend a garden, make a budget and stick to it, use a pressure cooker and other newfangled appliances we'd never had at home. I studied how she organized the family chores, how she packed a picnic, cut the children's hair, gave them pots and pans to play with in the tub instead of bath toys, traced the family's vacation route on a map in Magic Marker so everyone could savor the trip before they left and relive it after they were home. I watched her and Bernie together. I memorized their pleasure. I unloaded my despair about Mommy and Daddy's fights, and my anxiety that they might split up. When they were fighting downstairs, I called Betty from the upstairs phone. "They're at it again!" I would cry, and Betty would comfort and reassure me, even help me to laugh at their quarrels, as if my parents were naughty children and I the adult forced to tolerate their misbehavior. And when I needed some joyful noise to drown out my father's roar and my mother's tears, I called up memories of Betty's family dinner-times or the ruckus of her children's laughter. Because I had witnessed my sister's life I knew there was a better way.

I resolved to be exactly like her when my time came—except I wouldn't have four children, I'd have *five.*

Then Rena showed up. I had learned of her existence only three years earlier when the revelation of our family secret had literally knocked me unconscious and I'd awakened to my parents' guilty excuses and explanations. But it was one thing to know I had another sister out there somewhere in the world, and quite another to answer the bell one cold, crisp day and find her standing on the doorstep.

Rena, then twenty-seven, said she had come, reluctantly, because "our" father was a lawyer and she needed a court order, a marshal, some kind of legal help to get her belongings out of her mother's house. The mother, my father's first wife, was deranged and violent. Rena said she could not stay with her another day.

After a reunion with *our* father that can only be described as sedate, and a dinner during which my mother seemed to be trying extra hard to make her feel welcome, Rena stayed with us for a while, helping to care for Mommy, who was ill with cancer. I rushed home from school every day to be with my newly discovered sister, as if she was a visiting mermaid who might disappear with the next wave. We talked constantly, or more accurately, she talked and I listened as magnificent sentences poured from her mouth, every one of them polysyllabic and professorial.

She made obscure references to things like cybernetics, physiometry, and ethnographics. She corrected my mistakes. *(Secrete* means hide, not just ooze, and I've never forgotten it.) She sprinkled her arcane vocabulary into ordinary conversation and sent me rushing to the dictionary to look up words like "tautology" and "anima"—many of which I was tickled to encounter a few months later on the College Board exam.

Rena, it turns out, was a genius with an IQ of 180 and a Ph.D. in anthropology. She was the world's leading authority on Gypsy culture, a protégée of the great Ruth Benedict, and fluent in twenty Romani dialects. She'd been adopted by the Gypsy tribe that had been the subject of her doctoral thesis—by its king, no less, so she was a certified Gypsy princess. She wore Bohemian outfits and a thick long braid. She was exotic and eccentric.

She told me almost dispassionately how her mother heard voices and had hallucinations, and how she had beaten Rena mercilessly. Once the woman nearly blinded her with a blow to her eyes that broke her glasses; several times her mother attempted to strangle her, and once she dangled her out of a window, bragging, "I gave birth to you, so I can kill you."

"Why did you stay?" I asked, incredulous.

Rena claimed she had nowhere else to go. She said she regretted having to turn to our father for help but she had no choice.

"At this point, I'm interested in developing a compensatory relationship with you, not with him," she explained. "He could live without me all these years. I can live without him now."

"Daddy wanted to keep seeing you," I insisted, repeating the story my parents had told me when their lies caught up with them. "But he said your mother stopped the visits, poisoned you against him, and then threatened to harm you if he tried to get in touch or fight for you in court, so he stopped trying."

"My mother harmed me anyway," she said bitterly. "And

he knew she would because she was always violent. No, that's not what happened." Rena insisted that his court-ordered visitation rights were contingent on his paying child support, and when he stopped paying, her mother stopped the visits. Rena added: "He never fought for me. He didn't want me. He left me alone with her and I never heard from him again."

Suddenly, a huge, hot thought seared into a corner of my brain: if our father could abandon one daughter, he could abandon another. We're both his blood. Obviously, blood is no protection. Neither is time. She'd been with him twelve years; I was going on fifteen. I'm not safe. He could leave me too.

Then I thought of Rena, growing up without a daddy. My heart hurt for her. I must have seemed like her replacement, her father's new toy. Still, she had come back. She treated our father with icy propriety but she had forgiven me, the baby who started it all, and she had forgiven my mother. In fact, as Mommy's cancer worsened, Rena's kindness was one of her most endearing traits. She was helpful and solicitous in the manner of someone who had a lot of experience putting herself last.

She stayed over at our house for days at a time. Neighbors began to notice. Friends asked questions. Daddy told Rena he wanted to acknowledge her in the community, but rather than disentangle all of our complicated relationships at this late date, he asked if she would mind being introduced as a cousin.

To be disowned not once but twice, to be rejected after being rediscovered, to find her father more interested in the judgment of his community than the feelings of his daughter—how that must have stung. But Rena just nodded and said "cousin" was fine.

Soon afterward, she moved into her own apartment. I worked at our relationship, determined to make Rena a "real" sister like Betty. I marveled at her ways. She kept her entire wardrobe piled up on her ironing board and dressed herself from there. She wore sandals and dirndl skirts in an age of white gloves and matching shoes and bags. She was fascinating, intense, and utterly unique. As she revealed more and more about herself, I began to feel like an apprentice rather than a sister, especially when she took me to visit the Gypsies who'd adopted her. The tribe lived in a stretch of second-floor storefronts in upper Manhattan, but the king, a big man with a heavy black mustache, was right out of central casting. Most of the Gypsy women wore dozens of gold bracelets on both their arms; Rena told me they didn't trust the banks so they converted their life's savings into gold bangles and wore them day and night. I remember the evening meal, when everyone ate directly from the serving platters. I remember, too, how well they treated their children—like miraculous treasures. It was hard to know which child belonged to which parent because each was showered with love and attention by everyone. And I remember how the Gypsies adored their princess, Rena; my sister.

As did I. My adolescent crush, a fevered outburst of interest and affection that expressed itself in paroxysms of imitation. I wore sandals and black turtlenecks. I determined that I would become an intellectual. I would live alone. I might not ever marry. I believed I was a more interesting person just for having Rena as my sister. Meanwhile, Betty's life, happy as it was, suddenly seemed tepid, colorless, and conventional by comparison.

When I was fifteen—three days before Betty's thirtieth birthday—our mother died. That summer, I moved in with Betty and Bernie. I drove their car. I had no curfew. I went my own way. In the full flush of my grief, my teen rebellion, my awestruck adoration of Rena, my dumb risk-taking, my acting-out, Betty remained my most ardent booster. When I confided my inadequacies—small breasts, skinny ankles, mousy hair—she listened, took me seriously, then proceeded to counter my claims in her no-nonsense, English-teacher voice with the tenderness just below the surface, building my confidence and reiterating my strengths until I felt like Marie Curie and Debbie Reynolds rolled into one. Somehow, she gave me unconditional love and firm guidance without becoming my parent or disciplinarian.

How she communicated this fundamental regard for me, I really don't know. She just put it into the air we breathed—a sense of rock-solid sisterness, a respect for boundaries, an utter absence of condescension regardless of the disparities in our age, interests, development, and personal style. Somehow, she made me feel we were peers, and with that feeling, I was able to go off to college that autumn a surer, stronger person.

I have only two regrets about my relationship with Betty and both date back more than thirty-five years. First, that I never confided in her when I got pregnant in my senior year (it was 1959, abortion was illegal, and I couldn't face my respectable sister with my moral failure; I learned later that Betty had had an abortion of her own and would have been a knowledgeable and comforting ally in my search for an underground doctor), and second, that I may have caused her anguish during the years when I fell under Rena's spell and turned away long enough to take Betty for granted and betray her love.

The infatuation with Rena showed cracks after I graduated from college and started to see myself as a serious person with thoughts and ideas of my own. Though I still admired her greatly, I was ready to relate to her on more even ground while she seemed unable to approach me without the patronizing tone of a lecturing professor. The remarkable mutuality and respect that Betty had shown me throughout my childhood seemed out of Rena's ken though she was "only" twelve years my senior, not fourteen. The breach widened even more when she married a man who seemed so wrong for her that it was hard to square my remarkable Rena with her choice of mate and harder still to spend time with them.

We drifted apart. She had two children, wrote books and articles, and taught at a college in New York. I got married, had three children, wrote books and articles, and lived in New York.

Having things in common could not compensate for the imbalances between us. It could not fill the gaps in our past or give her back the fourteen lost years with "our" father, or relieve my vague sense of guilt. I always felt some complicity in causing Rena's suffering. What's more, I knew the family life I'd had and she'd coveted was far from the happy idyll she imagined. Still, she was the wronged one, the unacknowledged daughter, the secret sister who never quite fit in.

Over the years, Betty and I invited Rena to family gatherings but she almost always declined. Occasionally, she and I have lunch or exchange letters, but the wall between us has thickened with time. Today, to my regret, we are merely courteous acquaintances and I have resigned myself to the fact that I am a woman with two sisters—one who is cherished and close, and one whom I hardly know.

Having said that, I cannot pretend that the bond I have with Betty—wonderful as it is—is typical of other sisters. My twin daughters, now twenty-nine, have taught me what it means to enjoy bone-deep intimacy with another female and made me understand what Betty and I missed because of our age spread, generational differences, and separation over space and time. I've watched my daughters weave their lives together until they can read each other's thoughts, make each other laugh or cry, finish each other's sentences. Each knows the other thoroughly, historically, wordlessly, back to infancy and up to yesterday. Although both are married now, and each is a well-defined woman with a separate life, at some deep level, they have each other in a way Betty and I—for all our genuine love and equality—do not. Theirs is sisterhood of another sort, a sisterhood we could never have had.

Likewise, among my friends, I've seen sisters who talk every day and share the most minute details of their daily lives. It's a habit they fell into growing up and they've kept at it. Betty and I never overlapped in life long enough to develop such a routine. I rarely know what she's doing tomorrow and she generally doesn't know where I was last weekend. We don't go shopping together. We've never discussed sex. But we share the most important things—happiness, misery, family, politics, core values. From her, I still feel the same unconditional acceptance that sustained me in my troubled youth, and for her, I feel the same prideful love that I remember as a seven-year-old in the fabric store, beaming under my big sister's smile.

Writing this, I realize how sweet and slippery is this word "sister"—big enough to stretch beyond biology and across time; flexible enough to define soulmates and virtual strangers; precise enough to embrace me and Rena, me and Betty, my two daughters, and all the sisterhoods in between.

Louise DeSalvo

My Sister's Suicide

Early Summer 1993

MY BASEMENT IS a complete mess, and has been for years.

After my mother's death, when my father remarries, he sells the house that I grew up in, and most of its furniture, except for three pieces that I take. He packs up our family's mementos; and tells me that if I don't want them, he will dispose of them.

I am furious that he has chosen to bring very little from his first life—his clothes, his tools, a few photos of my mother (but none of my family or me or my sister)—into his new and happy life, though, in part, I understand. The last several years have not been pleasant ones for him. My sister's suicide. My mother's depression. Her terrible, inexplicable terminal illness.

I sense that he wants to leave anything that will remind him of those years behind. I would too. I tell him that I will take everything, go through the boxes, and decide what to keep, what to give away and what to throw away.

"My father goes off to Florida to get married," I tell my friend Kate. "And he leaves me behind to deal with all his shit." I make it sound like he's forced me into taking these discards. He hasn't. I take them because I can't bear to think of these boxes being heaved atop a pile of trash at the town dump. I will take what I want. Discard the rest. I will take care of it right away.

But that was three years ago.

Every morning, when I go downstairs to throw in a load of

laundry—a ritual that helps me think about what I will write that day—I pass the pile of cardboard boxes. I think that, someday, I will make time for sorting through them, I really will, but that, today, I don't have the time, or the energy, or the courage.

"Clean the basement." These words have appeared on hundreds of my "To do" lists.

"Today I have to deal with what's downstairs," I say to my husband, over coffee, almost every morning. Using a studied irreverence to mask my fears and feelings, I have started to refer to the boxes in the basement as "my mother's death stuff."

"When I take care of my mother's death stuff," I tell him, "we can put the Lifecycle down there, get some dumbbells, put down indoor/outdoor carpeting, make it into an exercise room."

What has stopped me from cleaning out the basement, I know, are the three cardboard boxes marked with my sister's name, "Jill," in the barely legible handwriting of the last months of my mother's life.

It is not that I expect that when I open these boxes, I will find documents—my sister's letters or diaries—that will explain the reasons for my sister's suicide some seven years before. I know my mother too well. Had these existed, she would have destroyed them.

What I know I will find, and what will be painful for me to see, are the few, trivial objects that my mother has chosen to save from my sister's thirty-seven years of life. The objects that will tell me what it was about my sister that my mother wanted to remember.

When I let myself remember Jill, I always see her in work clothes. In her country house in the Pacific Northwest. In the backyard of the tiny house she and her husband lived in for a year on Catalina Island, where the strains on their marriage had already begun to show. I see her bending over her potter's wheel, her long, honey-colored hair covering her face. I see her hands, red as raw meat from working with clay. A worker's hands. Remembering her hands is harder than remembering anything else about her. I see her arranging delicate teapots in the kiln. Preparing it for firing. Harvesting vegetables. Feeding her numerous pets—dogs, cats, and, once, a pig. She called him "Piglet," and let herself grow too fond of him, for he was being raised for slaughter. In those days, she and her husband caught or raised almost all the food they ate, they were living so frugally, so he could finish his research for his dissertation for his Ph.D. in wildlife management.

Summer 1983

MY SISTER IS living on the West Coast. Her most recent love affair has ended, and she begins "freaking out," as I phrase it in my diary. She wants to sell her house and move back East.

"I have no reason to stay here," she tells us.

I am worried about her, and my husband and I offer help. We'll find an apartment, she can take a job in my husband's company, and take some time to get her life together.

After my sister starts coming apart, I begin noticing, and recording, into my diary, disasters that I read about in the newspaper or hear about on the radio.

"People hurt when the ceiling of a shopping mall fell in. People hurt when someone doused them with gasoline in a supermarket and set them on fire," I write. My children start to call me D. E. W. "Distant Early Warning."

August 1983

"JILL HAS MOVED here from the West Coast," I record, "and it isn't as bad as I thought it would be. I've been keeping her busy and helping her out."

Against my advice, and for no good reason—she has plenty

of money from the sale of her house—Jill has moved back into our parents' house.

"A surefire recipe for disaster," I tell my husband.

December 1983

MY LIFE HAS been a shambles since soon after my sister's arrival. Several telephone calls a day, from my mother, my father, and Jill. My mother, insisting that I should include Jill in my life. Take her along when I go for a swim, have her over for lunch. My sister, complaining about my parents. About my father's condemnatory attitude—how he disapproves of her seeing this man or that one, how he gives her little lectures on how she can improve her life. About my mother's jealousy of the time she spends with my father. My father, telling me that Jill spends too much time in bed, telling me to call her, to give her a pep talk. Calling my husband for advice, and in exasperation. Watching the three of them deteriorate. Trying to help. But trying to keep my distance.

"What has come out so far," my mother tells me one day, after a family therapy session, "is how happy we were, as a family, and how close." What has not come out, I think to myself, is the violence.

I am teaching full-time at Hunter, finishing the editing of Vita Sackville-West's letters to Virginia Woolf, and *Between Women,* raising two teenage boys. I have no time for this, I say to myself. I wish they would leave me alone. "I have just about been worn out by everyone's needs," I write.

I believe that I have kept my sanity by keeping my distance from my family. My battle against depression has been an ongoing struggle that I finally believe I am winning with the help of a wonderful woman therapist. I don't want to be drawn back into their orbit. It's too dangerous for me. "The whole family is fucked up," I write into my diary, "and they want me to be fucked up with them."

Throughout the early part of December, my sister's moods vacillate wildly, the swings get wider and become more frequent. She is depressed and can't get out of bed. Then she has a great day. She meets a man she takes to immediately; she likes him so much she thinks she can marry him. She gets a job. She asks me how I'm doing, and seems to mean it—the first time in months. Then the man disappoints her, and she is very depressed.

In the middle of December, my mother is in very bad shape. She checks herself into the psychiatric ward of our local hospital.

My sister gives me her perspective of my mother's deterioration.

"She's doing it to get back at me." I listen. Wonder if Jill is exaggerating. What is happening with my mother and my sister seems connected in some dangerous way that I don't want to understand.

"Before she decides to go crazy," my sister says, "she writes out her menu for Christmas and makes a shopping list for food. She balances her checkbook and leaves a note about the bills that will have to be paid."

She also finds, and goes through, all my sister's mail. She reads the sexy letters my sister has written to a lover during her marriage. Then, according to my sister, she begins swallowing Valiums, goes to bed, and refuses to get up. (Just after my mother's death, as I am selecting a piece of jewelry to pin on the lapel of the pink suit I have chosen for her wake and burial, I find an article about adultery tucked into her jewelry box; women who commit adultery, it says, tend to have husbands who don't sexually satisfy them.)

At first, the doctors try drug treatment. But it has to be

stopped. My mother quickly develops a serious allergic reaction to the drugs. Shock treatment, the doctors say, is the only alternative. We find out, from my father, something we have never known: my mother has been institutionalized before, as a young girl. And she has received shock treatment before. When I find this out, I am not surprised that my parents have kept this secret. Mental illness, after all, is not something anyone discussed openly when we were growing up. My sister is furious that we haven't been told before. I wonder whether this was the reason that Jill and I were so often sent off to Long Island to spend our summers with relatives.

As my mother gets worse, my sister gets better. She seems more cheerful. Sure, now, that if she sets her mind to it, she can control her life and make it work. Craziness is a ball that is being passed back and forth between them.

My father comes to my house to spill out his sorrow, bewilderment, and rage. He tells me that what sent my mother over the edge was her finding my sister's love letters. That, and the fact that I am going away for Christmas. His rage spills over. He bangs my kitchen table with his fists.

"All your mother ever wanted from you," he tells me, "was a little love, which you never gave her." So, I think to myself, but don't say. Nothing has changed. Whenever anything goes wrong, he blames it all on me.

I control myself. Don't say much. My husband isn't home. He's caught me off guard, come over unannounced, when I'm home alone.

He talks about my sister. Weeps about how rotten her life is. Tells me what she's told him about her sex life with her first husband. It's not something she has revealed to me. "This isn't right," I think. "No father should know this much about his daughter's sex life." I wonder when my father and my sister have had such intimate conversations.

Christmas 1983

I AM IN THE Cayman Islands, with my husband and children, having the scuba-diving holiday that we had planned for months. It is a difficult time, and I shouldn't be here.

My mother has had an acute psychotic break and is in a psychiatric ward undergoing shock treatment. Every day, we make a call to see how she's doing. She isn't doing well.

My father is enraged at me for going away with my family at this terrible time. My husband and I have almost canceled this trip. I have almost stayed home. But my husband has insisted that I need to get away, that *we* need to get away, after the strain that we have been living with for months.

In Cayman Brac, my husband and I are waiting to hear how my mother's shock treatments are going. The last report was not good.

I try to relax, try to get some rest, but it's not easy. I walk to the end of the pier in the wind, and wonder if I'll fall off or be blown away. I have a moment of exquisite pleasure watching a sunset, but panic when I see a toddler run on the pier unattended. I am happy to see my sons together in a paddleboat, but worry if they'll run aground on the reef. And I can't enjoy my dives or my swims. I know there are sharks and moray eels and barracuda and spiny sea urchins. After a dive instructor tells a story of a diver swallowed by a seven-hundred-pound grouper (which everyone but me regards as apocryphal), I stop diving.

What soothes me is lying on my belly at the edge of the water, watching hermit crabs. I do this for hours, while my husband and sons dive. The sea grass is filled with them. They have red and blue bands around their legs. Their parade across the sandy bottom amuses me. Their fights do not seem connected to territoriality. I notice that they sometimes hitch rides atop one another.

I see a small one, struggling under the weight of a huge

shell. A large one, just barely protected by a small one. I wonder how they select the shells they haul around on their delicate bodies for protection. Is it accident? Some aesthetic sense? Do some feel a greater need for protection than others, and so, look for shells that are far larger than their bodies? Are there brave hermit crabs who don't mind being exposed? And timid ones?

I have taken my diary to Cayman Brac. Its cheerful cover of purple and white irises in bloom is out of keeping with the family tragedy I am recording in its pages, the family history of violence and insanity that I am trying to understand. Writing in my diary, as always, helps me immeasurably. It is, by now, a five-year-old habit—one that I have begun in deliberate, and self-conscious, imitation of Virginia Woolf.

"What I see clearly," I write, "is how, as a child, I was blamed for their bad times, how they expected me to make them feel good, and how unfair that was, and how impossible it would be for any young child to do what they expected." I remind myself of my mother's history of being unmothered, of its consequences in her care for me. Her mother died when she was two, and she was passed around from one inadequate (and perhaps abusive) caregiver to another. At times, she stopped eating (or wasn't adequately nourished) and nearly died.

I write, too, about my work. About how work, for me, is salvation. I wonder whether I have chosen to work on Virginia Woolf because of the similarities between her family's history and my own. In making out a work plan for my return home (which is an activity that always makes me feel good), I write, "Think about [Virginia] Woolf and incest." This idea comes as a surprise. I have vowed never to work on Woolf again. (Six years later, a book-length study about Woolf as an incest survivor, my most important work to date, is published.)

My sister, my father has told me in a telephone conversation, is returning to the West Coast. He's taking her to the airport. He's afraid that something terrible will happen if she leaves, but my mother, in her moments of lucidity, insists on it. She says she won't come home from the hospital if Jill is still there.

For a time, after I get this call, I feel bad for him, and for my sister. Feel bad that the weight of my mother's and sister's illnesses is all on his shoulders. But I am fighting to stay clear. In my journal, I write that I am fighting for my life.

January 1984

MY MOTHER IS HOME. She's not back to normal (and will never be), but she is functioning. She has begun to cook, and to clean. The last report from my sister has been good. She has gotten an apartment, and a job, and a car. Everything seems to be returning to what passes for normal in my life.

One morning, I am cutting an orange for breakfast. I am, as always, distracted. I slice a piece out of my finger, see the blood pour out, and lose consciousness. I have a history of blackouts. I've had them since childhood. They terrify me. I'm always afraid that the next one will be the last one. Afraid that I'll die. My family has always called what I do "fainting," but I'm not so sure.

(As I write this, and revise it, I can work only one or two words at a time before I feel like I'm going to pass out. I look away from the word processor. I look out the window at the backyard. Watch the squirrels. I try to center myself. I burst into tears. This last paragraph that I have struggled to write is the hardest, most personal passage I have ever written. I do it a few words at a time. It takes me days. But it's important for me to be able to say this.)

This one is scarier than most. My husband tells me that this time, I have stopped breathing for a long time, and he thinks he will have to resuscitate me. He knows that if he does, he'll break my ribs, so he waits through one, two, three interminable seconds to see if I'll start breathing on my own. Just as he's decided not to wait any longer, he tells me, I start taking deep, shuddering breaths.

The ambulance comes. My sons watch me taken away on a stretcher. The doctors, as usual, can't find anything wrong with me. "Stress," my husband says. "It's all the stress you're under."

This is a danger sign that I cannot ignore. I call my therapist and get back into therapy.

February 1984

A FEW WEEKS after the event occurs, I record into my diary, in very controlled prose, that my sister has killed herself.

"Jill killed herself at the end of January—January 29, to be exact," I write. "What to record here about it? The feeling I have, of having escaped. The distance I put between myself and my family, necessary, because it saved me. Sadness, certainly. But also . . . a sense of freedom, almost of euphoria, that I was no longer responsible for her, and that I had been responsible for her for so very, very long, as long as I can remember."

There is a family photograph of the two of us, taken when I am about thirteen, and when she is ten. I am sitting in my nightgown, in my mother's rocking chair. Jill is on my lap, pretending to be a baby. I hold a toy bottle to her lips. I pretend to feed her. My father is taking this picture, and we are posing for it. I look like I have been pressed into this against my wishes. My glassy eyes look past her, past the camera, and past my father, into the far, far distance. Jill looks straight into the viewfinder. She wears a phony smile, pretending she's having a good time. But I can see the sadness in her, the sadness that was always there.

"Did you have to bring her?" These words from one or another of my friends, or boyfriends, throughout my teenage years, whenever I arrive at a basketball game, or the park, or the Sweet Shoppe, where we all hang out. My parents don't allow me out of the house without my sister. I can't stand being in the house—a place where someone is always yelling at someone else—I need to get out of the house as often as I can. I nearly always accept my parents' condition that I take my sister with me. But I make her pay.

I race to wherever I'm going so fast that it is a terrible struggle for her to keep up with me. When we get to where we're going, I ignore her, pretend she isn't there.

She stands at the edge of the crowd. My mother hasn't wanted her at home. I don't want her with me. My friends think she's a royal pain in the ass. She looks the way she always looks, like she's on the verge of tears.

THE CALL COMES, as these calls do, around midnight, while I am sleeping. The phone awakens me. My husband answers it. He is in his study, a room that adjoins our bedroom. I can hear him talking and I know, from the tone of his voice, that something is wrong. The first part of the conversation is muffled. Then I hear him say, "Yes, I'll tell Louise. I'll tell her parents. I'm sorry, so very, very sorry."

I hear my husband's footsteps. I sit up in bed. Prepare myself. I know what his news will be, though I have kidded myself into thinking that because Jill seems better, I can have some breathing space, some time to catch my breath, until the next crisis. I can get on with my own life and not worry so much about hers.

MY SISTER HAS hanged herself in the basement of the apartment that she has shared for less than a month with the woman who has called us. She has used a belt to do it. She has killed herself early in the morning. "It is a beautiful, sunny morning," she has written, in the note in which she tells us that she can't go on and that she has decided to take her life.

This is not the first time this woman has found someone dead, she has told my husband. Her brother killed himself, and she is the one who found him.

When my husband tells me this, I feel sorry for her, and furious at my sister for putting someone so vulnerable through this again. But then I think, "I'm glad she didn't do it here. I'm glad I wasn't the one who found her."

My husband makes the telephone call to my parents. My father answers the phone. I can hear his screams. "No! No! No! No!" Then my mother's cries.

I get on the telephone with them. I don't remember what I say. My husband takes the phone out of my hand, and says we'll be in touch throughout the night. I hear him tell my father that, no, Louise can't come. He is protecting me. "She has to tell the boys. She has to be here with me and with them," I hear him say.

When I tell my friends about my sister's death, I tell them that the belt she has used to strangle herself with had been a gift from me. I don't know if this is true—I *had* given Jill the gift of a belt—but I am compelled to say it, and, at the time, I don't know why. Now, though, it seems to have been my way of taking responsibility for what happened to her, though I have never admitted to myself that I have felt guilty about her death. And there is this too. My telling the story in this way links us together, binds me to her, even in death.

1 February 1984

THROUGHOUT MY sister's wake, I remain detached and controlled. I don't cry. I store up incidents to tell my friend Kate, who comes with her husband and children the first night. It is the only way I can get through this.

When my parents, my husband, and I are brought up to the casket by the undertaker to view the body, my mother kneels down on the pew, looks at Jill, then turns to me and says, "Doesn't she look beautiful?"

"Mmmm," I say. I don't contradict her. Jill doesn't look beautiful. Her face is disfigured. Later, Ernie, who is a doctor, explains why.

My mother gets up. "See," she says to me. "She came home to us, after all. She came home to be with us on her birthday."

This is the craziest thing my mother has said so far. I can't stand it. But I tuck it away in my memory to tell Kate.

It *is* the first of February, my sister's birthday. She would have been thirty-eight years old. But, I think, wouldn't it be better if Jill was away, and still alive?

I REMEMBER something that happened with Jill in the autumn, soon after she came East.

She is walking away from me in the parking lot of the Y, where I have taken her swimming, toward her car. She is tossing something she is saying offhandedly, over her shoulder.

It is, I recall, a beautiful October evening. The sun is setting. The sky is glowing fuchsia, orange. In less than three months she'll be dead.

I don't want to hear her; I'm really not listening; I want to drown out her crazy talk. This day, she has gone on and on and on about the new man she has met, and how they have "clicked," and how she is thrilled that he has a daughter, how she's always wanted a daughter, and how, this time, she knows it's going to work, she's going to make it work. I've heard this before. I want to be alone; I wish she wasn't here.

"Who wants to be forty?" I'm forty-one, and think it's just a dig at me. Then she says, "Me, I'll never be forty." I think this is another crazy remark. Or Jill telling me she's afraid to grow old. When she's not wearing her overalls to do her pottery or her gardening, she still dresses as if she's fifteen. Cute little outfits. Foolish little-girl shoes. Proud when she's thin enough to buy her clothes in the preteen shop.

Jill is still talking. Now she is talking about my father, and how my mother hates them for spending so much time together alone.

"She's jealous of us," my sister says. "Jealous of how well we get along."

I don't answer. I climb into my car. Give a wave. She heads for hers. I am relieved that, inside my car, there is silence. As she walks away from me, I see, she is still talking. But now she is talking to the air.

Two dreams I have about this time. The surface of my parents' house is boglike; if you go into a room, you get sucked under and can't get out. I am in a house that is also a school, and someone is hitting me, and no one will come to help me.

NOT TOO MANY people come to my sister's wake. Mostly, our relatives. My parents' friends. My sister's life in the East ended when she moved West with her husband just after her marriage in 1968. Her ex-in-laws, who live nearby, don't come. My eldest son is not there. He has refused to come to the wake or to the funeral. Jill has killed herself during the week of his final exams. He has to get good grades to get into a good college, and he is angry at her for, as he put it, "fucking everything up."

I have picked out the casket. ("Make it plain," I say to the undertaker. "She was not a pretentious woman. Lived most of her life in overalls, at her potter's wheel, or out of doors.")

I have picked out the clothes that she'll be buried in. (An ordinary plaid blouse, and slacks, I decide. My parents let me have my way. They are barely functioning.)

I have picked out the flowers. (Daisies. She used to pick wild ones in the fields near her home when they came into season.)

I have chosen a few poems to read. I have said a few words about my sister's gift for working with her hands, for making pottery, and for turning humble things into works of art.

Before the undertaker closes the casket, he asks us if we want to say good-bye.

My mother takes my hand. She wants me to join her, and my father, at the side of my sister's casket. She wants us to say good-bye to my sister as a family. I pull my hand away.

"No," I say. "I want some time with Jill alone." My mother tries to grab my hand again, but gives up when she realizes that I won't give in, and that I am stronger than her and willing to make a scene to get my way.

At last, at last, alone, I kneel down and look at Jill. I try to look beyond the misshapen face in the casket to the Jill I remember. The Jill I shared a bed with for fourteen years because my mother, who practiced economies, determined that it was far cheaper to buy a double bed for the two of us than to buy each of us a bed of our own.

Of course, Jill is not there in the casket. The only place, now, that she will ever be is in my memory.

I reach into my purse and pull out an envelope. In it is a picture of her and the man who left her, when they were happy. They are clowning for the camera. It is Halloween, and she has carved a pumpkin. It stands beside them on the counter. As with everything my sister did with her hands, there is wonder and magic in her work. The pumpkin looks like a demon mask, the kind that is used to ward off danger and evil. In the envelope, too, is a card on which I have written the words "I love you," even if I'm not sure they're true.

I put the envelope, and one of the first pots my sister made, into the casket. I can't, I won't say good-bye.

Late Summer 1993

I HAVE HAD A good, work-filled summer. Finished a book about revenge I've been working on for years. Finished revising my second novel, about two teenage sisters. For its epigraph, I have chosen lines from Sylvia Plath's "Two Sisters of Persephone": "Two girls there are: within the house/One sits; the other, without. . . ."

I have cleared my desk. Filed away my notes and manuscripts. Sent everything off to my agent. For the first time since 1974, I have no writing to do, although I have some ideas about what I want to turn to next. This has been my plan: to give myself some breathing room.

My asthma, which has been disabling for close to a year and a half, is under control. My hard work—daily fast walking, meditation, therapy—is paying off. I feel better, in every way, than I have for years, though, of course, there are still problems. My terror of losing consciousness, of fainting while I am in my car, stuck in a traffic jam, so no one can get to me. (It has been a year and a half since I have lost consciousness, though I feel as if I am on the verge, often.) In therapy, we chip away at this, bit by bit. We look at the similarity between this and the way my sister has chosen to die. We develop strategies for me to try when the feeling comes over me. I can see myself making progress.

And on a day like any other day, I go down to do the laundry, but wind up, instead, in the basement, and I go straight to the back, to the boxes marked with Jill's name. My friend Kate has come over, and I have excused myself for a minute to run downstairs to throw a load of laundry in the dryer.

Sooner or later, I tell myself, I have to see what's in them. It might as well be now.

I call up to Kate and ask her to come downstairs. I tell her what I'm about to do and ask her if she'll stand by me while I do this.

The first box contains some clippings—an announcement of my sister's being "lady-in-waiting" to the high school prom queen, news items from her graduations, from her induction into an honorary society. The announcement of her engagement. And of her wedding. (In each picture, Kate observes, she smiles a forced smile.)

Underneath the clippings, carefully folded, and wrapped in tissue paper, are my sister's Girl Scout beret and her merit badges. We find it strange that my mother has saved them.

In the next box is my sister's collection of porcelain dolls. I take them out, and we look at them. "They're ugly," Kate says.

Under the dolls, though, are the clothes that my sister has made.

I can see her, in memory, bending over my mother's Singer sewing machine, her hair falling into her eyes, peering through her thick glasses, at the garment she is making. I hear the rat-a-tat-tat of the foot pedal, as she stitches along. All the clothes that my sister makes are dressy. Cocktail dresses with matching headbands. Evening gowns. The kind of dresses suitable for a life my sister will never know.

"Of all the things to keep," Kate says. "Of all the things to treasure," I think, "my mother has chosen these."

But in keeping these things, I know, my mother has tried, desperately, to hold on to the memory of the happy child. The happy child that my sister has never been.

When I find them, and hold them, I start crying. At last, at last, I am crying for my sister, I am crying for my mother, and I am crying for myself. I am glad that Kate is here for comfort. I know that I am ready to begin to give my sister up. I am ready to say good-bye.

Pam Houston

A Letter to My Sister Who Doesn't Exist

DEAR LONNIE,

I'm airborne again. United Flight 37 home to San Francisco, first-class and depending on what time zone we're in, I'd say it's sometime between ten and noon. The button-downed businessman at my elbow in seat 4B only wishes I'd stop crying, only wants to read his Plutarch in safety, thinks I may detonate at any time.

Below us there's nothing but leftover snow and cornfield stubble. Could be Missouri, could be upstate New York. I've told so many lies this weekend even I've lost track of where I am. I try to keep it simple when the stewardess asks me if there's anything I need.

I called Carter yesterday from a phone booth in Connecticut. When he asked where I was I said, "the bleakest place I've ever been." And this was true, but I made it sound like Nevada. I told him I'd run out of gas on one of those high desert stretches that have signs to warn you: next services eighty-seven miles.

I did run out of gas, in fact, but it was in Portsmouth, New Hampshire, at 1 A.M. and a freezing drizzle that's left me, it feels today, with the beginning of strep. Can you hear Momma screaming at me not to even breathe in her direction, Lonnie? I remembered that when Carter told me his favorite thing about our relationship: that we could snuggle as close as we wanted to the receiver . . . and not have to worry about exchanging germs. The Mobil station in Portsmouth was pretty close, down the block and over two small hills, the attendant friendly in that industrialized East Coast way.

But in the story I told Carter the guy's name was Reuben from Jean, Nevada (you know that place where the lights from the casino only compete with the lights from the jail?), and he drove a 1958 International Travelall and he had the backseat filled up with cases and cases of Tastykake fruit pies: peach-flavored, which I said was a mystery to me because I thought you could only buy Tastykake fruit pies within a hundred-mile radius of Philadelphia.

I know what you're thinking, Lonnie, and you're right, I still find all the smallest and most pitiful ways to dance on the ledge. Remember when we were kids and Momma was always telling me to look out for you. Did we know, even in those days, that it would become the running joke?

But Carter was sweet to me. He was doing the NordicTrack and reading me Stephen Dunn poems, and when he saw that wasn't gonna make me stop crying he picked up his guitar and we worked our way through that old Fleetwood Mac song "Landslide," and trying to remember the lyrics got me, for a little while, out of my head. He's an angel on earth that man and I try real hard to forgive him for not loving me the way we sometimes both wish he did.

Remember how Momma used to sing us that song where you'd be a farmer and I'd go to sea, and we'd laugh, the three of us together? I guess she wasn't far off, you raising those babies like sunflowers, and me, well, at sea would certainly be one way to describe it.

How I wound up at the phone booth in Connecticut, well, that was because of Jeff. I told him I'd be in Manhattan for the weekend so it wouldn't seem that far to go see him play music in

Massachusetts. I met him in January, in Chicago, after a concert and he gave me his number and a disc, every song about risk and absent fathers and unrequited love. I listened to it for two months before I called him, on the only day he was home in ninety.

He said, "There's no such thing as coincidence," and while I was talking to him, Carter left a message on my voice mail saying the same words exactly and that's a black hole even I'm smart enough not to look in.

One of the first things he asked me was whether both Mom and Dad were alcoholics, and I know you hate it when I talk about it, but in this case it's the thing that made me prick up my ears.

I said, "The next person who gets me really lucks the hell out," and he said, "What are you doing this Friday?" and the next thing you know I'd invented a wedding in Manhattan and cashed in forty thousand frequent-flier miles for a first-class ticket to Boston and back. My friend Peter, who took me to the airport, said the car would have the wrong plates on it, but when I got there Avis gave me a car someone had dropped off from Jersey. It scares me a little when the universe does that—when it facilitates my lies.

So I drove the ugliest rent-a-car in the universe to Westborough, Mass, changed my clothes in the parking lot of a Sunoco station, my bare feet on icy tiles, found the club, listened to his songs. He was shorter than I remembered and sweeter looking. He was nervous too, though it was hard to tell if it was because of me.

Later, at the Marriott something like lightning happened when our teeth came together, made the word canine come into my mind. We talk ourselves out of the things we need so easily, Lonnie, and I've done it well these months with Carter, but I remembered everything all over again when Jeff put his hands on me.

He said he was wild for me, Lonnie, said I was the freest thing he'd seen. He also said he wished I'd come with an instruction manual, I knew you'd like that one best of all. He said, "There was no wedding in Manhattan, was there?" and I said, "No," that fast, without blinking an eye. What's gonna excite me more, girl, than a man who might know me like you do. A man who's gonna wipe my lies away like another man wipes my tears, and then spit the truth back at me, hard, in my face.

He made time go away, Lonnie, with his voice and his hands, took me back to the side of the moon where it's something sweeter than logic that lets us decide. I don't know what I did to make him startle, but I was lit from within all weekend with the power of something I didn't understand and if the truth be told I even scared myself. My eyes felt like prairie fires when I looked down on him, and he was running before his feet hit the parking lot. He said, "Don't you let me back off from this," and I wanted to tell him *that* wasn't my job, but he was in his car and starting it, gone, I bet, for good.

I can hear your voice now, and I hate to tell you this but it's not unlike Momma's, asking me when I'll learn to stop chasing round the country, when I'll learn to stay home like a grown-up, tend my fire, do my work. But even Momma knew that the ink for my pen comes from the rain gutter on the balcony of the twenty-seventh floor of the building, and whatever work is in me, it's the same thing that chases these bad, bad boys.

I've always wanted to ask how you gave up the longing, Lonnie. Ask what it was in your way of living that let you put aside the ache. People call me brave daily, but you're the real survivor. You drew a circle around a life and planted yourself in the middle of it like a maple tree. The line I draw stretches into infinity. On the good days I can convince myself it's the road alone that's gonna make me wise.

My friend Peter says we live on the edge of wisdom for the

sake of love, but I always want to ask him, is that the incoming edge or the outgoing?

The older I get the simpler my fantasies. Two women sitting across a table from each other, two cups of coffee, strong as the love.

The stewardess just came by with a glass of milk and a double chocolate chip cookie. Again she asks if there's anything else I need. I need arms around me is what I want to say to her, and a few minutes of my life I don't make up while they're happening. What I really need, I want to tell this stewardess, is a little time to get a grip and a soft place to fall.

If you could write back to me, Lonnie, where would you tell me to begin the sorting? If I could make you real, girl, would you keep me from this edge?

I love you. Kiss the babies for me.

P.

Patricia Foster

*T*he Distance Between Us

ON THE DRIVE TO MOBILE, my sister and I sit together in the backseat of our family car, dressed in corduroy skirts and printed blouses with white socks and new Weejuns like the big girls in high school wear. My sister is talking about our elementary school, how Mr. Poake won't call on her when she raises her hand even though she *knows* that Montpelier is the capital of Vermont and that the major Axis powers are Germany, Japan, and Italy. Last month Mr. Poake wrote home to my parents, "Jean talks too much in school." My father wrote smugly back, "She talks too much at home too." I thought this the most exciting message in the world as if talk were a gift, a prize you could win. No one ever said I talked too much.

"But I'm only talking to my friends," my sister says, "and that shouldn't stop him from calling on me, because I *know* things."

I stare out the window as the car speeds along the causeway. From here I see grassy islands clumped together like sponges floating in the middle of Mobile Bay. Black men in overalls and flannel shirts fish from the bridges, their knees pressed into the concrete as they lean toward their poles, jars full of worms and crickets beside their feet. Gulls fly overhead, cawing, flapping their wings, making sudden, extravagant nosedives into the bay. While my sister and father talk, I'm pulled into the shimmer of light and air, smelling wind-salt and seaweed, catfish and mullet; before I can stop myself, I'm no longer in my body but floating outside the bonds of family life, vanishing as effortlessly as the lap of the waves against the shore. I *know* things too, I want to say, but they're secret, possibly shameful, things I can't reveal. When I look back at my family, I'm suddenly puzzled at our connection.

What does it mean, I wonder now, to be the daughter who separates from the family, not just physically but emotionally, coming to a place that questions the family myths? I'm not talking about the neglected child we read about in fairy tales, parented by a wicked stepmother and a weak or absent father, but a child whose parents are loving caretakers, whose stories of success simply make that child invisible. And of course, being an outsider daughter implies that there exists an insider daughter, one who is emotionally close, not just to the family but to the family's sense of itself, one who fits easily though not necessarily silently within that family skin.

It seems that as naturally as I assumed the former role, my sister was this second kind of daughter, the one who understood that the terrible struggle of childhood isn't necessarily to escape one's milieu but to find a deeper, more intimate route in.

I remember best the anticipation of her homecoming from Duke University the first Christmas of her college career, how we all waited anxiously in the kitchen, lingering over chili and salad, eating that extra piece of French bread, my father getting up each time he thought he saw headlights, then returning to the table with a sigh, picking up the napkin he'd dropped to the floor, while my mother, standing at the stove, said, "I hope she's not too late to eat this chili." College seemed about as far away as Paris or London to me, a place I might never reach, as if high school would drag on forever, subtracting substance from me until I became nothing more than negative space. Anxious, I dragged my fork across my plate, wishing she'd hurry. Before I could think another thought, I heard the click of the door, a rush of air, and she burst into the room, running toward us in her black leather miniskirt and boots, looking, really *looking* like a girl who'd been away to school. "Ooh, I missed you," she said, and hugged us all together, Mother still with the stirring spoon in her hand. *She's home,* I remember thinking, *and everything is different.* The crack in the Tiffany lamp no longer looks disfigured, but fragile, artistically flawed. The drip in the sink isn't annoying. The blare of the TV is only background noise. And yet, later when we put up the Christmas tree, each of us picking out our favorite ornaments to hang in a special place, what made me envious, so jealous I had to run to the bathroom to hide, was realizing just that: *she was our star.* I could see it in her face, the teasing mouth and darting eyes, the stories so ready to spill as she sat on the edge of a chair, a glass of white wine in one hand, her body leaning toward us as we huddled around her—my father bantering with her about her short skirt, her upcoming grades—until eventually she drifted away to see her friends. Without her, I didn't know what to talk about with my parents, as if I were a foreign visitor and had learned the form, but not the substance, of their lives. Alone, I retreated to an inside room, gray-walled and silent, troubled by an unspeakable envy.

I think now that my sister and I dutifully played out these shadow roles during our late teens and twenties, though neither of us could have acknowledged this in childhood or even in early adulthood when the intimacy of our childhood relationship was beginning to unravel. I wanted to say that we once saw ourselves as merged, fused together like emotional twins, and then the conflict/resolution of the piece would have been our separation, our independence. Yet if we were merged, it was in my original compliance with the family goal that we always succeed, that we climb to the very top of the heap. "Only A's," my father would tease when he saw our report cards every six weeks, his finger tracking the repetitious line. "Why not some A pluses?"

What I see is a child swinging higher and higher, her hands gripped tightly around the chains, her mind focused on going up, up, swinging deeper into the shadow of the trees while a tiny wedge of fear opens inside her. It's not, as you might expect, the fear that she will fall, but that she will never, ever go high enough.

I sat in the swing beside my sister, watching her succeed year after year, both socially and academically, and yet I was perplexed by the process of her success; although I followed in her footsteps, often repeating what she had done or what she advised me to do, I spun in circles. Still, my desire to succeed, to push myself to the front of the line, started quite early, this desire to be *like* my sister, who seemed so naturally to fulfill our mutual goals, to perform so effortlessly, so intimately, with the ease of a champion. In junior high I became outwardly competitive, going out for cheerleader three years in a row, campaigning for treasurer of the Student Council in ninth grade, going to all the clubs and dances, desperately trying to fit in, to enter the circle of popularity. While in high school, I went to Springhill College at night to study writing, even memorized the vocabulary records we'd ordered so I might score higher on the S.A.T. I think now I was trying to pry open the mystery of sequence, to decode cause and effect as if success had definite rules. I kept my eyes open for any clues my sister might drop, and yet my clinging to this heightened need brought all the phoniness of the mimic. Part of my faith in success depended on my naïveté and my unquestioning belief that others had my best interests at heart. And moreover, that we would agree on what those interests might be. Unfortunately, what I was learning was to ignore my interior nature, to hide the pull of my spirit while looking to others, particularly my sister, for the better direction. And in this peculiar way, I became an impersonator, nervously glancing over her shoulder to see just how it was to be done.

1965. It is my sister's senior year in high school, my junior year. I've lost the cheerleader bid, the Junior Miss bid; other than the honor roll, there's a large blank space on my high school transcript. I shut the piano lid in eighth grade, gave up dancing and clarinet in ninth. By eleventh grade I am clearly depressed and spend any free time in our shared bedroom staring at the ceiling, wondering how I will survive in a world I can't comprehend. And it's now during this bleak time that my sister sets herself up as my promoter, my social entrepreneur, my emotional trickster. Although this is never discussed between us, I know that if it had been, most likely I would have complied. I think though that it was probably an impulsive act on my sister's part, a moment of inspiration when she knew she could do the very thing that would make something happen for me.

I'm sitting in English class, staring out the window, waiting for Mrs. Jackson to finish reading "A Rose for Emily" when I see my sister walk by with several of her friends. They're out of class, strolling along, probably on "senior" business, but when she passes by my window, she sees me staring and stops with her friends, crooking her finger at me to come out. I shake my head no. I can't just leave class. Mrs. Jackson is droning on and on, poor Miss Emily getting her comeuppance from Homer Barron and then in the end, giving it back full force. I've already read this story several times, so I'm only half listening, my mind drifting like a lost ship at sea. My sister's friends beam happy smiles at me and I roll my eyes, thinking they're laughing because I'm stuck with the Peeper Creeper, the Elberta boy who tries to look up our skirts and sits right beside me. But when class is over, they're waiting at the door, arms open to encircle me. I don't know what's going on, why I'm being embraced as if something has happened, when absolutely nothing is happening to me. Then suddenly they're all talking at once, all laughing and joyous and to my surprise they're telling me I've been selected to the Key Club Sweetheart Court. Not the queen, of course, but even my sister isn't the queen. And it doesn't matter because my head is so light I believe I know how a snowflake must feel as it blows so whimsically, so gracefully to the ground. Then quite naturally, before I've had time to enjoy the full benefit of this pleasure, I know—though I can't remember if it's because she tells me or if I just figure it out—that I'm on the court, in this rare position of popularity, because my sister has gone privately to each boy in the club and persuaded him to vote for me. She stands beside me now, her hair a mahogany sheet that swings when she turns, her body larger but prettier than mine. At that moment I know in every fiber of my being the nothing of me without my sister.

And yet here is the important part, the part where I knit myself into the plot, swallow the narrative down whole: I don't say a word. I pretend I am still that snowflake, pretend that I am beautiful and graceful, that I can twirl in a spiraling eddy even if someone else is the wind. And in fact, there isn't a hint of surprise on my face when a month later my sister "nominates" and then "elects" me president of the Science Club, even though I hate science, with its dry reading, its stiff, precise rules, because this too, I know, is for my own good. When Mr. Bauer the chemistry teacher hands me the gavel, I accept it with unwavering gratitude.

This was the beginning, or so it seems to me, of an unspoken pact between my sister and me, an agreement that there could be very little, really, that was mine. And during those years it's my sister's generosity that I focus on, not ever my own cowardice, my own terror at living an imposter life. All I know is that I have to succeed, have to get into a good college, have to pledge a good sorority and find a way to drop the past like old garbage tossed into a sinkhole. All the pathological entanglements of the present must be subverted, denied, to secure this dream, for in my mind the future is everything, the present merely a way station, an absurd holding tank for the adult glory that's to come. Never do I see how the phoniness I'm accepting can hurt me, can warp my perceptions, because down deep, I believe there is simply nothing there.

I SIT BESIDE my mother inside a small auditorium at Auburn University. The chairs squeak as new people move into our row and fidget with their seats. On stage my sister sits at a table with four other students from her senior class, all part of the team competing in the High School Scholar's Bowl. On the other side of the room, five rival students sit quietly, sipping ice water, eyeing their opponents. I am nervous, not so much for my sister, who I know will do well, but because any competition, any battle of wits or memory, now frightens me. All my competitiveness has turned inward, become subversive; instead of increasing my attention, my awareness or curiosity, it only spooks me. I cross my legs and start swinging my right leg back and forth, back and forth, gently kicking the bottom rung of the chair in front. Mother quietly puts her hand on my knees, and for a moment, my jackhammer leg is still.

But once the Scholar's Bowl begins, my leg resumes its swing. Something in the agitation of that swing jars my memory and mentally I slip out of the auditorium, out of my present life to another day when this agitation is so great I can't seem to stop my leg's motion.

I'm in Mrs. Robinson's fourth-grade class. She's just read us William Carlos Williams's "The Red Wheelbarrow" and "This Is Just to Say" and told us that our assignment for tomorrow will be to write a poem. We make a list of words from our everyday lives, remembering a particular day when something important happened. But when I look at my list, I begin to sweat. I've written down: stilts, Christmas, sister, fall, driveway, air, happy—but I know I'll never be able to make a poem out of these words. I understand in some pocket of my brain that poems are openings, rips in consciousness, invasions of the self. My leg swings so fast, Johnny Mitchell raises his hand to tell Mrs. Robinson to make me stop.

At home that afternoon, I can't eat the peanut butter sandwich which waits for me on the table. Like glue it sticks inside my throat, the bread as dry as cardboard. Even the coconut cake, my favorite, remains untouched. I lick a finger of icing and walk into the living room to the piano. I feel hollowed out as if I've been erased. At the piano, I crash both hands on the keyboard, making a monster sound, the only poems I speak erupting through my fingers. I know I shouldn't talk about my family in school except in laudable terms and what I've thought about in class was the time my sister fell from her stilts on the concrete driveway and cried while I stood above her, high up in the air. I felt very tall, very strong, my head nudging the sun. From this height, my sister's head, bent down to her lap, her hands covering her eyes as tears seeped through the fingers, seemed quite far away. I wanted to smile.

When I begin to cry that night after sitting with my notebook spread out on my lap, a pencil in my hands rubbing round dots into the paper until the paper bursts from the pressure, my mother asks me what's wrong. I tell her I can't write a poem, though I can never reveal that it's a poem about triumphing over my sister, effacing her, even. Instead I say I have to write a poem about walking on stilts. My face must show my hysteria for Mother sits down with me, trying to console me by telling me that she'll help me. I hope she'll explain something about poems to me, but she's a scientist, and instead she takes my list and writes a rhyming poem.

My sister rings her buzzer to answer a question—"What is the term for a vocal performance without instrumental accompaniment?"—and I snap out of my reverie, back into the present. I am suddenly tired, my leg finally still. My sister answers the question correctly—a cappella—and sits back in her seat while the scoreboard records her points. I close my eyes, inhaling the dust of the auditorium, the mingled smells of perfume, after-shave, and garlic breath. We've eaten at the cafeteria, which featured Italian food today. As my mind quiets I put myself up on that stage but I know that what sticks inside my brain aren't the facts and details from a textbook but only a tangled black ball of confusion. And suddenly I'm furious, a writhing mass of envy churning inside my stomach, making me ill. Before I can stop it, the thought slips out as easily as a yawn. *I want her to fail.* I want to see the shock on her face, the slight trembling of her lips, the hard gasp of fear shadowing her eyes when the monitor calls out *Wrong!* This is the taboo I can never speak, must never reveal, this surely irrational desire that she will be down on her knees, degraded, ignored, while I walk past in the sunshine, my head held high. Of course to admit this would be shameful, heretical, a black stain on my familial soul. What I feel instead is a helpless guilt.

As if by magic, some angel's touch in the room, my mind lightens, slips off its critical track, and I'm running through soft, dusky light down the bluff to the creek. It's the summer I learn to water-ski, the summer I am ten, and we're visiting our next-door neighbors at their beach house at Soldier Creek. In the water, I start in a crouch, elbows pulled in, knees up near my chest, the motor of the boat seductively purring before me. The rope is still slack but already I hold the grip firmly, knuckles erect. All around me the neighboring kids are splashing and screaming. They've all had their turns, but this will be my first, perhaps my only, chance to skate on the water. I think of myself as a shirt flapping on the line, my body an effortless motion. Above me, the sky is bright blue with white streaks of jet clouds in loopy strings.

"If you fall, keep your legs away from the motor," my father calls from the dock.

"And don't fall into a snake nest," my sister yells, announcing our biggest scare. Last year a man skiing in Weeks Bay fell into a water moccasin nest and died a horrible death.

Before I can answer their fears, the boat roars forward, the rope straightens out, and I hear nothing, feel nothing but the subtle movements of my body rising, lifting out of the water as weightless as a piece of spaghetti. I'm up, stretching out, then swaying back, my body rhythmically moving with the motion of the boat, the flutter of the waves. It's like skating on glass, like Jesus walking on water. Free from family ties, I'm a natural. I can feel it. I float through the air, released into the sweet breath of rapture.

I SEE NOW that it would have been difficult for anyone who knew me to have helped me, for like many other children, I never spoke about what was going on inside my head. Even if someone had asked, I couldn't have explained it. I was getting lost in the way other children have gotten lost, through a veil of silence and confusion, weaving a cocoon of superficial normalcy, closing down, going numb, not acknowledging what was uncomfortable to know. And in a different but perhaps equally destructive way, my sister was getting lost, but her route was through attachment, her life pulled so closely into the family web there would be no way except through violence for her to escape. It's the perversity of both positions I'm interested in, the way distance and closeness become equal perils for young girls, both as daughters and as sisters.

Since my sister, growing up, was the closest to my parents, it seemed inevitable that she would take all her thoughts to them in cupped hands and open heart, wanting their reciprocal perfectibility as much as they wanted hers. In high school, she woke my father at five in the morning, begging him not to drink, not to split the family apart. She comforted my mother when my father ignored her, choosing instead rowdy friends who partied with him at football games, Mardi Gras, and the detested dog tracks. When my mother's loneliness seemed too much to bear she'd come into our bedroom and sit on my sister's bed to talk about her life. During those moments—when my mother was confessing her sadness—I always felt that I was looking on, observing rather than participating, feeling. Of course, I could mimic the emotions on my sister's face, simulating sympathy, but I knew—and my sister knew—that she was the reservoir of outrage and comfort within the family while I was simply waiting to see what part I'd play. Ironically, my part became the one-who-waits, the observer, until finally I realized I could escape, could become a different kind of "lost" by aligning myself with art—and the impoverished artist's life—a route no one approved.

When my sister wasn't busy with all her extracurricular activities at school and at church, she presented to us a running commentary on her life: her boyfriends, her girlfriends, her grades, her college plans, her editorials. I remember particularly one year when she was in a bitter struggle for dominance with another girl in her class, Sallie Greenwood, a girl who was smart and wily, smug in her perceptions. Sallie flirted with everyone's boyfriend, but demanded loyalty from her girlfriends. "Well, aren't *you* a good girl," she'd say when you didn't laugh with her at the Spanish teacher's, Mrs. Costello's, hairy underarms. "I ignored Sallie in the hall this morning," my sister would tell us at the supper table, "and I got a higher grade on the American history test, but then she interrupted me three times in Student Council meeting." My sister had never forgiven Sallie for winning the valentine box contest in sixth grade when Sallie's box was sentimentally wrapped in mounds of pink tissue while my sister had taken an artistic risk, decorating her box with black patent-leather paper accented with a dusting of red hearts. She'd cried that afternoon all the way to music lessons in a neighboring town.

While my sister confided in us, I kept all my stories under my coat. How could I tell the furtive pleasure I felt necking with my boyfriend as we drove down lonely highways in his dad's chicken truck, bouncing over potholes that left us with gashes in our mouths? The raunchiness I enjoyed with him seemed so inappropriate, so unsettling for its very promise of eroticism. Telling it would diminish it, would make me just another small-town girl gravitating toward heat. How could I tell about the night my best friend danced naked on the bed with paper tassels on her boobs, gyrating deliriously before us in celebration of her first French kiss? How could I explain that I was terrified of losing control of my body and thus would stand in front of the mirror, pushing my stomach in, in, in? The stories I valued seemed slightly abnormal, too private to reveal, though my sister blabbed everything, even once in college that she might need a pregnancy test. Instead of telling stories, I listened and waited, practicing my hiding skills.

Yet what is important to describe is what happens when the younger daughter takes leave, not off to Oz, but to a life of artistic quest while the older daughter stays put, not necessarily physically but psychically within the family realm. Does the plot reverse itself? Does the charmed daughter become doomed while the lost sister flies suddenly free, as would happen in fairy tales? Or is it merely a continuation, a furthering of what went on before, both sisters living out a drama whose patterns are embedded in personality and difference, in family roles they no longer can discard?

Fortunately, in our lives it was neither one nor the other, nothing so fixed, so immutable. And yet there is necessarily a split, a dividing that cannot be ignored. As it happened in my family, my sister married, became a doctor, made money, had children, and gained status in the world—the route of the family star—while I left by the back door, in shorts, sandals, and a tank top, driving to Los Angeles to try out a more bohemian life. I cut loose—I realize now—partly because my sister had already assumed the caretaker role, the one most responsible for the well-being of the family.

Even in exile I kept my thoughts to myself. There is something both remote and overly attached in my nature, some imbalance in my system. I've been either merged too closely with my sister and family or fighting tenaciously for separation. I've always felt this, as if I can never claim middle ground, but will always skid to the side, surprised, uncertain. When I left Alabama, I was clear in my desires: I wanted only to be separate. To study art. At UCLA I stayed late in the studio every night mixing dyes, painting abstract designs on cloth, waiting for the woman who lived with her dog in a hippie van to come into the weaving studio and set up her loom. Once Beth arrived, we'd talk about the work we were doing, about the teaching she did to keep herself and the dog alive. "I have to bathe at the gym at school," she told me. "But the weekends are really the pits. It's a real camping life then." I looked at Beth's dirty hair, her wrinkled clothes, and smiled as if she'd given me a gift, thinking how far I'd come from Alabama where women took such pride in their grooming. Here in L.A. I felt safe within such a diverse group of people. I could wander around freely, anonymous, and, at least superficially, autonomous. I had a sense of living on the edge, though in reality all I did was work in the studio and fill my free time with gallery openings and theater performances. Sometimes it was overwhelming, like the morning I stared at the dark saturated canvases of Rothko in his retrospective at the L.A. County Museum. Beside them I seemed about the size of a paper clip, weightless, irrelevant. After two hours of absorbing this mystic sadness, I felt such a heavy silence that I left in the middle of the exhibit, only to be stunned by the sun's stark brightness.

But art and my immersion in its chilly embrace wasn't the real story of Los Angeles. That story could as easily be told by my first attempts to find housing in this scattered, car-crazy city.

Because I was new and the rents were so much higher than in Alabama, I decided to answer ads from other women seeking roommates. I went forth optimistically, sure that I'd find someone compatible, preferably an exile like myself. The women I met with were cordial but distant (often women much older, women who made me feel my youth like a bloom not yet plucked, a fault potentially dangerous to them); there was a clear sense that—given no other takers—I would be allowed to live in the spare room and have kitchen privileges under a watchful, more adult eye. I would be tolerated. I might walk on tiptoe to the kitchen for a piece of cheese. I might soak in the bathtub on Sunday afternoons when my roommate went to the movies.

Back in my temporary room, what I told myself was this: had my sister been with me, she would have charmed these women, laughed with them, teased them, lifting the two of us into their welcoming lives. She would have insisted they go to the Boulangerie to eat chocolate-filled croissants, *forget about weight; we can walk it off later.* She had a knack for making other people feel comfortable as if she could be right there, under your skin.

Sitting alone on my single bed, I was puzzled, frustrated. The beginning of fall semester was imminent. I had to find a place. Get settled and unpack. And yet it's what I did next that changed me, set my life on a new course: I gave up my self-reproach. I stepped outside of my sister's shadow, dropped her mantle like discarded underwear on the floor, and decided on new terms. I would rent an apartment myself and advertise for a roommate. I understood for the first time that I could turn the tables, direct the story, could be the evaluator rather than the one evaluated.

IT IS DIFFICULT for me to know what happened to my sister during the fifteen years I was away. What happened in me was a broadening of perspective which allowed me to see more clearly not only my own troubles but also the difficulties in the role of the caretaker daughter, cross-yearnings I couldn't have seen as a child. And in some sense there has been a reversal, for it is my sister's suffering I see now as more critical than my own. My sister and her husband moved back to our small town before I left for Los Angeles, and it was no surprise when, a few years later, she went into practice with my father, following a predetermined pattern. Now she was as enmeshed with my parents in adulthood as she had been in childhood, and I understood that she needed my parents in a way that I never would. Perhaps having been the star, the one whose route we watched, she could never lose the stimulus of that original audience, that primal circle in which family approval is so hideously addictive. After all, family response was immediate; she didn't have to wait for the world to clap its hands.

She told me recently that she had never really wanted to be a doctor, had not wanted it with the deep conviction of her heart (that pulse which wakes you at three in the morning with prickles of desire and defiance), but had become a doctor partly to please my parents, who for separate reasons had always expected this of her. As a teenager she went on hospital rounds with my father, was active in the Future Doctor's Club, and when it seemed clear that my brother—who became sick at the sight of blood—wouldn't be a doctor, my father designated her as the one "to follow in my footsteps."

For my mother, my sister becoming a physician was more complex, a kind of retaliation for her own deflected plans. When my mother entered college at sixteen on scholarship from a small mining town, she had wanted to be a doctor, but upon admission, she was told it would be almost impossible since she was female. Because she was so young, from such an impoverished background, she thought she had no rights and she accepted her adviser's terms. Instead she became a nutritionist, an acceptable profession for a woman.

In her early twenties, my sister resisted studying medicine, getting a master's degree in counseling instead. But once she was away from the family, inside the professional world of social agencies, she decided rather quickly that medical school was the inevitable choice.

Last Christmas I went on rounds with my sister, following behind her like a witness, fancying myself the impartial observer who could see inside her working life. It was a warm glorious day, the sun shining through the windows, highlighting bedpans and oxygen tubes, exposing the flat, frazzled hair of the patients, the grayness of their hospital gowns. My sister stopped outside the first door and told me about the patient: Addie Rogers, a diabetic. "The last time I saw Addie, she said, *Dr. B., you're getting so stout!* Well, I had to tell her not to be so mean, and she assured me I was still the best-looking doctor she'd had so far." My sister laughed and put the stethoscope around her neck.

After looking at Addie's chart, my sister talked with her about her medications, her diet, about when she could expect to get out of the hospital and what consequences she might have from her recent hypoglycemia. At one point, my sister sat down on the side of the bed and answered Addie's questions, her fingers doing Hammond exercises on her leg while she talked. This one tiny motion sent a storm of static through my heart. I knew—as if I'd forgotten and suddenly remembered—that I loved my sister, as this hint of our former life of music lessons and practice intruded so persistently, so unconsciously, into her present world. For that one moment I understood her intimately, trapped by the *tap-tap-tap* of her fingers and the comfortable sound of her voice, like sand dripping steadily on stone.

Although my sister is a conscientious doctor with one of the largest practices in the county, when I see her in her home, I know the depth of her frustration; her natural recourse to the self is through color and composition, line and texture. Perhaps it's a response to the death and near death she sees daily in the hospital that her home is so vibrant with saturated color. Walking into her living room is like walking into a lush garden, a Matisse print: expressionist paintings of women—mauve faces, foreheads streaked with lime green and mustard—line her walls; wildly branching limbs shoot out of giant vases on her buffet. Her taste, like her temper, is vivid. I never see her so luminous, so animated, as when she's choosing colors, prints, designs, paintings. "When I'm redesigning the kitchen or choosing prints for the living room, I don't care where I am," she tells me. "My house is the place I enjoy." And yet I know her ideas are often thwarted, for she's not a practicing artist and her passion is dependent on having enough money to buy the perfect fit.

"I'VE NEVER REALLY wanted to live here," she tells me one day as we're driving around town, picking up her children. I look out the window at the flat farmland which spreads out around us. It is both beautiful and pedestrian with its wide green fields, its oak trees and scrub pines, its shacks and brick houses: a typical small southern town. When my sister first moved back, she had to submit to an old-fashioned system, a cultural tradition which placed women one step behind men. My father worried about her, said he was afraid the male doctors would resent her, would subtly punish her for daring to be among them. "She'll have to be tough," he said. "And she'll have to be careful." In essence, my parents closed ranks around her, supporting her, protecting her, yet at the same time restricting her response. They didn't want anyone to hurt her or to stand in the way of her success.

"Did you go see Mrs. Smith?" my father will ask casually at lunch when she drops in to pick up a sandwich.

"Not yet," my sister says. "I'll do it later when I make rounds."

"Well, don't forget. You've got to see Mrs. Smith."

"I know," she says, grabbing the sandwich from my mother and stuffing it into her purse. "I just said I would."

"You should see her first," my father continues, not willing to let the matter go.

Because my sister and parents see each other daily, there are few secrets among them. They know the habits and schedules of each other's lives, the food left uneaten in the refrigerator, the trips to Mobile for podiatry appointments and antique sales, the Little League games and Saturday afternoon shopping trips. Enmeshed in such dailiness, they feel free to give advice, to question each other's decisions.

"You're not going to wear that to the hospital?" my mother will say when my sister appears at their door on Saturday in a sweat shirt and pants, a scarf around her neck, decorative earrings on her ears. It bothers my parents if my sister isn't dressed professionally to go to the hospital (skirt or "good" pants, sweater and blazer), and it bothers my sister that my parents assume this responsibility. Of course, it's part of their old system of protection, wanting my sister to be safe within the public realm, free from even the most casual censure.

"I'm wearing it," my sister responds, a frown on her face. "Look, I have to hurry. I don't have time to worry about this." Then she hands my mother a shopping bag full of clothes. "I need you to return this to Ruff Hewn for me. It's got to be back today and I have to take the boys to baseball practice after work."

If the pattern of my young adult life has been one of control and restriction, a terror that I might fall into life, the pattern of my sister's life has been one of undefined boundaries, as if there is no sense of where she ends and my parents begin. They are all squished in there together, everybody looking around for seepage, for holes to plug up, for ways to make life safer.

• • •

NOW IN MY FORTIES, I study my sister at odd moments, ordinary moments that surprise me with their simplicity. I've lost some element of self-consciousness which kept me separate, microscopically self-analytical in my twenties. I can occasionally forget that I'm the younger sister, the shadow, the emotional monitor. This year at the beach I watch as my sister sits on the double bed, putting on her bathing suit. It's an awkward position and I wonder why she doesn't stand up, why she seems modest, even shy, about her body when we've seen each other nude many times in our lives. Today we're laughing about how seldom we shave our legs, and even more rarely the pubic hair that curls out of our bathing suits. I wonder why she would worry about the hairs on her legs since we're here at the beach tending children, the two of us relaxed under her maternal mantle. As my sister stretches her legs through the suit, she grimaces, knowing she'll have to wiggle into it. She's gained weight since her hysterectomy and usually wears baggy clothes, lots of overblouses and sweaters. Now she stands up, pulls herself into it, removing the T-shirt she's left hugging her upper body. I turn away to fix my hair in the mirror, some residual modesty provoking this deflection. In the mirror I notice how different we are, my blond paleness, my thinness accentuated by her darkness. I wonder briefly is she is ever envious of my thinness, my high metabolism which keeps me from gaining weight. I want to ask her, "Are you ever jealous?" thinking that I've always been jealous of her thick hair, her smooth skin. Yet the old shyness draws me back. I think instead about what we've been confiding, about family responsibility and the inevitable aging of our parents.

My father has had two open-heart surgeries, my mother endometrial cancer. At the moment they're both robust, working full-time, their comments ridiculously free of complaints. It's not unusual during the Christmas holidays for my mother to get up at five to go to the Winn Dixie grocery store; my father still plays golf, sees as many as fifty patients a day. "If we could just harness their energy," I say now to my sister as she puts the T-shirt back on over her bathing suit. "We could forget about sleep."

She nods. "But Daddy *is* getting tired. He goes to bed early now. Sometimes by seven-thirty." And she tells me that eventually she plans to build an extra wing onto her house so that when they can't take care of themselves anymore they'll have a place to live. "I'll never put them in a nursing home," she says, staring out the window where a rough surf pounds the shore. "I don't care if they need round-the-clock care. I see nursing homes every day. I wouldn't do that to someone I love."

I think about the many acres of land my sister owns, a pastoral farm graced with huge oaks and thickets of pine where horses and cows roam the pastures, where cats sleep in contentment on the patio in the sun. My father likes to watch the cows. I can imagine him sitting with the cats in the sun, watching the herd as it moves around the fields, munching grass. My mother would be in the kitchen, fixing iced tea, setting the table. And then more quietly I consider how inevitable it is that my sister will be my parents' final caretaker. *You want to live with me because you know I can put in a catheter,* she teases my father. *You live with Pat and she'll only write about your decline. But I can make you comfortable.* I feel relieved; it's consoling to know my sister has already assumed this responsibility.

Once we're suited up, ready for the beach, we walk together into her daughter's room to find three girls sitting one behind the other, stairstep fashion, combing each other's hair. "Oh, synchronized combing," I tease, and the three girls giggle. They are fourteen years old, two still with braces on their teeth, all with bikinis, suntans, and hour-long sessions with the bathroom mirror. My sister sits down on the bed, smiling at them, her fingers again doing their Hammond routine on her thigh. I realize that it was at fourteen that she became pretty, shedding the baby fat of middle school, growing taller, sleeker, no longer chunky but curved. I remember how good she looked in the high school beauty pageant, in the Speckled Trout Rodeo Contest, in her senior portrait. Almost instantly, I think about the summer in high school when we set up our bedroom as a beauty parlor, fixing up ourselves and our girlfriends to look like the models in *Seventeen,* the dancers on *American Bandstand.*

Until I walk into my niece Kate's room, I've forgotten how strongly my sister must have identified with this period, the time in many young girls' lives when they have power through the rites of seduction, when the world seems ripe with possibility. It was the time when she was closest to my parents, her life an open story of romantic emotion and impassioned opinions. For myself this period was the beginning of confusion, a time when I felt the horror of ambivalence as if it were a safety pin digging into my side.

I look at my sister watching these girls. Her face softens; she relaxes. I know that soon she'll start to fix them up, to suggest a lighter lipstick, a loosened ponytail. I can feel it in the chemistry of her smile. And almost before the thought surges through my brain, she says to her daughter, "Kate, bring me that comb. You need to pull your hair this way, not parted in the middle." At first her daughter frowns—what can mothers know?—but then she notices her mother's eager smile in the mirror and goes to sit beside her on the bed. When I leave, my sister is combing her daughter's hair.

As my husband and I drive home the next morning, we talk about family, about Daddy's recovery from open-heart surgery, about my mother's perseverance, her indefatigable energy, and as always, the continual dance between my sister and me. "Were you ever really close to your sister?" my husband asks, and I pause, surprised that despite all our differences, he doesn't think of us as close. Yet I know that for sisters, being close has so many meanings, so many repercussions. Being close for me meant emerging from the sticky web of merger, and ultimately, seeing not only my sister but also myself as a potential heroine. "I don't remember much about our relationship in early childhood," I tell my husband, and even telling it, I see myself running exuberantly down the grassy hill in our backyard or else being with my mother, my arm wrapped around her thigh. But when I turned seven, we moved to Magnolia Springs, and it's here that I become most connected to my sister.

I think about this as we shift from a county highway onto the interstate, worrying suddenly that my sister will be upset that I've written about us in a way that emphasizes our separateness, our difference. And it occurs to me that one can never grow up with one's sister. In some secret place we remain seven and eight. And yet we are always family, tied by bonds so deep, so invisible the soft blue noises of love rush through our bodies, surprising us, waking us as if from sleep.

As we speed into the darkness, cars rushing by, radios blaring, I reach back into memory and see two girls running and laughing as they rush down the oyster-shelled road in Magnolia Springs, arms swinging, hair flying as they compete for the first Popsicle at Moore's Store, and in remembering, I laugh out loud. "I won," I still want to say. "I won."

Meena Alexander

Letters from Flora

SCENES FROM A LIFE, Flora's and mine. They came like snapshots. Or postcards from across a border. The kind you hunt up, ever so slowly, from a large pile in a basket, in a little shop with window shades at the edge of the sea. And the shop by the sea is always in another country.

One rises up and its smoky surface, clarifies. Shot silk, tugged tight, in sunlight, stretched over the stubble field where millet was harvested, on a hillside not far from the waves, golden grains dashed to the side from the basket, sticking to the undulating surface.

So this is how it came: the white walls of the dining room, as a frame. Soft patter of rain in the courtyard, fragrance rising from the jasmine bush, earth soaked with rain under the roots of the mango trees. Peacocks crying out by the gooseberry tree, turquoise feathers shot with green, shivering. Servants in the pantry clattering pots, one with a sickle slicing the fibers of a new coconut. I hear the blade against the hard nut. A sliver, a scrape, a dark woodpecker, its high-pitched knock and trill.

She walked in as we were eating. I could tell by the high stride in her, the turquoise-and-green-colored skirts flouncing, that she was in one of her moods. Tiny feet shod in *chappals* of tooled leather. Hands with vermilion nails, delicate in spite of the plumpness that had stolen over her, the high angles of her cheeks lost in that nub of flesh.

"So come sit down, eat," Mama said.

Papa merely looked at Flora's face.

I watched her go to the brass urn, pour out water, wash her hands. Where the water trickled, the sand was dappled with the three pointed leaves of the passion fruit.

She came back, dragged a chair. It scraped on the tiled floor. She shoved it by the window. Sat down, crossed her legs, tugged her silk up ever so slightly so her silver anklet showed.

"So . . ." she trilled.

I noticed a fine hair that hung over the delicate meshwork of silver. A single hair on her ankle.

"Come eat, Flora. This fish is delicious."

Mama coaxing her, as if she were a child, lifting up a spoonful of the swordfish delicately spiked with coconut, seasoned with turmeric. I could sniff tamarind rubbed into fish flesh. Mama moved her plate, a fraction of an inch. Grandma's fine dinnerware and why the maid had laid it I couldn't tell. The golden plate caught the light. Flashed. Precisely at the flash of untellable light, Flora's voice rose as a *nautika* singer's might.

You have to imagine a bawdy voice out of a painted body, whirling in the hot season, drumbeats twirling arms and legs, breasts jiggling. Then somehow I thought of a mourner at a funeral—for there was a hurt in her she was daring us to take away. It was rage at the life stolen that racked her.

"Who do you think you are? Who? Who?"

"What do you want, Flora? Please stop this shouting." I thought my voice sounded entirely reasonable. I felt I ought to take some of the heat. Papa and Mama were growing older, as all the world could see. There were streaks of silver in Papa's hair now, though astonishingly his brow was still unlined. Mama's face was massed with laugh lines, a gentle double chin held her mouth upright. Flora was jiggling her right ankle a little, almost as if she were preparing for a dance.

"So who do you think you are?"

Her words were precise, as if she might hold a mirror up to us, outline our faults, reveal us naked on time's rack.

"If only you could see yourselves. How you live! So content. Cats smiling into cream. You know what I'll do. I'll kill myself. That'll serve you right!"

I saw Mama's hand trembling at the edge of the plate. Her wedding ring, heavy, covered in the fish sauce. How did Mama come to spill the rich sauce all over her hand? Oh Mama, I thought, why spill the sauce. And Papa, his face averted, his jaws clenched, the fine line of his head utterly erect, there against the back of the rosewood chair I see him.

"Eat, Mama, eat," I begged. But she couldn't. She was staring at her child. Flora's dainty head bobbing next to the window frame. Outside, wind blew the mulberry leaves into a silver blur. Her voice filled the room:

"I shall take my own blood and write on the walls of this house! Then what will you do? What? What?"

Thrusting the chair aside, she stormed out. The mulberry bush was utterly still. Smoke blew in from the kitchen. Perhaps one of the palm logs in the country stove was damp. Anya the maid, all dressed in white, brought in a casserole filled with dal. I could see the tiny scrapes of coconut, moist on the golden flakes.

"*Ammachi!*" She bent over Mama's plate, serving her spoonfuls. Nothing, Mama said, nothing. I saw her hands clench, the wedding ring heavy, cutting into her flesh. I saw her eyes pool behind the glasses she always wore. Papa did not look at Mama. He finished his dinner and stood up. He ate what he normally did, a few spoonfuls of rice, some fish, a little yoghurt. I waited till I heard the slow stream of water on the sand behind the verandah, water splashing the passion fruit vine. Then I stood up. I stood up and left Mama all alone as if Flora were her fault.

"Leela!" she whispered as she watched me go, but I pretended not to hear.

THAT HOT DAY IN MAY, before the monsoons fell, I walked behind Papa. His hands did not tremble. He held onto his cane, as if it were an ebony spear, part of his form. I used to imagine Papa as one of those ancient warriors in the service of Marthanda Varma. Sitting astride his elephant as the thunderclouds rolled, his spear in his hand. No more elephants now. The newborn elephant my paternal grandfather kept on his lands by the sugarcane fields had drunk itself to death. Death by arak visited on a tiny elephant. I used to watch its glowing form at night, darker than the stalks of sugarcane, more luminous than the barks of the surrounding rubber trees, Leela the baby elephant, named after me, fanning herself. Sometimes she sprayed herself with dust, and then the silver haze covered all her body.

I held the curtains open for Papa as he walked, ever so slowly into his room. Neither he nor I had anything to say to Flora. Papa sat at his desk and opened the Bible. Twilight swarmed off the bark of the *jamun* tree and entered his eyes. I heard the cries of the night creatures, owl and *myena* before the moon rose. And tiny rats scurrying into their holes in the tapioca patch. I could have stayed with Papa in his room, stood by the side of his chair all through my days. A daughter rooted in place.

At night a woman came to Papa, her eyes pools of mercury. In place of a sari, her head was covered with dead fish spewed from the southern coast. He knew it was his mother by the way she whispered his name: "Varki, Varki!" ever so tenderly. In her hands she held the plantain sheathe in which they had first bathed the infant Flora.

Papa sucked in his breath. He smelled the sharp fragrance of coconut oil, the tiny dark limbs wriggling, a moist green fruit cover, a foot and a half long, cupping the infant. He shut his eyes as his mother approached. He wanted her to put out her hand, stroke him on the head as she used to do when he was a tiny boy. "Varki!" she would call him, and when he came up running, she'd rub his head, ever so gently with her hand, and then from the silver dish on her lap, pop a bit of jaggery into his mouth. How sweet it was, coursing down his throat.

Ever so slowly, Papa approached his dead mother. But when he put out his hand to her, all he touched was the wet plantain sheathe she held out to him. He put his right hand into it and felt the damp glow of plant flesh.

"Flora," he whispered, "where are you?"

In the pitch-darkness his fingers tingled. He did not know what he could have done to have made the tiny child vanish like that. Instead he saw a moody woman of twenty-two, with a pointed chin and broad forehead. She was tossing her black curls, babbling. He tried to hold her back, but breaking loose of his frail hands, she picked up a small stool, flung it up, smashing the pots that hung above the woodfire in the kitchen. The spicy marinade darkened all the tiled floor. Papa woke up shaking.

PAPA WANTED to call her Flora. Flora rather than Pushpa, the Latinate name tripping on the tongue, quite odd in our circles. Exotic sounding. A lovely girl child with soft, curly hair, large dark eyes she used to make pictures in the mud, with her right index finger, mix henna and draw whorls on the patio: snail-like forms, forms with flaming hair, women with big bellies in saris. And all the while her ayah cooed over her: look at the child, the little child, God's blessing, Santa Marya bless her. And ayah made the sign of the cross, over and over, touched the conch shell at her neck.

"She'll be another Amrita Shergill," murmured Papa proudly, "my own daughter!"*

The next night I was sitting at the edge of Papa's bed. The rain was beating down softly, ever so softly. On the other side of the courtyard I heard Flora turn up the music loud, ever so loud on her tape machine. Edith Piaf: *"Rien, rien . . ."* Where did she get all that French music from?

Through Piaf's high wail I heard the fishman on his bicycle over the hill. He was whistling through his teeth, crying come buy, come buy my fish. Fresh fish from the sea, raw catch, kept on ice. Salt on the glistening fins, salt on the gills, eyes fixed to eternity. Through the window that gave out onto the courtyard I watched Mama race toward the road in search of fish. The hem of her sari caught in the mulberry bush and tore a little. She unbolted the courtyard door and raced past the mango trees. The fishman's whistle freed her to run, out, out of her life. Papa stayed in his room, the windows darkened, the Bible at his fist, open, ready. I saw the lines later. He was murmuring them, over and over again.

"Fear hath torment. Perfect love hath no fear. Perfect love casteth out fear."

Much later that very night I heard Papa breathing. Hoarse sounds as if bat wings had brushed *badam* bark. Then his breathing turned sharp, spurting. The nurse was on the other side of the courtyard and I had to cry out for her: *"Thankamma, va, ivideva. Va Thankamma!"* Flora heard first and she came racing, her silk blouse all askew.

"Papa," she whispered, "Papa, oh my Papa!" And she knelt by his bed, set her hands on his shirt, and tried to calm the jerkiness of his chest. It was as if a pile of dark fish held in the

* *Amrita Shergill is a celebrated Indian woman painter.*

basket of his ribs were slapping themselves up and down, fins dashing. Flora was so tender, she surprised me. Her hands moved over his chest, slowly, as if he were a small child. "It doesn't hurt, does it? Does it?" she crooned. I saw the wetness on his shirt from her eyes.

I drew Flora away so the nurse could lean over, adjust the metal rings on Papa's oxygen tank. I imagined Papa's chest, the live bronchioles inside turning rosy as oxygen rushed in. But it didn't help all that much and the next morning, before the sun rose, before the bats wheeled up over the *badam* tree, we had to take him to the hospital. Flora sat in the front with the driver and at the hospital steps helped Papa out; she didn't seem to care that her turquoise silk skirt dragged in the dirt.

Back home, that afternoon, I heard her yelling all alone in her room.

"Fools, bourgoisie. What do I want with you? You'll all die before me."

"Papa's so ill. She'll have to control herself!" I barely raised my voice. I was on the front verandah stitching a silk handkerchief, something grandmother Eliamma had left me. Its edges were worn and I thought I would hem them afresh, tuck in the worn threads, do a daisy stitch, the needle daring desire's dance.

"It's hard for her." Mama looked across the verandah at me. "She loves your father very much."

"Fools," I heard Flora yell. Her door was locked but her voice came through the rafters, the red tiles of our house: "Dead, you'll all be dead soon. And no man for me. Why can't you marry me off to a decent man?"

I heard her throwing something hard against the floor. Or was it the bookcase? I couldn't tell. Something rose in me. Bile. The stuff you want to vomit out but it's really your own juices. I held onto the window bars and would have made it to Flora's room where that voice was splattering syllables on the walls, the bed sheets, the white music box with the tiny ballerina she had set by the window.

"Bourgeois fools!"

I tried to shut my ears.

"Let her be. Please, Leela," Mama begged, holding tight to my arm. I felt her tired fingers on my wrist, right above the gold bangle she and Papa had given me when I graduated from school. Her fingers pinched a vein. Something started throbbing.

"Please, dear, she's sick, you know."

"Not that sick!"

I sat down, hard. I wanted to hold onto Mama's sari and cry. Instead I said in as normal sounding a tone as I could muster: "Has she been taking her pills regularly?"

Mama nodded.

"Maybe they're not working as they should?"

Mama just held onto my wrist: "We must pray for her, Leela," she murmured, "pray for her."

In the dark I saw the pigeons, high in the dovecote, flash their wings. I tried to imagine the prayers I had said as a child, floating upward to God. A great god with a white beard sitting high up on Parvatam Mountain. I looked out of the window and saw tiny points of moonlight flashing off a bird's wing.

That summer my parents tried faith healers. They trooped in with music and timbrel. One I remember. A woman large and dark. Plump as an elephant. She had an assistant who carried her harmonica. They wore blue saris. Blue, Mary's color. Blue for the petunias that grew by the wellside. Cheap blue cotton tucked into the large waists. Blue on the Bible covers. They started dancing, the words streamed out and music.

"OOO Lamb of God,
Jesu, Jesu Christu,
Let me be as Marya Magdalena to you!"

The fat woman twirled, the sweat gleamed on her body. On the station road, the dogs that lay curled in the dirt, by the huts of the very poor, started barking. Odd high-pitched howls as if the sky—turquoise in that premonsoon season—were about to fall on their head.

"O Jesu, have mercy, have pity, drive the evil forces from your daughter Flora's flesh!"

The fat woman moaned as she stamped her feet and the cymbals in the assistant's hands clashed. Flora was hidden in her room, behind three sets of doors. The spectacle, the noise and the neighbours flocking to the gates, Papa, recovered, sitting on his cane chair at the verandah's edge, Mama praying with the twirling women were all too much. Soon after, I left. I told myself I had good reason for going. What happened with Flora cast shadows in our house. It was difficult to see things straight with those dark outlines blurring space.

MUCH LATER, I saw the letters her hand formed on the walls. Flaming letters. Flora like Shadrach untouched by fire, while all the rest of us burned to cinders, flesh, bones, fine cotton, Papa's ivory-tipped cane, gold fillings in Mama's mouth all turned to ash.

Memory cannot save us. Drop us down into a well of life lived, from which we are raised, splints and lassoes knotted to our trembling bones, the past revivified through us, a gleaming substance that pours off our skin. Who can win another life for herself?

Perhaps the best one might do is enter a small shop with the waves pounding on the rocks, sift through a pile of bleached postcards, and as the sunlight glances off the metallic waves, glimpse scenes from a life: a whitewashed house with gracious verandah, teak doors quartered in four in the manner of the Dutch, stone steps leading up to the pillared portico and on the steps, a double shadow. Then one drew away, the smaller one, while the larger one stood firm. The two shadow heads still jointed at the base.

IT MUST HAVE been a whole year after I came to New York that Flora started writing to me. She used scraps of paper with a fine rice pattern. Bamboo paper, paper made of flax, paper from Pondicherry and Tibet, the rarest membranes of papyrus, nothing was too fine for her to search out. And on these fragrant scraps cut into odd rectangles and oblongs with her ivory knife, Flora wrote. For quite a while, seeing her long, loping hand on the envelope I was too nervous to slit open the letters. Nor could I show them to Janak. I imagined him screwing up his eyes, whistling through the gap in his teeth, uttering some inanity like "My, oh my, my . . ." As down below the young things strolled, gold hoops in their ears, boom boxes at the ready.

It was late fall when the letters started coming. A cold wind blew. I tried to imagine what winter would be like, the sharp glitter of cold, the alien snow. I bought a wool scarf and took care to knot it around my throat. It was a dun color, the closest I could find to my tinge of skin. I could never imagine my sister wearing a scarf like that. It would have been much too drab for Flora. I caught the bus to the East Side. I had joined Ganter College at Sixty-eighth and Park, part of the city system and the tuition was within my grasp. I had barely gone through a month of classes when her letters started coming. With so much to read, I couldn't manage her letters too. I set them in a little heap by the windowsill, pale, unstable things, and still I could not bear to cut them open.

What did I fear? That the sun and moon would fall on my head? That the sea would rise in waves, of precise indigo, screening out my face? That Harlem Meer, all dried out, would crack as if a tremor had struck?

Poor Flora and all the time I was making believe I had read her letters. The best I might have done was to tell her the truth:

"Dear Sister, halfway around the earth, I am scared of what you might say in your letters. I promise you not to throw them out. To quieten them I have put them on the windowsill, so they can catch what sunlight there is. Sometimes I look at the ink you have used to write my name and address. Brownish red. Where did you get that ink from? The little store on main street next to the Ladies Cool Bar?"

But of course I never wrote her. I tried to keep track of her through my weekly phone calls to Mama. But there was an anxious brevity to our back-and-forth, and an odd echoing as if neither Mama nor I knew how to tread right. We spoke of the cold, the sunlight on the kitchen eaves, the owl's nest in the *badam* tree, the high price of vegetables, how blue was fashionable now for silks so that even the Indian shops on Lexington Avenue carried ream after ream of shimmering green-blue, navy blue, royal blue, blue-black, indigo.

Then, after an odd silence, Mama spoke Flora's name. I was forced to echo it. I could sense that Mama was waiting for more. So unwillingly, I spat it out:

"Flora, how's she doing?"

"How's she doing?"

This was Mama, to make sure she got my question right. Or was there a tinge of coldness in her tone, a lack of surprise at my failure to care?

"Your sister is much the same."

"Ah . . . Tell her I called."

On another day, with snowflakes in the air, the soft sheen of light on the bare elm, I paused after my usual question about Papa's health. Mama murmured:

"Flora? She's seeing a new doctor."

"Why?"

My voice was abrupt. I did not want Mama's news about

Flora to spoil the clear space, the sunlit window where I could stand looking out onto stone steps, an asphalt road, an elm tree with crooked branches. I was irritated with Mama. I felt she had forced me into a foolish position. After all with Flora, nothing was new, it was one crisis after another, all in minor key, a scale of petty repetitions. Suddenly, though, I wanted my mother's voice to work miracles. She had given birth to us both, so surely in some sense she was responsible. I wanted her voice to spring me free of my sister, half a world away.

"Leela?" How tired she sounded. Had I paused too long? I let her go on. "Are you there, Leela? You asked about the doctor. We felt the last one wasn't working out. Your sister wasn't sleeping well at night."

She stopped short. Neither of us wanted Flora's news to stain the precious fabric of our shared time, mother and daughter each hanging on a phone, half awake, for it was early morning on the other side of the divided earth of our longing, voices pierced by uncertainties, imagining a touch or a tender glance that might assuage.

One day, though, Mama sounded glad, free even. Or was it the chill wind blowing in through my window? It was her dead mother's birthday.

"Remember how Grandma loved chocolate cream puffs, and coconut *barfi,* right till the very end." Mama laughed. "She always wore her white silk on her birthday, as she sat in her chair, receiving guests."

"Once Flora gobbled up all the *barfi* from the silver plate. Felt quite ill afterward!" I felt lighthearted, remembering my little sister in her pink lace dress. Then unable to go on, I hovered, waiting.

"She's gone away," Mama volunteered.

I was struck by the odd tone. Surely she was alluding to her mother. As if Grandma had taken off to see the traveling circus with its flying trapeze artists and double-headed child birthed in the Palghat hills—this last was widely advertised in the local newspapers—while the guests at her birthday were sipping their green tea.

"Away?" I felt breathless, imagining the double-headed girl, surely about my age, pulling on her dress, each head struggling through its own neck, two arms twined upward like a goddess, two arms bent earthward, struggling with the fabric. And there was Grandma in her white silks, staring in at the monster child through a hole in the circus tent.

"Flora, I mean. She's left us for a while, gone to an ashram near the sea."

"Ashram!" I mused, breathing softly. I picked up a cup of water and sipped at it.

"She's not gone to Kochi, has she?"

"How did you know?" Then she added: "Flora feels the distance from the family will do her good." There was a slight lilt to Mama's voice. A sudden sigh, a sorrow escaping.

I couldn't reply. In my mind's eyes I saw the leaves on the still waters of the temple tank in Kochi, the light on the surface of the water, with a few pipal leaves floating, the clock tower in the old synagogue across the white wall. And there was Grandmother, white hair loose, blowing in the breeze from the Arabian Sea. She was hobbling up the cobblestones up Jewtown Alley. I saw long doors to the side swing open, glimpsed rooms with red floors, old teak chairs, the sudden splash of a bare courtyard. A little shadow bobbed behind Grandma, tiny Flora bareheaded in the heat. And as I turned, feasting my eyes on the invisible source of sunlight, there in the distance were sharp indigo waves on the Arabian Sea.

"Look at your sister," Grandmother cried to me. "Hold Flora's hand, help her along, child. See how tiny her feet are!"

I saw my childhood self, pink skirt, flecked with mud, sandaled feet on the cobblestones, racing after Flora. When I vanished, she appeared, cheeks plump with milk and sweet cakes. Our shadows merged, two heads blurred into one. Two bodies too. I caught her by her tiny wrist, feeling the soft flesh, the whorl of baby fat. But her cries filled the air. She had already slipped, on the sharp cobbles, cut her knee.

There was a smear of blood somewhere I couldn't see.

I WAS TAUGHT in school that all the seas make one great sea. That all the bodies of water are one. The thought still confuses me. I prefer to think of great bodies of water as separate, various. Janak took me to a motel by the sea. We walked together by the rim of water. The Atlantic a mild silver, the waves in the distance foamy tipped. Staring harder I thought the waves were severed tongues, foam flecked with rose tints. Then the waves subsided. I looped my scarf over my head. I stooped over, touched the water to my hands, raised it to my lips. Bitter salt, sharp as a blade. Was this what Grandmother sought all those years ago as she walked with Gandhi on the Salt March? Was the salt different, warmer perhaps on the Indian coast? The sun's heat on her body as they walked was almost too terrible to bear. The thin cotton sari fluttered over her head. In her last years in Kochi, she had drawn us close to her, Flora and me, and spoken about those days. I wanted to slip off my boots, walk barefoot as she had done, but it was much too cold. The sand was white, glowing almost in that pale light as Janak and I walked away from the water and entered a little shop. It had green shutters, a little door propped open with a stone. The old woman behind the counter with shiny marcelled hair gestured at her wares: postcards, plaster lighthouses, magnets for fridges with LONG ISLAND inscribed on an oddly shaped bit of plastic. I touched a sepia-colored card marked fifty cents. A house somewhere by the water's edge with white walls, white pillars, wild grasses growing on the dunes. I felt a sudden shock. Flora, I needed to see Flora. Had I known something like this would happen? I had packed all her letters into my black bag, just in case I felt like opening them.

Back in the motel room, I waited till Janak went out for a run. I opened the curtains, looked out at the silken strip of water blurring into the greenish sky, a mast like a black stalk on the horizon. I picked up Flora's letters and one by one, laid them out on the bed. Then with a little knife, I slit them open, smoothing out the paper till the blue blanket was dotted with letters. The light off the Atlantic shone on my sister's letters. Between finger and thumb I felt their delicate textures. I should lie on this bed, I thought, cover my face with her writing, set my head to the east, to eternity. Such unreal thoughts of death came easy to me. But a disturbance forced me on.

Dates floated up, months and days all mixed up, October, May, June, 7, 15, 25, as if time had its provenance in our imaginations and words were as easy as breathing, sharp spurts, natural blossomings.

August 17

Dear Leela:

It's wretched in this place. I wake up in the morning, brush my teeth and sit for a while under the mango tree. I notice all the people who pass. Jimini comes by leading her cows to pasture. She waves to me. I don't go too close. Her breath smells of garlic. Just like that odd woman with chickens on the steps of Jewtown in Kochi. Did you see the man rush out with his knife to get the chicken? I saw his shadow, Leela. All I saw was his shadow and it covered me. At night when the sky is clear, and the seven sisters are visible, lighting the *jamun* tree, I lie on the ground, feeling the prickly grass. I press my fingers to the earth. I eat mud if I can. Bats swoop down from the *jamun* tree. They comfort my flesh. Papa and Mama have no idea of this of course. I have to be careful. You too have to be careful in what you do, living in America. Why not write to me?

With love from

Flora

October 12

Dear Leela,

Everyone says its high time for me to get married. Put in an ad for me in some newspaper. My friend Lalitha who once visited Wisconsin to see her aunt says the *Village Voice* would be the right place. Word it as you wish. Mention my love of poetry. I am reading Kamala Das again. Her "Old Playhouse"—that blue flash of freedom is what I am after. Say something like "artistically inclined." After all I draw as well. They should know that caste, creed, color are no bar. Or perhaps such an ad would do better in *India Abroad.* It has a wide readership, in Australia and Fiji too. Babu reads it when he can. I meet him for an ice cream now and then in the Cool Bar down the road. He wants to be a movie producer.

(What follows was scrawled on in tilting hand.)

You never met Rajan, did you? It was a long time ago. We loved each other. He offered to marry me. I told him I was pregnant. He came to my hostel room. He smoked a lot. I did too. Later I had to go to the hospital by myself. It was dusty on the streets. I passed the Halal Butcher's shop, red limbs hanging, making awkward shadows. Darkness raced behind the autorickshaw. "Faster, faster," I cried to the driver. I lay on that metal cot legs apart. I came back to my hostel room. Lay there all day till Romila put her head in. Romila and I used to go to French classes together. She brought me a cup of tea. Took my temperature. I have told no one this. No one.

(In a different-colored ink, a few days later perhaps?)

I lie on the grass, in the moonlight so that someone passing by might stop. A man, any man, a day laborer even, toddy tapper, woodcutter, someone passing in the dark. Papa says I am doomed. "To what, I might ask, dear sir?" I said this in a loud voice for all the servants to hear. "To the forces of darkness?" I ask, in a somewhat different tone, but just as loudly. By this time Mama is weeping and spills tea all over her lap and her cousin Bubbli visiting from Madras buries her head in *India.* It's a new magazine, have you heard of it, Leela? How could you, stuck so far away, poor you, in a cold country.

(Then followed a P.S.)

Our grandmother Eliamma thought she could change the world. Marches, fasts, love marriages. In those days people believed in doing things. Now? All we can do is blow each other up in the name of nation, or lie in the grass waiting breathlessly. I do not believe in God anymore. I want you to know this. Babu is making a movie. That's all my news for now.

Your loving sister Flora.

October 15

Dear Leela,

Why haven't you written me about the ad? No takers yet? I keep telling Mama to remind you on the phone. Better to marry than to burn. I keep reading that passage over and over again in the Bible. I have underlined it in red ink.

Write soon,

Flora.

November 25

Dear Leela:

I am not ready for anything. Marriage least of all. Something is burning up inside of me. I feel that even when I sit in the Cool Bar and have an ice cream soda.

The oranges in the bowl Mama had set on the rosewood table, their skins were crinkly, molten. Sunday, everyone else was still at church, only Papa and I were home. Through the rosewood table I saw three suns of inconceivable fire. Three suns burning up. I started choking. No one heard me. The recitation from the church flowed over the *casurina* trees: "O Lamb of God, that taketh away the sins of the world . . ." When I looked outside the tops of the trees were burnt. Later Papa told me there had been a lightning storm, two years ago, that struck the trees. "Did you not notice, Flora?" he said ever so gently.

Tomorrow they are bringing a man from Ranee for me to see. "Someone to possibly marry," Mama said, trying to be nice. She has laid out a sari for me. A pale pink thing, Katau voile. I will tie my hair back behind my head. Wear the pearl drops Grandmother gave me. Wish me luck, dear Leela.

Your loving sister

Flora

Janak and I got back from the seaside. It was late afternoon on Sunday. I did the little odds and ends I needed to do. Picked up my sewing things from the floor. Fixed scrambled eggs and toast for us both. Had some Tsingtao beer Janak brought in. He worked on his drawings. I too had an assignment. Started reading Blake's "Jerusalem" for a paper.

I wanted to write to her:

> *Ah me, Flora, running by my side:*
> *In childhood what wert thou? unutterable anguish!*

I wanted to write her in a way I had written to no one before. I wanted to tell her I felt her life flowing alongside mine. Felt her face and mine, held to the same dark body. Mama had given birth to us both. We had both drunk at her breasts. I needed Flora to speak to me again, as she did when we were children and Mama made me watch her, so Flora wouldn't fall off the guava tree and break her wrists, so she wouldn't tumble into the well. I was always the older sister, running after the little one's shadow, trying to keep her clear of harm.

Somehow I couldn't work on Blake. Nor did the letter come to me. It would be too forced, writing to her, after all the time I had kept her notes unread. I needed to talk to her. Pick up the phone, dial home, call for her. But it would be well before dawn on the other side of the earth. To calm myself I cleared up the lunch plates, stacked them neatly. Ran lukewarm water over the splotched surfaces, picked up a sponge. I heard a little cry and turned to the window. Saw old Marvin on his stoop with two little girls seated by him. Neatly dressed in pink, ribbons in their hair. The older one kept pulling at her hem, smoothing it over her knee. The other was sitting, quite happily on Marvin's lap sucking on a lollipop. From where I sat the two girls made a double shadow, awkward really, two heads, a body blurred into a shapeless bag. I heard that cry again, it turned into a giggle. The little one was sucking on her lollipop, wiggling her toes.

I leaned out the window: "Marvin, Marvin," I called, partly to ask him who the girls were, partly to distract Janak, who was rummaging in the fridge. I did not want Janak drinking too much beer.

"Marvin, hey Marvin, hello."

In slow motion the old man turned his head. The sanitation truck was grinding down brooms and all on the asphalt, sucking up an old shoe, a chair leg, a knot of plastic. When the truck passed I waved at Marvin and at the two little girls, who now sat, hands in their lap as if waiting for a photo.

I heard a pop—bottle top, the foam spilling. The two little girls, not budging. Behind them a crack in the door. The door creaked black. Hinges loose. A jagged crack between them who never should be severed. A louder shock. The old sanitation van blowing an exhaust, a short in the light system? Marvin grabbed the two, their pink all brushed with light, seven if a day, one slightly younger, hustled them indoors. Someone was crying on the street. He must have seen my mouth trembling.

"Here, baby, here."

He was gentle, my Janak.

"Here, sit. It's nothing. Some fool with a gun."

I sat down on the one chair we had, he knelt by me putting the beer in my open hand. It wasn't the shot I wanted to say. That night I called Mama.

"I was out by the water's edge," I told her.

"In this cold?"

"It's fine if you bundle up. I have a lovely scarf, a coat I got off the rack in a secondhand shop!"

"Oh Leela," I heard Mama sigh. The line was crystal-clear. A slow stream running the wellside after the moonsoon rain. A silver stream. One leaf from the mulberry bush floating on it.

"Leela, did you go alone?" Mama asked.

Janak was not official yet. I couldn't tell them about him. I wasn't sure myself how I felt. "How's Flora?" I asked instead. I really wanted to know.

The window was wide open. Marvin with the two little

girls, back on the stoop. One was calling to the other. They had little plastic skip ropes, neon green, looping their thighs. Their skirts were tangled in the rope. "Help, Elvira, help!" the little one cried. Elvira tried pulling at the end of the rope. Hard she pulled, harder. The little one started squirming.

"Listen, the meeting with the man from Ranee didn't go well. It was after that she ran away to Kochi. Not that anything happened in our house, you understand. Flora served the tea and pastries. Chatted politely enough about his business. Something to do with catering. His business caters for christenings, weddings, funerals. Big things like that."

Mama paused.

"What happened then?" I couldn't keep the tremor out of my voice.

"There was an accident. We're not sure what happened exactly. They gave her a room in the ashram but then her bed caught fire. The old mosquito netting. There was smoke everywhere. Your uncle Eapen was called. He was her local guardian as you know. He brought her home last night."

"Brought her?"

"Yes, in a car, with a driver. A nurse too, someone from the local hospital."

"How is she, Mama?"

I could not hear Mama's words for the noise from the window. Elvira was struggling with the skip rope as the little sister waved her hands up and down in the air, pink sleeves flapping as the rope bound her tight, tighter.

Mona Simpson

Sisters

MY GREAT-AUNTS were six sisters, each with the name of a jewel or semiprecious stone. But they didn't call each other those, they had nicknames. Goody, Heady, Girly, Slavey, Tom Tom, and Baby. Girly was fat. She gave me water once in her square kitchen, a maroon tall metal cup sharp on my lip. They said she went in for antiques. Baby was the wild one. She still wore frills at eighty. Goody could bake, Tom Tom kept a neat house. Slavey lost her hair at the end and had the handsome no-good husband, whom Tom Tom nursed for ten years. They visited each other's houses every day. They had no other friends. They are strangers on their tombstones: Opal, Pearl, Ruby, Sapphire, Coral, Amber.

WE KNEW A FAMILY with five sisters, steps besides. A widower married a widow. Two were tall, two less, two blond, two dark, one a redhead look-alike for Hedy Lamarr. If you met them in their sixties you would still know which was the beautiful baby. She'd tell you. They all would. She was still beautiful then too, but not more so. Perhaps in a more regular way. At her wedding, two of the sisters fought. They pulled hair, a lamp was thrown at a head. They bit, scratched, kissed laughing the next day. The steps were mad because the bride wore one of their mother's old dresses she'd found in the basement for her going-away outfit. It was *their* mother's, not hers. Even though they'd never fit in it. The steps were big girls, all. And the bride did. Fit. She still did the year before she died. She wore it for the costume ball at the home.

When one's husband bought a gift, three or more of the sisters went along.

They eat with each other several times a week, at each other's homes, although there, too, fights erupted over something like a nickname or a shoe or an implication that someone got more fifteen years ago from one parent.

One drove all night from Chicago to reclaim the silver from her mother's attic another had taken home and polished.

You weren't using it.

But it is mine. Still.

The mother, who happened to be kind and fair, one of the beloved women in the world, promised each of the girls silver then, but in time. She needed to buy it on time. She herself worked, baking wedding cakes and taking the festal photographs.

They competed, those girls, all their lives, they envied each other's wardrobes and husbands and houses, but most of all they fought over her.

She had little time with each alone.

They each wanted her only.

SOME DISTANT RELATIVES on the Arab side, were four sisters. They were aristocrats. I never knew them well. But I studied the way they were with men.

The oldest was the hook, a dangerous beauty when she was young, one side of the mouth curled down in an almost-sneer. Her lips were big, full, oversized, as if they'd smeared over the border. She lured the men for them all. Men fell for her, mooned over her in a drift and the sisters worked together, laughing at him, at all men. The youngers bided their time.

Three men in turn came to appreciate slower, consoling virtues. The eldest saw her three young sisters married and finally had a baby out of wedlock with an elderly, famous Italian.

The youngest sister died first. The eldest, by then home again, married the husband. By then it wasn't a case of long finally requited love. Any sister would have done. They each knew how to make his toast.

MY COLLEGE ROOMMATE was one of three sisters. She was a distinct oldest, there was a middle and a baby. The oldest was Dad, a brilliant but daffy ornithologist, the youngest Mom, a stylishly reckless younger wife who knew one thing and that was how to have fun in life, and the middle was neither which has given her a life of trouble.

WE ALL KNOW two sisters who are opposites and live miles or a continent or oceans apart. Our town had many of these. The one who stayed and the one who left. My mother and my godmother were each one of these. The one who stayed tended to end up taking care of the aged mother; fathers tending to die first. The one who left did something else and had a life. The one who stayed tended to offer services: the groceries picked up, the odd errand, maybe scrubbing the kitchen floor, picking up a cake on Sundays. Just company. Daily, every day, weather; the other, being. Children. Grandchildren. Arriving in a boisterous mess for a rare holiday when the house was taken apart. Generally, they were represented evenly in the will.

I NEVER HAD a sister and only sometimes wanted one. Not a younger.

If I had a sister, I would want her to be older and knowledgeable, flippant with her dark secrets. I imagined a room full of underwear and sophisticated underground music, bras on the shower rod.

My old college roommate on the phone to her family, now at thirty-three: a classical lament, everything wrong. How they're wearing pants this year and hers all too wide, sigh, problems of health, her grandfather fell again, oh no, could she do something? Of course he could stay, the couch pulls out. Prices of things.

I listen to her portrait of yoked overworked people and recognize nothing. We've just come in from running. Even her daughter is overburdened in this account, under a melancholy umbrella. "But we're fine," she says at the end. They all did that to each other, each of the daughters, and the mother too. They competed not over joys or accomplishments or even purchases, but over pain. Slights and wrongs of twenty years earlier easily slid into the conversation. What each one got from the father, they came to always at the end of fights, each telling her, the oldest, she got more. She couldn't bear to be alone, but she did love him. "He didn't ask me one question either!" she screamed. Then, later, a hard staccato, "But I call. I call him and I tell him straight, Dad, you didn't hear me."

I whisper to calm down. She holds the phone out for me to hear: "You can ask, that's because you know that he loves you, you were given that sense of entitlement!" Her sister, the always-aggrieved middle.

It was never ending their fight about who got least and they will wage it, I understand, for the rest of their lives.

She is quite snide about her in-laws and their politer conversations.

"Bragging," she calls it. "They brag. That's what they do." Her mother-in-law chronicles the honors and accomplishments her children brought her, starting when the participants were two or three. "Did you hear what Matthew said . . . Three years old," the story always finished.

I envy her family, their bickering and plaintive weeping. My own family assumes a fair evenness in life. Parents set out their children as to sea, at a certain age, with prescribed provisions and from there they expect little. It was assumed your fortune or misfortune, with the exception of dire illness, was your own business.

The sisters compete to suffer because if anyone prospered she would be generally held to owe tithe, they were understood to be on a communal journey, not of their own choosing.

Erika Duncan

What Is Cinderella's Burden?

WHAT IS CINDERELLA'S BURDEN? What is it that she is carrying, really? And what is the meaning of the pumpkin? What is the crime of staying away from the one whom one serves past midnight, beyond the hour when the one who is wicked and abandoned must be bedded down all alone?

Cinderella, daughter, sister of ash. We were opposite sides of our mother's self-love and self-hatred. The self-love never picked up by any other in my mother's own childhood was really only a loneliness longing for reflection, which was why, perhaps, my sister was always so distant. But my sister was ever so beautiful to my mother and me.

The self-hatred was so precious and hidden at once, it must be given away to another. As the oldest daughter it was I who was chosen to carry it to safety. As a child, so carefully bearing the self-hatred my mother couldn't bear, when I looked at my freer and lovelier sister, how could I have known that there was no room for my sister in that mission, and that my sister's seeming freedom was not, originally, a choice?

It was only much later that I began to be able to look at my sister objectively, and to see what it must have meant for her to adapt herself to an exclusion from a dance going on between my mother and me, already so complicated that no newcomer could have entered it even if she had tried.

Although there were only twenty months between us, those twenty months made all of the difference.

"By the time I came along, there was simply no room," my sister said simply one day when we were thrown together in caring for our mother, who had deteriorated so suddenly, all battles were gone.

During a nightmarish four months my sister had been my mother's main caretaker for a variety of reasons. The two most immediate ones were practical. Although her work required frequent trips to very far away places, when she was actually present she lived in New York City, a subway ride away from my mother, while I lived in eastern Long Island, one hundred miles away.

The second had to do with my youngest daughter's illness, which happened to coincide exactly with my mother's losing of competence and health. From August until December my daughter would spend fifty-five days in the hospital and undergo three major surgical procedures for a rupture of the colon that should never have assailed someone so young.

But beneath this: choices patterns, as old as we were old, as deep as we were deep. When my mother, a few months earlier, had announced that she had willed my sister an "extra" house, partly because my sister, who didn't already live in the country, had promised not to sell it, but also as an expression of her closeness to the one "who had been more available," because I had had others to care for, and "having children was a choice," it had been the end of a certain cycle of thinking of giving and getting, of caring and fleeing, of who had cared most, and who was more drained.

And now we like the players of the next generation in the tragedies of Shakespeare, left standing in the rubble, to make it all right. I thought much of the ends of the tragedies of Shakespeare, and how different it is with women than with men.

In the fairy tales of sisters, where the issue is fairness/unfairness, and chosen and unchosen sister, no queen must die, no sister murder must take place. Once the unchosen sister has been shown a way to show the fairer outside world her unfairly hidden inner beauty, the bad queen or bad stepmother simply disappears from the story. The previously maligned sister has no desire for revenge against the sister (or sisters) who were more fortunate, but now that there is enough to go around, and the evil enchantress' previous powers have been made irrelevant, she shares her bounty equally.

No one can remember what happened to Cinderella's mother once the inequality among the daughters was rendered irrelevant. It is as if the relevance of the bad stepmother is only active when there has been daughter splitting, and once that is conquered she can quickly lose her powers.

Is that a wish? Is that a true reality?

IN WRITING THIS ESSAY I am very interested in splits and reversals, in the way that patterns come back over generations, even when we attempt to undo them, and the depths of the feelings of real mother/false mother and real daughter/false daughter that make for the fairy-tale splits. I am interested in mirrors, and in ways of breaking down the mirrors, and giving the shards equally to all. I am interested in beauty, in the fact that so often the fairy-tale-tortured and hidden one, whose own beauty is hidden, finds her redemption in washing the face of a death's head or troll. I am interested in knowing what would happen if we all shared our ugliness, beauty, our good and our bad, our hopes and our hatreds, our fears.

IN OUR FAMILY it is possible to begin with the Cinderella version proper, for my mother based much of her understanding of her own psychology upon it. Her real mother had died. And her stepmother preferred her real daughters and was cold and was cruel to my mother, so cruel that when my four-year-old mother, at her stepmother's arrival, had gotten frightened and had wet the bed, the stepmother had dipped her head in the bed urine.

When my oldest two daughters were tiny, three and a half years old only and five, my mother took them to see *Cinderella* and told them that she too had a wicked stepmother who had favored her real daughters, and that was the first thing my daughters ever learned about their grandmother, that she was an abandoned and unloved child.

In my situation, since I was my mother's real daughter while my mother's real mother was gone, the configuration was supposed to have been an absolute reversal. My mother's divine gift to me, made doubly potent by our family's extreme and deeply practiced atheism, was that great somethingness that had come out of the passed-on nothingness, the manna of the perfect mothering that had no precedent and no remembered flaws, since it had come out of the void.

Like the Christ child given to the virgin, I had come where there was nothing, no seed planted. My father, our father, in the configuration was irrelevant.

It would be later the irrelevancy of fathers I would notice as I looked at the patterns in the good sister/bad sister tales. Or else it would be the relative weakness of fathers.

In the fairy tales sometimes Cinderella is one of two sisters, more often one of three, as if the perceived goodness, entitledness, must be doubled, multiplied, to double the weight of the "bad" one abandoned alone.

Sometimes she is the true but hated daughter of a bad queen or unnatural mother. But more often she is the daughter of a good, often dead other mother, the one the new stepmother hates. Sometimes she has in her imprint more of man than of woman, and is the daughter of the good but bullied male creature who cannot defend her against the stepmother's jealousy of the preferred, beautiful dead. She is the preservation of the remembered love that the man bears for his first perfect dead wife, who is so often, at least mythologically speaking, his mother.

The younger she is, the more chance there will be to trick her; if she is beautiful, to exchange her beauty for ugliness.

As I think back over the fairy tales, I am assailed by the reversals, wondering what does it mean that the rejected stepdaughter is so often the youngest, the innocent princess, while obviously, biologically the stepdaughter would have to be first?

And in that moment of my mother's mental disappearance, my sister wept and my own eyes were dry. If I could have given it all up, all of the wishing for reparation and revenge, for the gentle mothering I never would receive, now knowing that it was too late, for just one of my sister's tears, I would have prayed the deepest atheist prayer I knew.

"My task was different," I said softly to my sister, "and it was one at which I had to fail."

And then, perhaps for the first time, we both embraced each other and we cried.

Only much later was I to learn that the good daughter/bad daughter split was not so uncommon.

I SHALL TRY TO go backward. But how strange is the locked cage of memory. And how many the reasons to lock it. Virginia Woolf knew this when she put so much stock in the single stopped image, in its brightness and dullness, the large and the small of it, trying to determine her age on a journey (either to or from Cornwall) by the size of the red flowers on her mother's dark dress, to determine how close or how far she was held by the contrast, to make up for the sensation of Being almost totally lost, and even the memory of motion, accessible only through the most stopped and stilled silence. And along with the sensation of Being, almost all accurate notions of what was the actual relationship she had with her mother, irreparably lost.

In my mind, when I think back as early as I can, I see not myself but the pose of my own shyness, in a classroom, in a school yard, never liking it too much when I am away from my mother. I see a pose that already prefigures the curvature that will not come for almost a decade, as if body and psychology already are linked . . .

And then I see my sister with her arms spread wide open, rolling fast, rolling freely toward the neighborhood children who are not like the children in our public school, but go to the Catholic school nearby. I have a strange fondness for these children, and a curiosity about them. But they do not like me, for I have so many more words than they do; and even when I try not to use them, they come out. I have a strange way of using them, with a sort of shame.

My sister is wearing the roller skates that I helped her to put on, but I know better than to go along with her. Four freckled boys, all happy brothers with the simple name of Baker, smile at her. And she smiles back. Although she is a bit shy, her shyness is of the endearing kind. And other children like her. Adults also like her.

I know that something about me will make these children shy away from me, and I both show it and hide it as I come running home to my mother and she showers me with kisses, making me, for that moment, feel very special. I do not know just when it is that she tells me that very special people often have a hard time in the world, but that they ultimately are the ones who do great things. Although she doesn't say so directly, I begin to feel that I have just been told a very special secret, that for all my sister's seemingly charming qualities and skills she isn't quite this thing that links me to my mother, that for all its woes, will never become interchangeable.

Because I am the oldest and the first, she will take me upon her knee and tell me about the very special relationship that mothers have with their first daughters. And later, when in early adolescence I will start to show a very special rage, she will tell me that that too is part of the mother and first daughter intensity.

In the fairy tales sometimes the chosen/unchosen child is sent out into the world to be harmed, and in the gift of her compassion for the underdog she will prove herself by washing the faces of the hideous trolls her stronger and more cared-for sisters shun. Sometimes she is kept at home, like Cinderella, completely hidden, until she is discovered by the Beautiful. What is it that the mother/stepmother is fleeing in keeping hidden the "other" child? What part of her own self is it she shuns?

There is a largeness, and an isolation, already in this drama that it will take a lifetime to undo. But here perhaps I must talk a little bit about what it meant for me to be an atheist, communist child. I was one of those children who, although a devout believer in the fact that there were no forces anywhere beyond the human, yet yearned for communion and the sharing of God. I loved always the singing in churches, especially the singing of little tiny children who were giving over their trust to a bigness they could not yet reasonably fathom, yet felt. In my world the only bigness was my mother. Years later when my second novel was published, my most autobiographical, and my father asked "Who am I?" I replied "You are the dead musician because you always played a music that I could not hear."

I think often how the communion with God, with a power much bigger than one's mother or father, must preserve, at least to some extent, the sense of a self separate from that of the mother or father, with which to commune, how it must more easily translate, later on, to a communion with nature and music and art. I think it is different for those who have acquired atheism later on, as a phenomenon of adult choice, or for those who never take their childhood atheism quite so seriously.

The communist chunk went very well with the atheism, and had to do with the enormity of human responsibility. But my mother was also a psychotherapist, and would often try to substitute understanding for feelings. Feelings existed, in fact they abounded, larger than life, all around. But they were there to be conquered. I think that the conquering of feelings, like the conquering of the yearning for God, early on became a contest.

Our favorite toys, my sister's and mine, were my mother's thematic apperception tests, cardboard placards with drawings of houses, half peopled, over which one would superpose the remaining cutout people to make stories. They were all, they were so designed, to be family relational stories, of mothers and fathers, of sisters and brothers, and such. And then there were the pattern blocks, used, normally with a timer, for the I.Q. tests. We knew that our mother had tested our I.Q.'s some time ago when she was practicing, and that one of our I.Q.'s was higher than the other. Only she wouldn't tell us which was which. For years I was tormented by imagining that my sister's I.Q. was higher and that my mother knew.

Competition, difference, how little they matter if each can feel loved and unique. Less than ten years after my mother reassures the seven-year-old who is me that it doesn't matter if the other children like her, because I am specially unique, and moreover I belong to my mother, I will find myself sitting on her bed with her long into the night. My father, who was never enough, who never seemed to fill her up, has tired finally of being reprimanded for his smallness. He has found his affirmation elsewhere, and has left her.

I am now fifteen, and at the age of first boyfriends, at the age of first loneliness and first knowledge of betrayal. But no, over and over again I have had this in earliest childhood with girlfriends. And my mother is crying to me about how lonely she is, and I on her bed, way past my own bedtime, am trying to reassure her that her uniqueness and strength is a wonderful, beautiful thing, that "even if it frightens all the men away, [she] wouldn't want it any other way."

Was there a way that I knew even then, or before that, when I was a child first left all alone in a school yard, that my mother was painfully hard to like? I have no memories of experiencing my mother as a rejected person when I was a very young child, but can only reconstruct my own thinking that because I am more intense it is harder for children to like me. Somewhere along the line I have learned the word intensity, and I know that it is something that describes both me—my "nature" and the thing that makes me similar to my mother—as well as my relationship with my mother. It is the one thing that my sister doesn't have, and over the years, as my jealousy of her grows, I will learn to cherish it. The child in the school yard stands alone, the child who moments earlier was excelling in the classroom, or perhaps the child who was the unknowing victim of anti-Semitism. Later on she will be the one who bravely refuses to salute the American flag, who will be so happily praised by her mother the minute she comes home.

Because I am frightened of the other children, more and more I will stay with my mother, who will pretend to comfort me, even as she assuages her own loneliness. And as my insight, my vocabulary grows, as she is able to confide in me more and more, and I in her, we will know that we are together in this specialness that alienates other people.

We will watch my little sister be liked by her classmates and teachers. And my mother will be proud of her and I will be jealous of her. And my mother will reassure me that jealousy is a natural emotion, that I shouldn't feel bad about feeling that way. And I will try to overcome my jealousy by becoming my little sister's teacher. And she will learn fast.

Almost before I have learned how to read, before I have had

the pleasure of watching the words dance on the page, and entering a magical world all alone, I will teach her to read. And then my mother and the teachers who love her will have her skipped a year in school, so that she is suddenly almost in my grade. And I will have to watch more carefully than ever to be sure that my friends do not find her, and discover that she is far more likable and better than me. And even when I am watching, ever so carefully, there is no way that I can keep people from discovering how wonderful my little sister is.

I HAVE NO MEMORY of my little sister's birth, which came a year and a half after mine. All that I know is what I had been told as soon as I was old enough to comprehend such things, if not much sooner, for always the fact that I had many words deceived my mother into talking to me as if I had been much older. My mother, so the story went, had wanted desperately to conceive. And yet, while all the others "who wanted children far less" easily conceived, she had great troubles for ten years.

By the time I finally came, she was so afraid that the pattern would be repeated that when I was eleven months old she started trying again. Although, as she was often to tell me, she would have wanted us at least two years apart, as often happens in these cases, my sister came immediately, breaking whatever separate bliss my mother had anticipated with me. Later on I would repeat this pattern with my two oldest daughters, panicking because at the age of nineteen it took me all of three months to become pregnant, starting immediately again when my oldest daughter was eighteen months old. And my sister, seeming to evince no curiosity, would stay very far away.

I remember very little of the first six years of my life, which surprises me, because I was, to all accounts, a very verbal child, although only my mother was able to understand me. According to the stories passed down it was suggested that I have speech therapy so that others would be able to understand me also, and even my father went along with this suggestion, but my mother won out because she was the psychologist of the family, and she "didn't want to make me self-conscious so young."

I suspect that the absence of earlier memories has a great deal to do with the way I learned to turn over all of my conscious thinking to my mother. For as long as I can remember, in my childhood and my adolescence, I told her everything that I thought. In my childhood, I suspect that I didn't have any thoughts that she wouldn't have liked, for I have no memories of anything other than perfect harmony and happiness with her. Later on, in my adolescence, when I spoke thoughts that she didn't like, there were brutal fights between us, that lasted on and off for over twenty-five years.

WAS IT FROM our father that my sister learned her separateness? I remember a recurring scene at dinnertime. My mother was worried that my father was always looking at me and ignoring my sister. We had one of those booth-type seating alcoves in the kitchen, where two people could sit on two facing benches in an enclosed space, and the people on the inside would have to wait for the people on the outside to get up, in order to be able to move. I remember that my mother kept changing our seats, so that my father would be forced to look at my sister, but no matter which way she arranged us, she was never satisfied that a change had occurred. I have no memories of my sister's or my father's expressions during these sessions, but only of my own embarrassment for them both, my own desire to protect both of them.

My sister later confided to me that it was partially through watching me that she learned separateness. She saw me over and over again getting into trouble when I told my mother too much about what I was thinking. I was the child who drew and wrote, and of my earliest childhood writings and drawings my parents were both very proud, until I separated from them, and there came into my work a darkness that they felt vaguely responsible for, and didn't know how to handle, a grief that could make certain sorts of jagged rough edges that they were embarrassed for with their friends. It was as if my sister always knew that she should not reveal herself, so much so that once, when she was about ten years old, or so my father's story goes, my parents found a beautiful drawing that she had made tucked under all of her clothing in her bottom dresser drawer. When they took it out and admired it, several hours later they found it crumpled up in her garbage can.

What had my father meant to tell me when he revealed this to me, he who had always hovered as a gentle spirit yet could never reach me?

When parents are much too large, and their children don't yet know how to cut them in half, I suspect they must cut themselves in half. Was it really a smallness that my mother felt inside, that made my father so easily disappear for her, and made us help him disappear, even as we severed ourselves from ourselves?

My mother had such a terrible fear of disappearing, if ever her children should meet. She had given us eyes, two very different sets of eyes, and had pasted them onto our heads, but then, as the fairy-tale mothers did, bewitched them into not being free.

We never really looked at each other, my sister and I, and yet I remember a single occasion when my sister crept into my bed and she wet it, when we were staying in a motel, while we were traveling cross-country. And she got to sleep with my mother, and I with my father, and my father had to change the bed.

I remember some times when my parents had fights, and we would huddle in the backseat of the car together. It is the only memory of physical contact I have, except for my sister's wetting the bed. And when my parents were getting along, and there was a suitcase between us, it would be jolted from one to the other while the car hit the curves, and we would be very unhappy with each other.

And then I remember my parents' shocked and hurt expressions once when I was found holding a Coca-Cola bottle over my sister's head, a gesture so completely out of keeping for me that none of us knew what to do with it, for generally, perhaps because I was so encouraged to talk to my mother about my jealousy of my sister, I never acted it out. My mother was so proud of this system, this manner of touching the feelings that kept us from acting things out, that keep us in the eyes of the world, ideal sisters, ideal daughters.

I search in my mind for the time when the tides switched, when I was no longer my mother's good little daughter, but suddenly I had become the evil one. Somewhere between preadolescence and the age of sixteen this must have happened, this "acting out" as my mother would call it in her psychological jargon, the time when my need for a separate perception began, and yet I couldn't keep quiet, I needed her approval so badly. It was mainly over the right of a separate perception that the fighting began, I remember, and who could wound whom more deeply, and it happened, not suddenly, but gradually, gradually over time, with many periods of intensified closeness and make-ups that were almost sexual in between.

When I try to remember the doors, it is in this period that they first become important, the fact that my sister seemed to be able to close her door without conflict while I only closed mine with great guilt, and mine could be easily opened if my mother was angry or just needed to talk. My sister's somehow was inviolable. Even now I do not know whether I am more frightened of other people's doors or my own.

It was during this period that I first began to resent the fact that my sister was able to keep secrets while I didn't seem to know how. If ever I would try to talk to her about something that upset me (especially about my new problems with my mother) I would feel that she was beginning to look down on me, as someone who didn't know how to handle people, that she had shut the door to her heart. It was during this period, when so many sisters begin to gang up on their mothers and begin sharing their secrets, that I remember feeling consciously for the first time the sadness "of not having a sister."

This would be a feeling I would keep for most of my adulthood, so that it was possible for people to know me for years without knowing that I had a sister. We rarely did anything together, although we shared many interests to a much greater degree than most sisters. Good daughters of our parents, we continued to share our atheism, our political beliefs. We shared certain aesthetic tastes, and could continue to get each other the right books for our birthdays, even when we didn't see each other all year long. We heard about one another mostly from our mother, and I remember, for years, everything that my mother would say about my sister's achievements had come into my heart like a dagger, something about the way she did it obliterating who I was and creating an aura of deep inner blackness in me, through which my sister shone. How exactly this happened, this feeling of irrelevance whenever my sister was mentioned, I will never know, only that it became a pattern that was repeated on and off with other women for years to come.

My sister became an anthropologist, going away to far-distant places, and often for long periods of time, so that when she came back everyone in the family dropped everything in order to see her. She stayed single for a long time, and her reasons for being away were so good no one could have faulted her for them.

I was always around, if not always available, especially during the years between twenty and thirty when I didn't know which to take care of first, my children, my mother, or my art. Because I had dived into my choices recklessly and deep at age twenty, with all of the reckless belief of a twenty-year-old, I often found I had gone in beyond my water level and I tended to need help that wouldn't come, for my mother herself was too needy. And since I had a man while my mother had none, a fact that she would often remind me of in echo of her complaint from my childhood that I had had a mother while she had none, she felt that it was only right for me to continue as her comforter.

She saw me, at the age of twenty-two, already with two children, not as a frightened and overextended child mother but as a grown woman with two children herself, who surely had room for the mother who had raised her and loved her so dearly. And so the dance began of my withholding myself, dreaming that her money might help open the doors toward a separateness I had relinquished too early, and she, with a will as tough as her atheism, withholding even the simplest offerings. And so it was that my time and concern became my currency, her money hers, the issue of who could withhold what might have helped the other the battleground. Because my mother had never had a mother, the fact that mothers and daughters should expect different things from one another never came up.

My sister had made a professional choice that not only allowed her to travel away but also allowed her to be financially independent. Was it out of a secret fear of losing my mother that I took on her own mother field of psychology and became immersed in exploring "mother wounds" and imprint? Or was it because imprint was handled so strangely in our family? It was different now that I wore the perverse pride of being more difficult and thorny than my sister, and in failing at impossible tasks, as I waited for the fairy-tale moment in which my years of being my mother's little confidante while taking care of three children, while my sister wandered free, would be rewarded and I would wear the golden crown.

If my pattern was to rush into the most complicated and impossible situations I could find, my sister's pattern was to move more slowly and to wait, protecting herself until she was ready. My sister only very gradually approached the intimacy I had shared with my mother, never coming close until sometime in her thirties when she was a fully formed adult and I was starting to move away.

Was it her return that allowed me to withdraw, in this period when I suddenly began to be aware that money would not come from trees, or from my mother, and I must begin to concentrate on making a more viable life for my children and me, when I began to know that my husband would not fill in where my mother would not? Or was it the withdrawal that I had been too fearful to dare—like the doors—that finally allowed my sister to become the daughter of my mother's deepest dreams? For those who have been caretaker children never move away gracefully. Their retreat is always seen as a betrayal.

IT WAS AS IF we had always moved in an opposing rhythm, my sister and I, taking turns, filling opposite spaces, so my mother would never be left all alone. It wasn't until after I had separated from my husband that my sister got married. It wasn't until I went away to college that she began to go out with boys.

The issue of children was a bit more tricky, since it was one in which we couldn't take turns. So I had my children very early and my sister had none. My sister stayed very far away from my children, all the years of their growing.

Was it because her choices were so different, or was it the way I did it that so frightened her, in echo of my mother's self-consciousness and intensity, as I struggled both to repeat what my mother had done and to undo it?

I only went to college for one term. It was right after my father had left my mother. The summer right before that I had gone to Europe on my father's ticket. When I came home for

Christmas vacation my mother and I got into a talk that lasted all night long. I only remember a few words, my own "the hollowness of academia" and "I want to talk about life and *they* want to talk about Faust's masks," and hers "Then why do you want to travel three thousand miles?" and "I am not invested in your going to college the way so many other middle-class parents are." But I remember well the tone and intimacy, so like the all-night talks in which I used to comfort her, or those in which she used, much earlier, to comfort me.

So I stayed home. I remember very little about my sister from that period, only that after a while my mother and I fought very brutally, and that my sister avoided both my mother and me. Within a month I had met my twenty-four-year-old husband-to-be, and he made me a beautiful piece of sculpture, stopping very often to make love to me while he worked. As soon as the sculpture was finished, my mother commissioned him to do one of my sister.

I remember how I cried and wept, feeling that I didn't have a chance, that once he had stared at my sister and molded her forms, all would be lost. Nothing could comfort me, nor reassure me that my sister wouldn't somehow triumph and begin to push me out of beauty, love, all things. But I didn't have to worry. In another few months my sister went off to college, where she stayed four years, and then continued on through graduate school. By the time she finished graduate school, I was already the mother of three children.

Later on, whenever I would talk about what it had meant to allow a not-yet-seventeen-year-old to enter a life of no security, my mother would talk about the importance of choice, and what she would call "the strength of my will," which she had "heard" and honored.

And of my secret desire to be there in order to comfort her, the pattern of leaving school which I would later see when I taught college freshmen, following a divorce? To experience this along with me would have meant journeying to a place she would not go.

The college story, among the stories of my childhood, is one I have never been able to share with my sister, for her version of it is so much closer to that of my mother. And she gets angry at my sense of the burden I bore in staying home.

It is strange, I am thinking, how little revenge comes into play in the fairy-tale stories of sisters, or the thought of making a cudgel out of one's own pain to wield over the head of the one who was spared, how little the slaughter appears that one finds in the stories of brothers and princes, and even of mothers and daughters alone. For Snow White's cruel betrayer queen does die quite violently, and we do not have trouble knowing how she died.

I wondered a great deal why the desire for slaughter is so absent from the fairy-tale stories of sisters, when in real life the sister who is slated for badness and failure feels so strongly the desire for revenge against both mother and better-loved sister, or she feels how the wishing to murder turns in toward the wish for self-slaughter.

The story of my adulthood is one of not a single but of many, many turning points, toward that desire and away, a slow voyage toward acknowledgment and reversal, in which writing and the making of art would occupy a crucial and a saving place.

It has always been easier for me to write about mothers and daughters when I have deliberately omitted my sister. For I see now how much more difficult it is to sort out the pieces when one's could-have-been self is portrayed in one's own tabooed voice. It is easier, I suspect, to give ourselves a voice when we are writing about our mothers, because the obvious inconsistency in our sizes saves us from feeling that we are usurping a voice where it should have been equal. Also perhaps the fact that we are starting the story later, that our mothers have the head start of a whole generation, saves us.

It is harder with sisters, where the roads forked so closely, to be ever a symbol of a self never made or a road never taken. And the knitted, knotted threads: whose triumph becomes whose sacrifice? All that we accomplished by not being the other, and all that we couldn't accomplish. They are the face of our opposite possibility, and of our impossibility, our longing and our shame.

AS IF I COULD redo the mother and daughter conundrum that so haunted me and get it right, I had my daughters and I had them strong. So serious, such an old young mother was I at twenty and at twenty-one. And then again at twenty-four, as if each child might hold the mystery. I watched three girl children learning how to be sisters, learning how to love and fight. And I was never still. At first I painted, then I wrote. By the time I was twenty-two and had two children, I had given up painting and turned to writing permanently.

My three girl children grew so differently. There was nothing in their relationship I took for granted. They hated in a way I didn't remember. They also were attached in a way I didn't remember. How still, how very still it was for me when my three children were very small. Aged I haunted the playground where already I could not make small talk with the mothers ten or fifteen years my seniors. I was once again the small child in the playground. Rachel, the first, was shy, and Gwynne the second was not. In a world of emptiness and repetition I sat, and wrote of old, old people trapped on park benches, and wrote about two sisters, "opposite halves of women lost," in a first novel about four very old people, dying alone. Where then bury my sadness?

In a world of happiness at home, so like the first remembered world I had shared with my mother, I was the hidden beauty whom my husband with his sculptor's tools and princely artist's eyes alone could see. And he would render up my portrait endlessly, and make me beautiful, making me all that I had ever wished to be. Gone were the days when my mother had had him carve a likeness of my sister's face, her flowing hair.

My sister almost never came to visit us. She was busy with college, with being young. Then later on she was busy with working. When my mother was living in Chicago, my sister came for a while to live and work in New York. But it didn't matter. We almost never saw her. Then my mother returned to New York. Soon afterward my sister left for Cornell, to take a second degree. The dates, the exact chronology is blurred. Somewhere along the line, between my leaving college and my having children, my mother remarried, and thus her move away. Somewhere along the line, my mother and her husband returned, and then her husband left her. Somewhere along the line, my sister decided to study anthropology, and then the trips began, to Alaska, to Indonesia, the rare dramatic photographs that lined my mother's bureau tops, the rare Indonesian rugs, a softening, stories, golden earrings for me . . .

Life moved, life moved in fits and starts. I was more tired in those years than I could know, more worn than I could know from mothering. My first book took its shape so dark, so sad, my parents and my sister turned from it. My children grew, not simply. They were sensitive and wore my tensions well. They were not "good" children in the way my sister and I were.

How then to tell the rest of the story, my separation from my husband, which came after twelve years of happiness with him, despite the other inner sadnesses that no one could break, my going over to women in a search of some lost perfect communication I remembered from my childhood, my husband's heartbreak and our years of rough fighting, years of disappointments with women, sometimes the children shying away from me, sometimes their coming back, years sometimes of happiness, or temporary happiness, a more permanent living relationship in which finally to settle and a friendship with my husband rekindled in hardship and sorrow, and the years of hard knocks that had come to our third.

How to tell the story of beginning to work with women, of beginning to teach other women, and the feelings of jealousy that were kindled when the other women were able to use what I had to offer, perhaps better than I could, when they seemed to know how to say, more than I, what others could more easily hear, years of loving other women, of being close to other women, and enjoying the communication, looking always for the lost sister. How to tell the story of gradually coming out of jealousy and beginning to appreciate from the inside my own imprints, of beginning to enjoy the challenge of working with them and with my own particular history, of beginning to enjoy working with other women.

How to tell the story of my three daughters, of watching them be sisters, watching them know that it was all right to fight, and even to hate and be sisters, and not being frightened.

It was my youngest, my third, who showed me how it can be when the riches are unevenly distributed. While Rachel and Gwynne overcame the obstacles of a divorce and the poverty of being daughters of two artists who had less separately than they had together, coming out of it all with only "normal-sized" wounds, Jane had the sorts of physical problems for which there are no easy solutions. She went through years of wearing a heavy metal brace that went from a leather hip girdle that pulled in her small belly to a plastic chin rest holding up her small chin. From the age of eight until she was twelve, when it was clear the bracing had not worked, she bore the brace in silence, trying too hard to be brave. If only I had known then how to help her cry. But I was not a child who had been taught to cry. The cries came only very slowly, and were part of her healing.

"If only this curve had been given equally to my sisters and me, with one-third each, none of us would have had to worry," she said, at twelve, when finally she had to undergo spinal surgery.

Eight years later, at the age of twenty, as she lies in her hospital bed with a ruptured colon, railing at her unfair hand, I am trying to honor her outcry, not to silence or squelch it, as I speak of what it means to have been dealt an unfair hand and yet to have to cope with it, to know it is the only hand you will be given, as I try to talk about the time lost, even in my own life, in wanting a sharing of fate that is, alas, no matter how much we might wish it, impossible.

And as I tell her how I would wish to take this burden from her or at least to be able to share it, knowing that that wish alone can't ease her burden in the secret of our separateness, a sorrow, but also a relief for separateness in general washes over me, as if at last I have come back into my skin.

As I look forward and backward from my daughter to my mother, in this moment of realizing the limitations of my own mothering, I am coming into the knowledge of what it means to accept what is given. There is something religious in my sense of the knowledge being given to me, so that increasingly the word prayer enters my vocabulary, although still it is only a longing. Even in my awareness of my own helplessness in the face of a new kind of mother love, I am coming into a loving so different from that of the rescued and rescuing loves of the fairy-tale dreams.

But the events do not seem to be affecting just me alone. Among my own children, Gwynne, who has always been closest to Jane, is now veering away. As if in echo of my own relationship with my mother, she is realizing that nothing she has ever done for her sister has felt like enough. Rachel, who has protected herself from her two younger sisters in order to grow old enough, is coming into the picture with enough now left over to go around. Although geographically she is a continent away, she is suddenly the one who can be called up at two in the morning, New York time, and kept on the phone for hours. She is suddenly the beloved of the youngest sister in her trouble, for whom, just months earlier, there was so little space in her heart.

TIME PASSES. Jane is well once again. And the time has arrived for the others to feel sorrow, exhaustion, and anger. My mother is well once again, and is settled in a place where I can only wish her health and happiness, wishing for her all the dreams that she never did realize, that here in this place where there are others who are also alone now and there not by choice, but through a breaking down of the body that will come eventually to all, she will not be abandoned, she will not be alone. It is a Quaker retirement community that my sister and I have found for her together, working cooperatively as sisters, perhaps for the first time.

And now it is time for the next generation. Gwynne is painting and studying acupuncture. Jane is weaving. And Rachel, a graduate student in chemistry, is going to get married. She is entering an intact happy family in style. Her sisters will be bride's maids. They are both happy, amazingly happy for her. And even my sister, and even my brother-in-law—as shyly we begin to admit that we mean something to one another, that we want to mean something to one another—show shyly that they are strangely happy about this, that they too are wanting to come.

In a telephone conversation I remind Jane of what she said when she was twelve, about wanting to divide her curve equally among her sisters, and she grows silent for a minute, for she has just told me that she "never wished what I went through" on her sisters, "although often I would wonder why it was me."

Now she says, "Then maybe I did wish it on them, but I

don't remember thinking anything like that." She hesitates, then asks, "And if you could have given each of us a third of the curve, would you have done it?"

"Yes," I say, "for a third of the curve wouldn't have caused any of you any problems."

"And if you could have given us each one operation, instead of my having three?"

But here it is my turn to be silent. I try to explain that with the curve it is different, because I wouldn't be giving anybody any pain. (The stomach surgery caused some of the most deadly pain that I have ever seen.)

"But you would also be taking away pain," she counters.

I finally have to confess that her question is unanswerable, as I lead her into other safer, more general areas of thinking about sisters and she tells me in a speech that runs on and on, that is both formal and quaint, and reminds me of the little girl coping who wore the body brace all those years, and the little girl hiding her pain, that "siblings are important because you know them the longest. You will probably outlive your parents and you don't meet your friends or your husband until later, but your sisters are there for almost the same time that you are. And you don't have to take a vow, and you won't ever lose them; they are just a given, which is why it hurts so much if something bad comes from your sisters. They are the only people who will be at equal levels, and not be responsible for you or try to control you."

And I think that for all of the ways I had worried that the "unfairness" would wound her, she knows something deep and permanent that my sister and I are only now beginning to discover.

Then, remembering my image of the golden crown, I ask her whether she expects to be somehow rewarded for the time when she carried a heavier burden, as I explain my own fantasies and my own reactions to the fairy tales, how so often the one who suffers most wins in the end. She seems to smile for a minute, even through the distance of the telephone line, as I hear her soft laugh, and perhaps a moment of relief. Then she says:

"No, I never think I'll come out better off than they are. But if I can get through it—and often I doubt that I can—if by the time I'm thirty I can have a normal job, a boyfriend and a cat, a home. And if I will be living alone, or with a friend, or with a significant other . . . If I can have all of this [which Rachel and Gwynne now have], I know that I will appreciate it more than they do, that it will mean more to me."

All three of my daughters agreed to talk to me about sisters, but in the days Rachel and I spend together we are so happy in planning her wedding, there is a way in which we don't want to look back. "Rachel has found something that is very special, and I don't want it instead of her. But someday I would like to have it too," Jane has said. And I feel that in sharing that "something," in reaching out to her sisters, she is making her statement. Knowing that such pomp will mean more to Jane than to Gwynne, she has decided to reverse precedent, and has asked Jane to be the maid of honor.

Gwynne has told me that she is eager to talk about her sisters, and has even suggested I formally interview her. She brings in a bowl of cereal and finds a batch of pillows so that we may sit at right angles to one another on my bed. She is the daughter with whom I have had the most intimate conversations over the years, although she will tell me, early on in our talking, that she doesn't remember any of them, that she doesn't remember that we ever were close.

It is awkward, this interview, for we are too close to talk things over like strangers, too involved to reveal the real secrets, yet neither of us desires to stop this. For a long time I cannot find the right questions and she cannot find the right answers, as she explains how it felt to be "stopped" and "kept from growing" by her younger sister and "detached" from her older, how she feels very guilty about the violence with which she has tried to break free.

I see in my mind as we talk, Jane very little and sitting on a stairway, on the bottom step of the stairs that lead to her sisters' downstairs rooms, waiting for one door or another to open. I see a little girl, so sad-faced, so lonely, waiting to be let in.

And then I realize that she is my own self in a playground, at the rim of a classroom, and her sisters my demons. I realize my fear of her sisters, even as I realize my fear of her, how much I have raised the three children in fear and in sorrow and how in many ways I was afraid to be a real mother, but hid down among the cinders, and yet slowly, with their own striving and their sorrows, they taught me how to be a mother and love.

And out of the fairy tale wishing to share the bad mother and break the bad mirror, I look back at my sister, that shy girl of barely eighteen who brought to three children in twenty-six years a single pair of white cotton lace-trimmed rubber panties, that I loved, strangely, and used for each little girl in turn, she a shy little sister of eighteen, and I a shy new mother of twenty, and our own mother not knowing how to teach us how to be either sister or mother.

Now, twenty-six years later, I see her reaching out to my children, who are finally older than we were when I first had them and she first went away. I see her shyly reaching out her hand to me.

We will be silent, my sister and I, on the matter of the will that rewarded her for coming back healed as the appropriate adult daughter and punished me for being burdened and worn. Made in the height of my mother's anger which preceded her temporary amnesia, it is what we will leave to the future.

And I for the first time will leave it to my sister to determine, what is willed, what is stolen, whether what has been wanted in madness, and carved into being in madness and need, has validity, substance, once the madness is done.

And my sister and I, as together we hold up the puzzle, what was willed, what was chosen. Did we choose? Were we chosen? Now I choose once again to become a good daughter, as I did in my childhood, never mind what was given, never mind what was lost. I choose to take good care of my mother, along with my sister, and to let *what was* rest, at least for a while . . . I realize, slowly, slowly, that I will never undo what my mother has done to us, but that I would like to get to know my sister, and perhaps it might be possible.

There is so much left to be discovered about sisters, about how to bond late if one didn't bond early, about how to undo, or make gold out of what has been lost . . . or how to redistribute the gold and the frogs. And perhaps so much consists merely in seeing more clearly, without the black and white imposed divides, what was gold, what was frogs.

There is a time that goes beyond anger, that goes beyond blame, that becomes, as I learned from my daughters, the moment to play one's own hand, to make sense of the false distribution, the false mirroring and allotment of tasks, and go forward, taking with us the separate experiences, and the memories that will bind us at last.

"It is funny," Gwynne says to me as she sits there on my bed, "Rachel, Jane, and I don't agree on anything, practically, but we all remember our childhood as a time when we wandered hungry and uncared for and alone, and we had to figure out what to do for ourselves, because you didn't know how to be a mother."

And I think to myself, *yes, it is in the right to demonize me together that these three girls, despite everything, have been linked.* And I think of how free Gwynne is to tell me these things, and how frightened my mother was of my perceptions, of the fact that my sister and I might dare separately talk.

I am thinking, as Gwynne demonizes me with such ease and I listen with something that is also relaxing in me, about how surely there is a reason for the invention of witches and wicked stepmothers, even among those who have been naturally mothered and well, in the community of daughters in their search for a same-sized shared fate.

And then I remember, and I do not know why, how when she was a very little girl Gwynne was so frightened of witches that every time one appeared, even in a most innocuous puppet show, we'd have to go away.

"It is funny," Gwynne says, "despite everything, I think we all knew that you loved us."

In the fairy-tale stories there is always the waiting for a rescuer, the waiting to be seen.

Is there a moment, I wonder, when we stop caring about being seen, and then suddenly, like diamonds, the eyes of the others, each seeing their own world, their own fears and dreams all around the shared histories that we couldn't quite share, will come clear?

"It is strange," Gwynne says to me softly, "I don't think I have been jealous of either Rachel or Jane, or wanted to be like them, instead of being me."

In the time that intervened between the writing of this article and preparing it for publication, my sister and I have become closer. My sister and brother-in-law traveled to China to adopt a baby girl.

However—and this time it was my sister who pointed it out!—the pattern of her waiting for me to finish doing something before she is able to begin remains unbroken. It was not until my three daughters had moved fully into adulthood and the oldest one was married that she could make the choice to have a child.

Contributors

Meena Alexander is a poet, novelist, and memoirist. Her most recent work includes *Fault Lines, Nampally Road,* and *House of a Thousand Doors.* She is a professor of English at Hunter College.

Robin Behn, a poet and essayist, is the author of *Paper Bird* and *The Red Hour* and coeditor of *The Practice of Poetry.* She is chair of the Creative Writing Department at the University of Alabama.

Louise DeSalvo is the author of *Conceived in Malice: Literature as Revenge, Virginia Woolf: The Impact of Childhood Sexual Abuse on Her Life and Work, Casting Off,* and the forthcoming memoir *Vertigo.* She is a professor of literature and writing at Hunter College.

Erika Duncan is a novelist and journalist. Her novels include *A Wreath of Pale White Roses* and *Those Giants: Let Them Rise.* She is the author of a nonfiction collection, *Unless Soul Clap Its Hands: Portraits and Passages.* She writes a monthly "Encounter" column for the Long Island Weekly section of the *New York Times.*

Maria Flook is a novelist and short story writer. Her recent work includes *Family Night, Open Water,* and the forthcoming collection of short stories *Human Shores* and memoir *My Sister Life.* She teaches in the core faculty of the Bennington Writing Seminars at Bennington College.

Patricia Foster is the editor of *Minding the Body: Women Writers on Body and Soul.* She is the winner of the 1993 PEN/Jerard Fund Award and teaches in the nonfiction writing program at the University of Iowa.

Bonnie Friedman is the author of *Writing Past Dark: Envy, Fear, Distraction, and Other Dilemmas in the Writer's Life.*

Donna Gordon won a PEN Discovery Award and a *Ploughshares* Discovery Award. She is an essayist and short story writer who lives in Cambridge, Massachusetts. She has recently completed a novel and a book of nonfiction.

Lucy Grealy, a poet and essayist, is the author of *Autobiography of a Face.* She teaches at Sarah Lawrence College and Amherst College.

Joy Harjo is a poet whose books include *Mad Love and War, Secrets from the Center of the World,* and the forthcoming *The Woman Who Fell from the Sky.* She is a professor of writing at the University of New Mexico.

bell hooks is a feminist critic and essayist. Her most recent books include *Outlaw Culture: Resisting Representations* and *Teaching to Transgress: Education as the Practice of Freedom.*

Pam Houston is the author of *Cowboys Are My Weakness,* which won the 1993 Western States Book Award.

Jesse Lee Kercheval, a novelist and short story writer, is the author of *The Museum of Happiness* and *The Dogeater.* She is a professor of creative writing at the University of Wisconsin, Madison.

Lori Hope Lefkovitz is the author of *The Character of Beauty in the Victorian Novel* and is the editor of a forthcoming collection of essays on the body. She is currently working on a book about the representations of sisters in literature and film. She is an associate professor at Kenyon College.

Kathleen Norris is the author of *Dakota: A Spiritual Geography* and *Year of Common Things.*

Letty Cottin Pogrebin is one of the founding editors of *Ms.* magazine. She is the author of many books, including *Deborah, Golda and Me, Among Friends,* and the forthcoming *Time Lines.*

Mona Simpson is the author of *Anywhere but Here* and *The Lost Father.* She is currently at work on a new novel.

Debra Spark, a novelist and short story writer, is the author of *Coconuts for the Saint* and *The Tail of the Dog Star* and editor of *Twenty Under Thirty: Best Stories by America's New Young Writers.* She is a professor at Tufts University and Colby College.

Joan Wickersham, a novelist and short story writer, is the author of *The Paper Anniversary.*

Joy Williams is the author of *Taking Care* and *Breaking and Entering.*

PERMISSIONS

BELL HOOKS: "Girls Together: Sustained Sisterhood." Copyright © 1995 by bell hooks.

PAM HOUSTON: "A Letter to My Sister Who Doesn't Exist." Copyright © 1995 by Pam Houston.

JESSE LEE KERCHEVAL: "Earth." First published in *American Short Fiction,* vol. 4, no. 13, spring 1994. Reprinted by permission of the author.

LORI HOPE LEFKOVITZ: "Leah Behind the Veil: Sex with Sisters from the Bible to Woody Allen." A version was first published in *Hebrew University Studies in Literature and the Arts,* vol. 18, 1990. Reprinted by permission of the author.

KATHLEEN NORRIS: "Borderline." Copyright © 1995 by Kathleen Norris.

LETTY COTTIN POGREBIN: "Sisters and Secrets." Copyright © 1995 by Letty Cottin Pogrebin.

MONA SIMPSON: "Sisters." Copyright © 1995 by Mona Simpson.

DEBRA SPARK: "Last Things." Winner of a 1995 Pushcart award, first published in *Ploughshares,* vol. 20, nos. 2–3, fall 1994. Reprinted by permission of the author.

JOAN WICKERSHAM: "The Shadow of the Mountain." Copyright © 1995 by Joan Wickersham. A version first appeared in *Glamour.*

JOY WILLIAMS: "Traveling to Pridesup." First published in *Taking Care,* copyright © 1982 by Joy Williams. Reprinted by permission of Random House.

About the Editor

Patricia Foster received her MFA degree from the Iowa Writers' Workshop, and completed a Ph.D in women's literature from Florida State University. The editor of *Minding the Body,* an anthology of narratives about women and their physical selves, she teaches in the nonfiction writing program at the University of Iowa. She lives in Iowa City.